HIGHER GROUND

HIGHER GROUND

HOW TO TRAVEL
RESPONSIBLY
WITHOUT ROUGHING IT
RHIANNON BATTEN

First published in Great Britain in 2007 by
Virgin Books Ltd
Thames Wharf Studios
Rainville Road
London
W6 9HA

A catalogue record for this book is available from the
British Library.

ISBN 978-0-7535-1279-1

The paper used in this book is a natural, recyclable
product made from wood grown in sustainable forests. The
manufacturing process conforms to the regulations of the
country of origin.

Designed by Design Culture

Typeset by Phoenix Photosetting, Chatham, Kent

Printed and bound in Great Britain by
Mackays of Chatham, Chatham, Kent

1 3 5 7 9 10 8 6 4 2

Contents

INTRODUCTION

You've bragged to anyone who will listen that you won't be in the office for a couple of weeks. You've begged, borrowed or bought a killer holiday wardrobe. And, with the grace of a sumo wrestler, you have pressed your suitcase into submission. Yet, now that you are being toasted by the sun, brushed by soft white sand and lapped by water as clear as the vodka in your flirtini, something is holding you back from revelling too blissfully in the holiday spirit.

Maybe it is the suspicion that your hotel is diverting water resources away from the local population? Or that the flight you took to get to your tropical idyll pumped out over a tonne of carbon dioxide? Perhaps it's the worry that, by giving away a stock of Fruit Pastilles to the local children, you might be inadvertently encouraging them to beg?

Holidays used to be about escaping the daily grind, an instant rescue remedy for frazzled souls where you could indulge in all the misbehaviour you wouldn't dare consider back home. Over the past few decades, as we travelled to ever more exotic destinations, few of us thought very deeply about the effects our travels might be having on the places we were visiting – or on the troubled seafronts we had abandoned back home. But in this era of increasing ethical awareness, where it is the norm to buy local, opt for organic, recycle and choose iced decaf triple grande skinny lattes of the Fairtrade variety, many of us find ourselves taking guilt trips, not holidays.

If you're heading off by plane, the self-reproach is likely to start before you've even arrived at your destination. With air travel the fastest growing source of the greenhouse gases that lead to climate change, there is no longer any doubt that flying costs the earth. According to a recent report by Oxford University's Environmental Change Institute, aircraft currently produce almost 6 per cent of the UK's carbon emissions and, unless government policy changes, are predicted to account for about a quarter of the national total by 2050.

Flying isn't the only aspect of our holidays that can have an impact on the environment. Flushing non-biodegradable toiletries into local sewage systems, buying mineral water in plastic bottles in countries which have inadequate waste (let alone recycling) facilities, hiring a moped to speed off on your own instead of taking public transport, and encouraging the development of golf courses or ski slopes in arid or ecologically sensitive destinations can all have a harmful effect on local ecosystems. So too can careless behaviour at ecologically fragile sites such as nature reserves or coral reefs, or unwittingly buying souvenirs made from endangered species.

Then there is the social impact of travelling. Will your holiday be funding an oppressive regime? Is your hotel locally-owned and community-spirited or will all the profits from your bargain break be siphoned out of the country and into the pockets of a large, multinational company? Does your tour operator employ local guides? And, however worthy a volunteering holiday sounds, will you be leaving people in the lurch after they've come to depend on you if your placement is only arranged on a short-term basis?

Sometimes there are even more subtle ways that travelling, and all that goes with it, can have a negative impact. That shiny new rucksack you've just bought may be made with sweatshop labour, for instance, or the local speciality you've guzzled might be the end result of cruel farming methods. Even buying travel insurance requires serious consideration if you don't want the profits of your purchase to be funding unethical investments.

If we take all of these worries to heart, the obvious course of action might be to stay at home and feed a passion for international travel with re-runs of 'Big Cat Diary' and a flick through the latest *Hip Hotels* guide. Those who take a fundamentalist stance, particularly when it comes to air travel, are doing this already. If your job is based in one place, you have no friends or family living abroad, you don't have to take your holidays in short bursts and your ethical beliefs are strong enough to resist the combination of wanderlust and a bargain flight on a wet winter's day, this approach might be viable. But avoiding all journeys simply isn't feasible for most people, who are about as likely to stick to their promise as they are to pack a hair shirt in with their swimsuit. For better or worse, medium- and long-haul travel is part of modern-day life.

A zero-tolerance approach to travel also ignores the positive impact holidays can have. Backpacking around southeast Asia may not compare to studying for a PhD in international politics but its educational nature is irrefutable (even if that stretches only to being able to order a beer in sixty languages). There are other, stronger arguments for keeping on trucking, bussing and train-hopping round the world. For one, you might think that it is a good thing to give up flights altogether but what about people in India or Bali or Greece? What impact will it have on them when the tourist dollars stop flowing?

Somewhere between those who believe that we should only holiday close to home in tents that we have knitted ourselves from organic angel hair and those who fly off to Malaga on a whim so that they can spend an unplanned day off in the sun, there is a middle way: travelling responsibly without roughing it.

This is not a difficult philosophy to follow. Flying less is a good way to start. So, too, is staying in small, independently run hotels, caring more about the people you meet at your destination than whether they can mix a decent margarita and refusing to join a herd of safari jeeps as they ambush what appears to be the only animal in sight.

As for not roughing it, *real* luxury today doesn't mean having a personal pool attendant or checking into a penthouse suite. It means seeking out unique experiences that veer towards the low-key and local. Travelling responsibly can be just as stylish and indulgent an experience as any other trip. Some of the world's most decadent hotels have showers fed by solar-heated rainwater, grey-water irrigation systems, designer compost toilets and sustainable food-sourcing policies in partnership with local communities (it hasn't taken hoteliers long to cotton on to the fact that people will be more easily persuaded by the responsible travel philosophy if they are having a good time than if they are being nagged into submission).

Likewise, how much more luxurious is it to cross Europe by sleeper train than join the scrum for a seat on a budget airline? Or to wake up to a lazy al fresco breakfast on the sun-dappled terrace of a shabby chic guesthouse than to be queuing up for greasy sausages and reconstituted eggs in a characterless chain hotel restaurant?

Responsible travel is also fun. Unless you have the kind of heart that is moved only by surgery, it is deeply satisfying to return from a holiday knowing that your actions – and your money – have helped rather than harmed. That's not to say that travelling in this way is always straightforward. Just as the ethical shopper sometimes has to choose between loose, local, unorganic vegetables or organic ones that have been flown half way round the world and cocooned in plastic, the responsible traveller faces some tough decisions. At times balancing green, social and practical considerations can seem trickier to calculate than Michael Palin's travel expenses. But that doesn't mean you have to be some kind of eco-saint to be a responsible traveller. I own a car. I have ordered chips on all five continents. Sometimes I forget to turn the lights off when I leave a room. If I can change my travelling habits, anyone can. How far down the responsible road you want to go, if at all, is your business. But, if you want to give it a try, I hope that this book will help you find your way.

CHAPTER ONE

GETTING THERE

Sky's the limit

Robert Louis Stevenson wrote that 'to travel hopefully is a better thing than to arrive', but you need an awful lot of optimism to enjoy travelling by plane these days. Clampdowns on baggage, rigorous airport security, overstretched facilities and the threat of terrorism have turned what was once an exciting escape from everyday life into another of its grinds.

For the responsible traveller, these negatives are superseded by an even greater problem: climate change. Trains, planes, cars, buses and ships are all major emitters of greenhouse gases, but air travel is the most damaging. While a single person travelling in an average car is responsible for emitting roughly the same as they would if they travelled in a full plane over the same distance, air travel pips motoring to the post as prime offender – because we tend to travel further by air and because aircraft emissions are rising faster than those of any other sector, and because of the heights at which planes burn fuel.

Rising emissions are largely linked to the increasing affordability of flights, in particular the success of budget airlines, and the resulting increase in the number of people taking short-haul flights. In an era when more and more people can afford to fly to Mallorca for the day (or to Hong Kong or India for a long weekend), staying at home seems wildly unadventurous. In this climate of binge flying, travelling by air has gone from being a rare luxury to something almost as prosaic as deciding what to have for lunch.

A lot of hot air

According to figures released by flight information company OAG, there were more than 2.51 million flights scheduled in May 2007, about seventy thousand more than there had been the previous year. Much – but not all – of this growth is taking place in emerging economies such as India. Delhi may have been the world's first capital to convert its entire public transport fleet to run on compressed natural gas (CNG), but there hasn't been such clear-sky thinking for its aviation industry. In May 2007, India's domestic airlines were offering consumers 8,600 more flights and 1.7 million more seats than they had in May 2006 (partly due to a massive 62 per cent growth in the low-cost sector), while the number of international flights in and out of the country doubled between May 2001 and 2006.

It's a similar story in China, where passenger numbers have doubled since 2000. Between May 2006 and May 2007, the country's domestic airlines were offering 22,900 more flights and 3.2 million more seats while international flights were up by 17 per cent. The bad news for anyone living below a flight-path, or beside a runway, is that this trend is likely to intensify.

Here comes the science

When sunlight reaches the Earth, some of it is reflected back through the atmosphere into space while the rest is absorbed, with the help of greenhouse gases. This absorption results in a warming of the atmosphere, a naturally occurring process that fluctuates over time. However, current levels of greenhouse gases are worryingly high and increasing rapidly.

In 2001 the Intergovernmental Panel on Climate Change (IPCC) predicted that by the end of the century global temperatures would have risen by between 1.4°C and 5.8°C. The IPCC also believes that levels of greenhouse gases in the atmosphere must peak by 2015 if a rise in global temperatures of more than two degrees above pre-industrial levels is to be stopped.

James Lovelock, who founded the Gaia hypothesis (an ecological hypothesis which, basically, proposes that living and non-living parts of the earth should be seen as a single organism) has written that the earth is now 'trapped in a vicious circle of positive feedback. Extra heat from any source, whether from greenhouse gases, the disappearance of Arctic ice or the Amazon forest, is amplified, and its effects are more than additive. It is almost as if we had lit a fire to keep warm, and failed to notice, as we piled on fuel, that the fire was out of control and the furniture had ignited. When that happens, little time is left to put out the fire before it consumes the house. Global warming, like a fire, is accelerating and almost no time is left to act.' It is this urgency that has brought the issue of climate change to wide attention.

If scientists' predictions that temperatures are likely to rise over the next century are accurate, the likelihood is that there will also be an increase in sea levels and in extreme weather events such as hurricanes, droughts, heatwaves and floods. These in turn may result in phenomena such as outbreaks of infectious diseases (warmer, wetter weather might enable diseases such as malaria and yellow fever to spread to new areas) and in the mass displacement of people living in low-lying coastal areas.

Why the big focus on aircraft emissions? Because planes run on kerosene, which, like any fossil fuel, releases greenhouse gases into the atmosphere as it is burnt (namely water vapour, nitrous oxide and, most significantly, carbon dioxide, or CO_2). Not only are emissions of greenhouse gases from aircraft rising faster than those of any other sector but aviation's impact on the climate is exacerbated by the fact that these gases are mainly being emitted high above the earth's surface, in the upper troposphere (the troposphere is the lowest part of earth's atmosphere) and lower stratosphere, where they can do more damage.

Experts believe that at these altitudes the nitrogen oxides from jet-engine exhausts play a part in the formation of low-level ozone, another greenhouse gas, while the contrails planes leave behind them may help trigger the formation of cirrus clouds, adding to the warming effect. Because of these additional factors, the IPCC has estimated that the burning of aviation fuel has a 'radiative forcing ratio' (essentially a greater warming effect) about 2.7 times that of carbon dioxide alone.

Air traffic in Europe is no exception to this pattern. *Sustainable Aviation*, a publication put together in June 2005 by the UK aviation industry, stated that air travel in the UK supports 675,000 jobs, adds £14 billion to the economy and generates incoming visitor spending of around £10 billion. Given these figures, it is no surprise that growth in the aviation industry isn't being curbed. A white paper published at the end of 2003 underlined the British government's attitude to the situation. It stated that demand for air travel 'is projected to be between two and three times current levels by 2030. Some of our major airports are already close to capacity, so failure to allow for increased capacity could have serious economic consequences, both at national and at regional level.'

The industry has taken this statement and run with it. Current expansion plans being considered include a third runway at Heathrow, and new runways at Stansted, Birmingham and Edinburgh airports. In Glasgow, a £25 million terminal expansion is expected to provide for a predicted boost in annual passenger numbers from nine million to twenty-four million by 2030. This is in addition to the fifth terminal currently being built at Heathrow. Set to open in March 2008, this is designed to cope with an extra thirty million passengers a year.

The anti-jet set

The predicted environmental impact of all this airport expansion is staggering. In October 2006 the Stern Review on the Economics of Climate Change was published. This seven hundred-page document, commissioned by the British government, is the largest and arguably most significant discussion of the effects of climate change and global warming on the world economy. It found that aviation currently emits around 600–700 million tonnes of CO_2 each year, or around 2–3 per cent of global CO_2 emissions (in the UK, aviation is believed to account for almost 6 per cent of the country's emissions). However, as passenger numbers increase, emissions are likely to soar. The United Nations predicts that this figure will increase to 6 per cent by as soon as 2030.

An even starker message was conveyed in a 2006 study by the Tyndall Centre for Climate Change Research. This stated that, based on continued aviation growth of 6.4 per cent per year (its current average), by 2050 aviation would be using the UK's entire carbon emissions allowance if the country is to stick to the government's target of cutting emissions by 60 per cent by the middle of the century. Everything else, from ground-based industry to domestic heating, would have to be carbon neutral.

Why I *Do* Fly

'No one has been able to explain to me how a few empty seats on scheduled flights are going to make any difference to global warming. I am more disturbed by the fact that scientists believe that deforestation has a much bigger impact on climate change than aircraft emissions. The worst deforestation is in the developing world, largely as a result of increasing population. Tourism is one of the two pillars that support the economies of these impoverished countries. The other is mining. Without the former, cash-strapped governments will rely on the latter, with its inevitable consequences for the environment.

'Some of the greatest hardship I have seen in the developing world is when tourism has suddenly ceased because of a natural or man-made disaster. It is then that you realise just how many people depend on tourism to make a living. I think we should stop feeling guilty about travel and rejoice in the positive contribution we can make. Simply being there helps.

'But there is much more that travellers can do than follow the responsible travel guidelines on using local services and so on: they can get involved in improving the lives of the underclass. The charity Stuff Your Rucksack (*see chapter five*) links tourists and local organisations that need "stuff" brought to them.

'Here's an example of just how well this can work. A young couple visiting Peru brought a bag full of baby clothes knitted by elderly women in Britain. They delivered the clothing to a charity in Lima which works with young pregnant women in prison; when their babies are born they have nothing to wear. In return the women make handicrafts which can be sold to raise money. The tourists bought some handicrafts to take home to England as presents. Result: the knitters are happy because they're doing something useful, the tourists see a side of Peru normally closed to visitors, and the teenage mums in prison feel valued too. Everyone is a winner.'

*Hilary Bradt is the founder of Bradt Travel Guides
(www.bradt-travelguides.com)*

Predict and Decide, a 2006 report commissioned by the Environmental Change Institute at Oxford University concluded that: 'The implication is that the UK will be unable to meet its targets for reducing climate change impacts without action to curb the demand for air travel.'

There have been some efforts in this direction. While calls for taxes on aviation fuel continue to be ignored – they are prohibited under international law and would be difficult to implement unless they were introduced globally – Air Passenger Duty (APD) for anyone flying out of a UK airport doubled in February 2007. The move was designed to make the aviation industry confront its environmental costs. However, the general consensus has been that the rate rise – the new rates range from between £10 for economy class flights within Europe to £80 for business and first class long-haul routes – was not a significant enough increase to stamp out binge flying (it has been calculated that if aviation fuel was taxed in line with petrol, the average long-haul plane ticket would be £500 more expensive). Instead, campaigners have called for a tax per kilometre, increased annually in line with inflation and collected in a similar way to APD, as a kind of atmospheric congestion charge.

There is a well-worn argument that increasing aviation taxes is undemocratic because this is likely to make flying an elitist activity again. However, according to the Civil Aviation Authority (CAA), 55 per cent of budget airline passengers have a household income of more than £35,500, with two-thirds of that number coming from households that earn more than £46,000. This implies that much of the increasing demand for flights, in the UK at least, is not the result of more people flying but of the same, relatively well-off, people flying more.

The appliance of science

In early 2007 Richard Branson, chairman of Virgin Atlantic, announced a prize of $25 million for anyone who could come up with a system for removing one billion tonnes of carbon dioxide or more from the atmosphere every year for at least a decade. It would be a brave soul, however, who was willing to gamble that technological innovation alone might provide an answer to the problem.

Attempts to improve the efficiency of aircraft have been successful at reducing their emissions up to a point. The new superjumbo, the Airbus A380, is 12 per cent more fuel efficient than the Boeing 747, for instance, while turboprop planes, though only suitable for short flights, are said to use only 64 per cent of the fuel per passenger mile that jets do. Likewise, lowering the weight of planes, improving aerodynamics, fine-tuning engines and towing planes by electric vehicles to starting grids on runways may all help reduce emissions. However, these advances do not go far enough to produce the massive cut that is needed.

In fact, all these savings are likely to be outweighed by the predicted increase in passengers in the years ahead.

It's a similar story when it comes to improvements in efficiency in areas beyond the aircraft themselves. Reducing the level of airport congestion that leads to planes spending time in holding patterns, or streamlining air-traffic control are both useful indirect ways of cutting emissions. IATA, the International Air Travel Association, is currently pursuing an initiative aimed at trimming detours around national borders, or military training areas, from international air lanes. IATA has recently implemented an initiative aimed at trimming detours around national borders, or military training areas, from international air lanes. Over 350 routes have been improved so far, one of the most significant being the inauguration of IATA-1. This new route, inaugurated in April 2006, cuts 30 minutes off flight times between China and Europe, saving 2,860 hours of flight time, 27,000 tonnes of fuel, 84,800 tonnes of CO2 emissions and 340,000kg of nitrogen oxide emissions each year.

Cuts such as these still don't leave enough room for aviation to keep growing at its current pace, however.

Neither, so far, have been experiments to produce alternative aircraft fuels (to kerosene, which is currently used to power most flights). Hydrogen fuel cells may provide a realistic emission-free fuel for buses and cars but the heavy tanks and fuel-cell stacks they require make the idea impractical for planes as we know them, and developing a new type of aircraft from scratch is prohibitively expensive.

Research at Imperial College London has shown that it is possible to fly currently available planes with a mix of 95 per cent kerosene and 5 per cent biodiesel. But that is still a lot of kerosene, and biodiesel comes with its own set of problems: as well as causing deforestation, growing crops for fuel is likely to create what green campaigner George Monbiot and others have described as a 'competition for food between cars and people' (see chapter six).

'Synthetic' fuel, or synfuel – a liquid fuel made from coal, natural gas or biomass – is one functioning alternative to kerosene. In comparison with other alternative fuels, synfuel appears to be a realistic substitute. Its raw materials are easily available in large quantities, it's pretty straightforward to produce and it works with most current engines as they are (it is already being used on some aircraft in South Africa). The US government projects that its domestic consumption of synthetic fuel will rise to 3.7 million barrels a day by 2030, as oil prices rise. However, the attraction here is one of economics rather than environmental concern; at best, CO_2 emissions from planes running on synthetic fuels are estimated to be only 1 to 2 per cent lower than those burning kerosene.

And there's the rub. Developing planes which run on low-emission fuels is only going to happen if the price of running them on kerosene or high-emission synthetic fuels becomes more expensive than producing an alternative. Or if the oil wells run dry.

A get-out clause?

With airport expansion continuing in the meantime, the aviation industry is likely to place its faith, instead, in the European Union's Emissions Trading Scheme (ETS). This is designed to put a cap on emissions, by allowing companies that emit more than an agreed allowance to buy carbon credits from companies that have reduced their emissions below a fixed target, rather than reducing their own emissions.

So far the scheme only covers ground-based industries but in December 2006 the European Commission proposed that aviation should be included. According to the proposal, aircraft operators would be obliged to hold CO_2 emission allowances for all flights between airports within Europe from January 2011 onwards; in 2012, membership of the scheme would be extended to include all flights arriving at or departing from airports within the EU, thereby including airlines from outside the EU. At present the EU ETS is the only multi-sectoral emissions trading scheme in operation – there are currently no other regulatory trading systems that cover aviation.

Dangerous Liaisons

Besides environmental concern, there is another reason why some travellers choose not to fly: most passenger aircraft are produced by Boeing or Airbus, both of which are arms manufacturers. If you hold an ethical bank account, or investments that consciously avoid the funding of arms producers, it might go against your principles to then jump on a plane made by such companies. Noam Chomsky made a more provocative connection when he wrote that many passenger aircraft are just modified bombers.

According to a report published by Amnesty International in 2006, the market for the global arms trade is expanding: 'Some of the increased military spending is in countries least able to afford it. In 2002–03, Bangladesh, Nepal and Pakistan were among those governments that spent more on their military than on healthcare.'

Reports state that Boeing's annual turnover of US $50 billion has been, in part, recently generated by the sale of arms to the governments of Indonesia, Israel, Kuwait and Saudi Arabia, while Airbus is owned by the European Aeronautic Defence and Space company (EADS). The two companies are currently in the process of lobbying for a £100 billion contract with the US armed forces.

No fly zone

In June 2006, the Bishop of London, Richard Chartres, provoked a livelier debate than he had bargained for when he told the *Sunday Times* that 'making selfish choices such as flying on holiday or buying a large car are a symptom of sin.' This seems a pretty extreme view. Yet, especially where air travel is concerned, given the information we now have about the environmental and human impact of aviation, it doesn't seem completely unreasonable to suggest that there are moral implications involved in choosing to fly. Indeed, many people believe that travelling can never be truly 'responsible' if plane tickets are part of the package.

To put this into perspective, a typical return flight from London to Cape Town emits over two tonnes of CO_2 per person. This is around one fifth of the average person's current annual carbon footprint. However, according to the UK charity the Climate Outreach and Information Network (COIN), if everyone on the planet were to take personal responsibility for avoiding climate change, rather than leaving action to industry and government, we would have to live within a personal, annual emissions limit of 2.5 tonnes of carbon dioxide. To stay within this, therefore, flying is impossible unless you ration yourself to a once-a-decade splurge.

These figures can appear so daunting for the average person that they run the risk of making us view action as pointless. If this is the case, it can help to focus on the more general message the statistics present. What they illustrate more than anything is just how disproportionately large our transport emissions are. No matter how conscientiously we turn the TV off standby, kit out our house with energy-saving light bulbs or eat only locally grown produce, we will not manage to substantially lower our carbon footprint if we continue to fly with happy abandon.

If you're seriously committed to reducing your impact on the environment (you can do a quick carbon calculation on the Best Foot Forward website – www.bestfootforward.com), you can say goodbye to spur-of-the-moment shopping trips to New York, hen weekends in Prague or second homes in Ibiza. The best way of driving down emissions quickly is to take the low-flying principle to its logical conclusion, and vow never to step on a plane again.

'Why I Don't Fly'

'I'd been working on climate change for years before I helped set up Plane Stupid. I'd read and researched a lot about aviation and had come to the conclusion that it was one of the biggest threats to the climate but, at the time, there was little high-profile work going on in the area by the environmental movement. This seemed to be a gaping hole so we decided to try to fill it.

'In the last five years I've taken one return flight to Greece. Since I started working with Plane Stupid I haven't flown at all. There are many distant places I'd love to see – the Amazon being one example – but I don't think it's worth killing millions for. Whenever the consequences of not flying are worse than the consequences of flying, flying is justified. This is probably the case in 1 or even 2 per cent of flights. However, as the consequence of flying is the destruction of the planet, missing a meeting or even a wedding isn't enough.

'Flying on holiday is neither responsible nor justifiable, at least for the next few decades. No amount of offsetting changes this basic fact. Punching someone in the face and then paying them £50 compensation doesn't make punching people in the face "responsible". If you're delivering organs for transplant or attending cease-fire talks, then fine, I'll wave you off at the airport – but not for holidays and, 99 per cent of the time, not for business.

'We need leadership. We're trapped by materialist individualist thinking and a system which promotes a status quo. This is going to kill us. We need a leader with some balls who can just say, "F*** consumer choice, I'm banning short-haul flights and 4x4s in cities and patio heaters and every other stupid waste of energy, because otherwise we're all going to die." We wouldn't have defeated Hitler if the best Churchill could do was put an extra 10p tax on sauerkraut.'

Graham Thompson helps run the Plane Stupid campaign, which aims to 'bring the aviation industry down to earth'.

The third way

Abstaining from aviation altogether is an admirable choice but it is not a simple decision for the majority of us. The very fact that flying has become such an integral part of modern life means that, even with video conferencing and camera phones, more of us than ever have work commitments or families living in destinations that demand we travel abroad by plane (Satish Kumar, the editor of *Resurgence* magazine, which focuses on environmental issues, has described his annual flights to see family in India as 'love miles'). Promise not to fly in a moment of eco-diligence and all but the most resolute, or time-rich, will fall off the wagon at some point.

There is also an argument that continuing to fly for holidays that support sustainable tourism projects can help lift people out of poverty, create jobs, fund sanitation and education projects and promote the protection of wildlife. So, a more realistic target for many of us is to fly less, swapping short-haul flights for trains or other modes of transport, dramatically restricting the number of long-haul flights we take each year and staying longer on each trip.

If you feel you want to make a more public commitment to avoiding what the campaign group LowFlyZone describes as 'flights that are only possible because they are cheap, flights that are disproportionately polluting because most of the fuel is used getting to cruising height and then almost immediately landing, journeys that can easily be made by rail', its website (www.lowflyzone.org) asks people to pledge to limit the number of flights they take each year to either 'gold' or 'silver' level.

The first means you promise to take no flights for a year, except in a personal or family emergency, while the second means not taking more than two return short-haul flights, or one return long-haul flight, over the same period. The service is free, but it asks for donations to cover its costs (those who sign are sent a certificate to remind them of their pledge).

Carbon offsetting

Rock stars do it. So do car companies, hair salons, schools, film producers, villages and governments. In China, there are even plans for the world's first carbon-neutral city. Carbon offsetting has now become as ubiquitous as owning an iPod. And it is big business. Do a quick web search and, among other choices, you can find everything from offsets for a year of washing machine use charged by text message to those sold as a package with car insurance.

The Great Escape

On 1 September 2006, Barbara Haddrill set out to travel from the UK to Brisbane for the wedding of one of her best friends. But, believing that air travel is environmentally damaging, she decided to go overland.

Previously employed at the Centre for Alternative Technology, in Wales, Barbara gave up her job to do the trip. Her route took her by bus to Moscow, train to Beijing, train to Vietnam, train, bus and boat to Cambodia, bus to Thailand, train to Malaysia, bus and boat to Singapore, cargo ship to Australia, plane to Bali, bus and boat through Indonesia, boat to Singapore, cargo ship to Italy, train to Paris and bike to Wales.

You'll notice there was a flight in there.

'Here is the great dilemma,' she wrote on her blog In February 2007. 'Ever since I got to Australia I started looking at how I was going to return. I searched high and low for shipping companies, fishermen, sailors, anyone who I could get a lift with. Without paying lots of money to get a cargo ship I decided my best bet was to head to Darwin, the nearest place to any other country, and check it out. Unfortunately due to timing I arrived in the middle of the wet season.'

Cyclones were a risk and no one was going anywhere soon on a sailing or fishing boat. There was a huge sailing rally in July, when she might have been able to crew her way from Darwin to Bali, but her visa for Indonesia was due to run out in April.

'I feel like this trip is bigger than me now and bigger than the wedding I came to,' she continued. 'I am running out of cash and I miss my friends and family and home.' She weighed up her options and eventually decided to fly to Bali. 'There are no ways to justify my decision but I am only human and unfortunately have had to break my own commitment and take a small flight,' she wrote. 'This flight will produce 0.4 tonnes of CO_2, which I take full responsibility for – and still keeps me below my limit of 2.5 tonnes a year.'

Going overland wasn't fast – her trip took eight months in total, including a three-month pit stop in Australia and other diversions along the way – and it was expensive. Haddrill estimated that it cost her over £2,000. Yet, in terms of reducing the environmental impact of her journey, it was a huge success. The calculations Haddrill made showed that her trip had created around 3 tonnes of carbon dioxide. A return flight would have generated 10.7 tonnes.

No consumer group has embraced the concept quite as wholeheartedly as the contemporary traveller, however. A twenty-first century means of having your cake and scoffing it, the basic premise is that you can 'neutralise' the CO_2 emissions you generate through travelling either by planting trees to absorb CO_2 and lock the carbon away in forests (this is known as sequestering), or by investing in other carbon-reducing projects.

Simple. But what exactly does carbon offsetting involve, and is it really the responsible traveller's instant rescue remedy, a licence to carry on flying?

One common misconception of carbon offsetting schemes is that they all work by planting trees, which then re-absorb CO_2 from the atmosphere. This is not the case. Other offsetting projects typically involve investing in renewable energy projects, which aim to provide alternatives to the burning of coal, oil and gas in the first place, or energy efficiency schemes. The latter aim to reduce the amount of fuel used, for example by supplying energy efficient light bulbs in countries where they are either unavailable or prohibitively expensive, or building stoves that will work using only half as much wood as traditional open fires. Other schemes work by buying up emissions trading credits and taking them out of circulation.

So far so straightforward. But, how do you actually go about offsetting your carbon emissions? Myriad companies now offer online offsetting services. Two best known of these in the UK are Climate Care and the Carbon Neutral Company (formerly Future Forests), though there are many others. Log onto one of these websites, type in your flight, car or train journey details and the company will calculate the CO_2 your trip is likely to produce and tell you how much money you need to pay to offset your travel through one of its schemes.

According to the Carbon Neutral Company website, for instance, a typical return flight from London Heathrow to New York's JFK airport would produce 1.2 tonnes of CO_2. The cost to offset these emissions through the company is £12.90. Pay up and you can take off with a clear conscience, or so the argument goes.

Fans of carbon offsetting schemes also argue that simply by making these calculations we increase our awareness of the amount of CO_2 our travel habits are responsible for producing. Although you can also make the same calculation without buying an offset – the Choose Climate website lets you click from point to point on a world map and gives you a whole host of data for a comparable plane journey, from the amount of fuel used to the height of a tree containing an equivalent amount of carbon, or the extra amount you would pay if aviation fuel were taxed at the same rate as petrol.

Too good to be true?

The more that carbon offsetting projects have become mainstream, the more the companies that provide them have come under attack. There are several reasons for this. The first is a problem with the basic equation that suggests that you can swap fossil carbon for carbon absorbed by trees. Measuring how much carbon dioxide is being produced by a flight is a relatively straightforward process – although a truly accurate figure could only be reached by taking into account variables such as the age of the plane, how full it is, what time of day you travel and so on (this variation might also explain why, if you search for an offset for the same journey on different offsetting websites, they will often come up with different figures – and a different price – for the transaction).

Measuring how much carbon is absorbed through offsetting schemes is harder to compute. Though it is widely accepted that trees and other plants act as a carbon 'sink', there is an argument that, if you plant a new tree, it won't soak up the kind of levels of CO_2 being promised until it is fully grown. That might take 60 years, or more. In the meantime, trees are also susceptible to disease, fire, timber harvesting and natural decay.

Adding further to concerns about how much carbon can be absorbed by tree planting, a six-year study published in *Nature* in 2006 suggested that plants may not be as effective at removing increasing amounts of carbon dioxide from the atmosphere as had been hoped. In a classic example of feedback spiral, the report concluded that rising atmospheric CO_2 levels affect the availability of nitrogen and other nutrients in soils and thus restrict the ability of plants to absorb carbon.

Even if you accept that planting trees is generally a good aim in terms of reducing the amount of CO_2 in the atmosphere, critics of offsetting schemes have argued that the setting up of large plantations can have other effects that should be taken into consideration. In some cases there have been claims that local communities have been dispossessed of their land by big plantation companies, and that monoculture developments of non-native species have adversely affected the local environment in some places by depleting water tables, increasing soil acidity, contributing to biodiversity loss and introducing pesticide contamination.

Not all tree-based offsetting schemes work on the basis that saplings are being planted, either. Some projects pay to keep existing trees from being cut down, even though some of the forests you can buy sequestration rights for may have little chance of being felled anyway. For all these reasons, many schemes are turning away from tree planting and focusing more on energy efficiency and renewable energy projects. These are more clearly based on 'additionality' – where the savings in emissions are additional to what would have otherwise occurred without the offset funding.

Seeing the wood for the trees

A further criticism levelled at offsetting schemes – and a valid one, bearing in mind that many carbon offset companies are profit-driven, rather than run as charities – is that they are not always adequately monitored. The making of Coldplay's 2002 album, *A Rush of Blood to the Head*, for example, was claimed to have been carbon-offset by the planting of 10,000 mango trees in the state of Karnataka, in India. Proving that even genuinely well-meaning tree-planting schemes can go awry, however, a report in the *Sunday Telegraph* in 2006 found that, of the 10,000 trees that were given to small farmers in the region, only a few hundred were still alive four years on. The rest had perished through lack of water and inadequate financial and infrastructure support.

This isn't just a problem for famous bands funding large-scale projects. When you pay to offset a flight, your money will often trickle down to small-scale local charities, under a complicated chain of command. Not only can this mean that responsibility for the success of the project gets shifted around from one part of the chain to another to the point where no one organisation is ever fully accountable, but also the high levels of administration involved mean that valuable funding is sometimes diverted away from the projects themselves and eaten up by bureaucracy.

One good way to ensure that the project your carbon offsetting company supports is fulfilling its promises is to check that it is independently monitored. The British government has published a consultation paper on establishing a voluntary Code of Best Practice for the provision of carbon offsetting to UK customers, and aims to have the Code operating by late 2007. In the meantime, the 'Gold Standard' carbon credits certification scheme, based in Switzerland and backed by WWF, recognises the best renewable energy and energy efficiency projects. It doesn't cover tree-planting.

If you're booking a trip through an accredited tour operator or travel agent, you can also opt to offset your journey through the new Tourism Industry Carbon Offset Scheme (TICOS). This industry-wide initiative has an agreement with UNESCO and the IUCN (World Conservation Union) World Commission for Protected Areas to develop projects around World Heritage sites, and each project is monitored by the scheme's science and research team and reported on through its website.

Creating a smoke-screen

One final criticism of carbon offsetting outweighs all the others – the fact that it tackles the effect of the problem rather than its cause. By offering us a way of assuaging our guilt about travelling, there is little reason for us to try to cut down on our air or road time. In fact, there is an argument that carbon offsetting tells us that we can carry on flying, driving and polluting with impunity. If we believe the hype, the pressure on us, and on governments and companies, to instigate change is lessened.

Friends of the Earth director Tony Juniper has stated that 'carbon offsetting schemes are being used as a smoke-screen to avoid real measures to tackle climate change', while the spoof Cheat Neutral website suggests the practice is as misguided as paying to assuage the guilt of infidelity. Kevin Smith, the author of *The Carbon Neutral Myth*, goes further, making the analogy between carbon offsetting and the medieval practice of selling 'indulgences' for the remission of sins.

A counter-argument has been made by Paul Monaghan, head of ethics and sustainability at the Co-operative Group: 'To say offsetting should only be progressed after all other options have been exhausted is daft: it's like saying waste recycling activities should be discouraged as they encourage people to duck the higher imperative of waste minimisation.'

Covering your tracks

Where does all this leave the responsible traveller? The answer seems to be a qualified acceptance of carbon offsetting, albeit acknowledging that contributing to carbon offset schemes doesn't offer a licence to pollute. We should only carbon offset in addition to reducing our emissions, not instead of, and we should choose carbon offsetting schemes with care – ideally projects which are monitored under schemes such as the Gold Standard or TICOS.

In a study by *Ethical Consumer* magazine in June 2007, the following offsetting companies came out on top: Atmosfair, Carbon Counter, Equiclimate, Global Cool, NativeEnergy and Pure. If you decide to offset your emissions, make sure you do some research before you sign up and encourage the company to be more accountable. Ask whether the projects in question are independently selected and verified, what proof there is of the stated environmental benefits, what guarantee there is that every tonne of CO_2 claimed is offset and whether the company has a policy of annual auditing and verification.

If you want real responsibility for getting the job done, you could always do it yourself. This isn't a budget option: the author of *How to Live a Low-Carbon Life*, Chris Goodall, estimates the cost of establishing 1,000 saplings at £2,770, working on the assumption that an acre of broadleaf trees will capture up to 2.6 tonnes of CO_2 a year.

Table 1: Guilt trips: How the major UK carbon offset schemes stack up

Provider	Website	Non-profit?	What it invests in	What you can offset	Gold Standard projects?	Calculations for a typical round-trip transatlantic flight (London to New York)	
						Tonnes	Offset Cost
Climate Care	www.climatecare.org	No	Forestry, Renewable Energy, Energy Efficiency, Certified Emissions Reduction, Voluntary Emissions Reduction	Flying, Driving, Household	Pending	1.54	£11.55
Carbon Neutral Company	www.carbonneutral.com	No	Forestry, Renewable Energy, Energy Efficiency, Certified Emissions Reduction, Voluntary Emissions Reduction	Flying, Driving, Household	Pending	1.2	£12.99
World Land Trust	www.carbonbalanced.org	Yes	Forestry	Household, Flying, Driving, Train, Boat	Forestry not covered by the scheme	1.22	£11.91
Carbon Clear	www.carbon-clear.com	No	Reforestation, Renewables, Energy Efficiency, Certified Emissions Reduction, Voluntary Emissions Reduction	Driving, Flying, Household, Nappies	Pending	1.5	£11.25
Pure Trust	www.puretrust.org.uk	Yes	Renewable Energy, Energy Efficiency, Certified Emissions Reduction	Household, Road, Flights	Some	1.5	£15.43
CO2 Balance	www.co2balance.com	No	Forestry, Energy Efficiency, Certified Emissions Reduction, Voluntary Emissions Reduction	Household, Several types of transport	No	1.22	£11
Carbon Offsets	www.carbon-offsets.com	No	Forestry, Renewable Energy, Energy Efficiency, Certified Emissions Reduction, Voluntary Emissions Reduction, EU Allowances	Flying, Driving, Ship, Train, Household	Pending	1.17	£8.22

Most of us don't have a spare acre of land or the time to care for 1,000 saplings, though. A more realistic alternative to paying offsetting companies might be to make individual charitable donations to worthwhile environmental projects such as Trees for Life, a Scottish charity trying to restore the native Caledonian forest, which also offers volunteering placements. Or to join a local Carbon Rationing Action Group. A bit like a low-carbon answer to Weight Watchers, these groups work towards an agreed reduction in personal emissions, and pay for any excesses (each group then decides where the money goes).

HOW TO MINIMISE THE IMPACT OF FLYING

- Airlines with younger fleets tend to be more fuel-efficient than older ones (you can compare companies on the Air Fleets website). Unfortunately, many of these also happen to be no-frills operators running an increasing number of short-haul flights

- Choose direct flights, rather than those with stopovers, since a high percentage of fuel is burnt during take-off and landing

- Some experts suggest avoiding night and winter flights altogether, although you would need super-powers to be able to do this when crossing different time zones and travelling from one hemisphere to the other. While a plane will emit the same amount of carbon whatever time of day or year you travel, a study published in 2006 by the Meteorology Department at the University of Reading suggested that the warming effect of a flight's contrails is increased at night because they trap heat from the earth but don't reflect radiation back into space as they do during the day. Because planes produce more contrails in cold temperatures and high humidity, the study also found that flights between December and February, during the Northern hemisphere's winter months, are responsible for half of the aviation industry's average climate warming effect, even though they account for less than a quarter of annual air traffic

- Be waste aware in the air. *Trash Landings*, a 2006 study by the Natural Resources Defense Council (NRDC) in the States, reported that: 'the U.S. airline industry discards enough aluminum cans each year to build 58 Boeing 747 airplanes. And aluminum waste is just the tip of the iceberg: the airline industry discarded 9,000 tons of plastic in 2004 and enough newspapers and magazines to fill a football field to a depth of more than 230 feet.' It went on to say that most of this waste is currently sent to landfills and incinerators, rather than recycled

- Consider voluntarily offsetting your journey's carbon emissions through a reputable scheme

- Think about buying flights through North South Travel, a travel agent whose profits are given to charitable projects in developing countries. Set up in 1967 by Terence Khushal Singh, a former Director of the Indian Tourist Office in London, it aims both to provide competitive fares for travellers and generate funds for worthy causes

The end of the road?

Flying isn't the only carbon culprit. Despite congestion, high petrol prices, the threat of road accidents and an ever-smaller chance of finding space to park, more of us than ever are travelling by car. According to the Department for Transport, the average Briton now drives around 8,400 miles a year. That's around 1,000 miles less than the average annual mileage a decade ago, not because we are driving less, but because there are more cars on the road making shorter journeys (the proportion of households without access to a car fell from 38 per cent in 1985 to 25 per cent in 2005 while the proportion with two or more cars rose from 17 per cent in 1985 to 32 per cent in 2005). In total vehicles now contribute around a fifth of the UK's current greenhouse gas emissions.

Most of this car use takes place as short everyday journeys – the 2005 National Travel Survey found that nearly a quarter of all car trips are shorter than two miles in length – but plenty of us also set off on holiday in our own vehicle, lured by the freedom of the open road and a free rein on luggage.

Emissions per passenger mile are roughly the same for cars and planes. According to Airport Watch, 'as a rough approximation, flying has the same climate changing effect as each passenger in the plane driving their own (smallish) car the same distance'. However, we don't tend to drive the same distances as we fly – it's not often that you see a car with British number plates in Sydney or Shanghai – and emissions from cars aren't released high up in the atmosphere where they can do the most harm. While a lack of filling stations and poor long-distance range are holding back otherwise significant developments in alternative fuel-powered cars, a future of low or zero carbon driving is less of a pipe dream than it is for aviation.

If you want to lessen the impact of your driving in the meantime, one of the best sources of information is the Environmental Transport Association. As well as campaigning for greener motoring, its website has a useful news section, outlining developments in sustainable transport. The organisation also sells alternative breakdown cover, handy for those who take ideological exception to the AA and the RAC, with their history of lobbying for road expansion.

Pimp my ride

Better still, leave the car at home, travel to your destination by public transport and, if you need a set of wheels at the other end, hire them. Hertz recently launched a 'green collection' of its more environmentally friendly cars, available at

50 of its outlets in Europe. According to the publicity, they all do 40–65mpg and meet the EU's 2008 voluntary target of a maximum average CO_2 output of 140g/km. City slickers can hire even more environmentally friendly electric cars in London through Future Vehicles.

The down-to-earth City Car Club is another sensible idea for occasional car users. While its vehicles aren't all low-emission ones (it currently has 30 new hybrids on order), the concept wins serious greenie points for encouraging people to cut down on road time. If you're a regular visitor to one of the cities the scheme covers (currently London, Edinburgh, Bath, Brighton, Bristol, High Wycombe, Norwich, Poole, Portsmouth or Reading) and you only need a car on odd days, you can pay the club a one-off joining fee of £75 and then pay as you go, rather than having to hire a car for the whole day. Prices start from a reasonable £3.60 per hour. Similar car clubs, such as London's Zipcar are appearing all the time, so it's worth checking local websites for the latest in your area.

Car sharing runs along similar lines. Designed to help cut down on the number of cars travelling around with only one person in them, it's a bit like organised hitching. Usually free to use, you register online and are then put in touch with people who are driving the route you want to cover. Passengers share the cost of the journey with the driver.

Companies offering national and international schemes include IsAnyoneGoingTo, Liftshare, Lift Pool, My Lifts, Share A Car and Compartir. The website of Car Plus, a UK charity promoting responsible car use, includes a long list of other schemes. For security, make sure that whichever scheme you use offers some way of checking that drivers and passengers are genuine. Most provide guidelines on this to members.

While every city worth its salt now seems to have a plan to convert its taxi fleet to alternative fuels, specialist green taxi and chauffeur firms have also been popping up faster than you can say 'Follow that car'. These include: PlanetTran in the US, which serves New England and California with a fleet of hybrid vehicles; Eco Limo, which does roughly the same in Melbourne, Australia; and Bio Beetle, which rents out VW Beetles converted to run on biodiesel in Hawaii and LA.

In the UK, Green Tomato Cars, Climate Cars and Ecoigo both offer similar services in London. The latter styles itself as a more decadent green motoring experience; as well as offsetting emissions and using the obligatory hybrid vehicles, it offers customers Belu water in biodegradable bottles and copies of *New Consumer* magazine to enjoy during the ride. CNG-fuelled tuk-tuks are also providing a (slightly slower) alternative to mainstream taxis in some UK cities, as well as further afield.

LOWER CARBON DRIVING

Check your tyres Under-inflated tyres create resistance when your car is moving, which means your engine has to work harder, so more fuel is used and more CO_2 emissions are produced. Check and adjust your tyre pressure regularly, especially before long journeys; driving with the correct pressure can cut 10 per cent off your fuel use. Strike a balance, though, as over-inflated tyres can be dangerous.

Ditch the clutter Extra weight means your engine has to work harder, burning more fuel and increasing CO_2 emissions, so unload any unnecessary detritus from your boot before you set out. It's estimated that you lose 1 or 2 per cent in efficiency for every extra 50kg. Likewise, remove roof racks, bike carriers and roof boxes when not in use.

Woah there Staying at, or within, the speed limit is not only safer, it is more economical. At 70mph you could be using up to 9 per cent more fuel than at 60mph and up to 15 per cent more fuel than at 50mph. Most cars attain maximum efficiency between 30 and 55mph.

Keep it smooth Stopping and starting means the engine will be using more fuel and therefore producing more CO_2. If the traffic ahead looks like it's coming to a standstill, ease off the accelerator and try to time it so that the traffic in front may have started moving again by the time you reach it.

Don't be a boy or girl racer Modern car engines are designed to be efficient as soon as they are switched on, so there's no need to rev up, Grand Prix style, when cruising the local high street. It will only waste fuel. Instead change up before the counter reaches 2,500rpm (petrol) and 2,000rpm (diesel).

Don't idle When the engine is idling you're wasting fuel and adding to CO_2 emissions. If you're at a standstill for more than two minutes, switch off the engine and restart it when the traffic moves.

Keep a natural cool Running air-con reduces a car's efficiency, but then so does the drag caused by open windows. If it's not unbearable, switch off the air-con and use the vents and fan.

Don't drip and drive When you're re-fuelling, avoid overfilling the tank. Spilt fuel evaporates and releases emissions.

Consider offsetting your emissions Some car insurance companies now offer quotes with offsets included, but shop around to make sure you – and the planet – wouldn't be better off buying each part of the package separately.

LA-based Evo Limo goes one step further in the bling stakes. Its fleet of SUVs has been converted to run on CNG. All seat six and come with professional drivers and (presumably not very eco-friendly) mini bars and DVD players. If you really wanted to cut down on emissions, it would be better to pull up and party off road, of course.

It's a similar story with the Hitchsters website, which pairs people up to share taxi rides to and from airports in New York and Boston. Though it might marginally cut down on road use, a service which only covers routes to airports – and which you could do by public transport anyway – is never going to be way up on the green scale.

On the buses

According to George Monbiot, if the average car user travelling on the M25 were to travel by coach instead, it would increase the road's total capacity from 19,000 to 260,000 people and reduce carbon emissions per passenger mile by an average of 88 per cent.

This is a powerful argument for switching to public transport where possible. If these vehicles were powered by alternative fuels (trials of buses run on hydrogen fuel cells and electricity have already been successfully carried out in several cities), coach travel would be an even greener form of transport. And, while it may not be as comfortable, or as fast, as other forms of transport, going by coach is usually cheaper.

For journeys within the UK, National Express operates the largest coach network, while Megabus runs a growing network of super-cheap intercity services (if you're heading abroad, it also now operates in the US). Other coach companies include Scottish Citylink north of the border and Ulsterbus in Northern Ireland.

Further afield, the biggest long-distance coach operator in Europe is Eurolines, which is owned by National Express. Eurolines runs a network of routes linking around five hundred European destinations, from Amsterdam to Zurich and across the Med to Morocco. Adult fares from London to Amsterdam, a journey of around ten to twelve hours, currently start from £30 return, including ferry crossings.

The company also runs popular services to various French ski resorts in winter and sells Eurolines Passes. These run for either fifteen or thirty days and start from £115 for under-26s or £135 for adults for the fifteen-day version. You can buy these online at the Eurolines website, although, to buy standard single or return journeys online, you will be redirected to the 'Europe' page of the National Express website.

A useful service for anyone planning a cycling trip within Europe who doesn't want to pedal all the way to their starting point, is the European Bike Express. This will shuttle you and your bike by coach (with a special bike trailer) from various pick-up points in the UK and take you to drop-off spots in France or Spain, before picking you up again on a specified date. Return trips start from £192.

KEEP ON TRUCKING

'Overlanding neatly puts into perspective the classic debate of how you can square the environmental consequences of your visit with the social benefits it might bring.

'Trips normally last for anything from a couple of weeks to nine months. That's hardly doing the planet a favour – according to carbon footprint consultants Best Foot Forward, a typical purpose-built truck carrying up to 20 passengers on a 28-day trip from Nairobi to Victoria Falls emits about 3.5 tonnes of carbon dioxide. Most trips also start in the host country, so you have to fly to get there before you do anything. But travelling this way can also bring benefits to poor areas in developing countries, generating income for remote villages, which wouldn't otherwise see tourists.

'Trying to weigh up these issues is a bit like comparing apples to pears. How do you compare two such different things? Travellers have to make these kinds of decision all the time. It usually comes down to how the tour is managed. If you go with a company that has been operating in an area for a long time and has well-established local links, the chances are that your trip will be beneficial. Two of the best-known overland tour companies – Guerba, in Africa, and Dragoman Overland in South America – have strong responsible tourism credentials.

'What does that mean? It means that both companies employ local guides, local mechanics and parts suppliers and spend money at locally owned hotels, homestays and campsites. They also support long-term community projects which tourists can get involved in during their trip. You can have a great time travelling but it's also good to get out into the local community and put something back.'

Richard Hammond runs the Green Traveller website, which gives advice on how to have greener holidays.

THE WORLD'S GREATEST ROAD TRIP?

After the US invasion of Afghanistan, the Asia Overland 'hippie' trail – the greatest journey of the 1960s and 1970s – was reopened for the first time in a generation. In 2003, author Rory Maclean spent five months following the classic route through Turkey, Iran, Afghanistan, Pakistan, India and Nepal by bus and train. He 'saw an opportunity not only to capture the spirit and stories of those heady years, and to compare youthful idealism then and now, but to understand why the Sixties cast such long shadows over our own fearful and protective era'.

Things weren't quite as they had been thirty years earlier. In an article for *Resurgence* magazine, Maclean said that 'in Cappadocia, where hippies once dreamed of the dawning of a new age, everyone was sending text messages home. In Isfahan, the former Persian capital and the most splendidly proportioned city in the world, every second tourist planned to write a travel article after their holiday. In the shattered remains of the Kabul Museum, I found an overworked guide-book writer. Most revealing of all, virtually every one of the global nomads I met had reached their destination by air.'

Yet, from a practical perspective, Rory's journey hadn't been difficult at all. 'Those countries are not as wealthy as ours, so people are more reliant on ground transportation. The buses are all very modern and easy, and it's the best way to travel because you're travelling with local people and getting to know the country through them. In the 1960s and '70s, the vehicles were neither as regular, or as comfortable, and there were many more Western buses and cars making the journey. But then, before the oil crisis, people had much more time. For all the luxuries we have today, we don't have that.'

He concluded that we have much to learn from those who followed the original trail. 'Like them, we need to favour ground travel, to limit our flights, to stay longer in a single spot rather than dart between scattered destinations. Above all we need to learn to move away from our culture of immediate gratification and choose trips where we can value the journey as much as the destination. Getting there should again become part of the adventure, galvanising us to live in the moment or – in the Sixties' imperative – to Be Here Now.'

Rory Maclean's book, Magic Bus: On the Hippie Trail from Istanbul to India *is published by Penguin (www.magicbus.info).*

There are also numerous private hop-on, hop-off bus companies operating across Europe, mainly for the use of backpackers. While standard public transport is almost certainly a more responsible way to get around, some of these services can be a useful way of reaching more off-beat destinations. Ze Bus, for example, runs twice a week from June to October between a network of towns, tourist attractions, music festivals and surfing spots in the west of France.

For more inspiration on coach trips, the websites No Fly Travel and Eco Friendly Tourist both give some listing information on routes and ticketing companies for coach and other forms of surface transport.

How low can you go?

Comparing emissions for different forms of transport is difficult to do accurately since the data tends to vary according to how many people are travelling in each form of transport, the exact length of the journey, the age and type of vehicle (diesel trains are more polluting than electric ones, for instance, and hybrid cars are less polluting than standard models), the speed travelled at and so on.

However, the figures below, which are based on the carbon calculators from offsetting website CO_2 Balance, give a fairly clear representation of how transport emissions stack up:

Journey	Kilometres	CO_2 emissions by plane (tonnes)	CO_2 emissions by car (tonnes)	CO_2 emissions by LPG car (tonnes)	CO_2 emissions by train (tonnes)
Southampton to Inverness	947	0.11	0.18	0.17	0.04

On the right track

The message this table gives is pretty clear: where possible, let the train take the strain. Because train journeys generally take a lot longer than planes, they're not always going to be a practical alternative to flying, but they are a feasible lower-carbon substitute to some car trips and short-haul flights. Many modern trains now run on electricity and, in June 2007 Europe's first biodiesel train, operated by Virgin Trains, set out on a successful trial trip from London Euston to Llandudno in north Wales.

Train travel may not seem such an attractive option in an era when the British railway system seems to be overstretched and struggling with old technology, a lack of high-speed lines and the legacy of Dr Beeching's track closures. But a 2006 report by the Tyndall Centre for Climate Change Research predicted that the British rail network will grow by 25 per cent by 2030, with capacity boosted by the introduction of double-decker trains.

The popularity of train travel in much of the rest of Europe, however, is already steaming ahead. Speed across France or Germany by train and it's rare that you will get stuck in a traffic jam, be held up by rigorous security screening or have to scramble for a seat.

Travelling by rail also allows you to go straight from city centre to centre, avoiding time and money spent getting out to airports. It can be a creative exercise: J K Rowling thought up the idea for the *Harry Potter* books while on a train between Manchester and London, and Alexander McCall Smith regularly writes on trains to and from his home in Edinburgh. If you're taking time out to travel further, you won't have jet lag to contend with, either – or that Lost In Translation feeling you get when a plane tips you, blinking, into a new destination.

Railways are also the most romantic way to get from A to B, C or Z. Would the classic Inter-Railer's call to arms, the film *Before Sunrise*, have been quite so poignant if it had been set onboard a Ryanair flight to Frankfurt Hahn?

Channel hopping

Anyone starting their journey in the UK will now find crossing the Channel easier with the launch of Eurostar services from St Pancras International along the UK's first high-speed line. A 2006 report into air and rail competition prepared for the European Commission found that 68 per cent of people travelling between London and Paris already choose to travel by rail. That figure may increase as the new line from St Pancras cuts journey times from London to Paris, Lille and Brussels – and, in summer, Avignon – by an average of 24 minutes on each route. This gives new average times of 111 minutes to Brussels and 2 hours, 15 minutes to Paris – much less than the journey would take if you took travelling to the airport and check-in times into account.

This line is the second and last stage of the Channel Tunnel Rail Link and includes the opening of a new station at Ebbsfleet, just off the M25 in Kent. This is designed to soak up most of the 'stopping' trains that currently serve Ashford International, leaving the latter with just three daily trains to Paris and one to Disneyland Paris. Fares start from £55 return from London to Calais.

As well as opening up traditional destinations, this fast track also means British skiers will be able to head to slopes in the Alps more easily by rail, cutting times on winter 'snow train' routes to Moutiers, Aime La Plagne and Bourg St Maurice. Return fares on these routes start from £179.

Life in the fast lane

There have been other dramatic new developments in rail services across the Channel, also. Transport expert Christian Wolmar neatly described how the introduction of the Train à Grande Vitesse (TGV) revolutionised train travel in France, stating that 'the high-speed train service has destroyed much of the domestic aviation market and stimulated the economic development of those regions lucky enough to be served by these elegant trains which have become a symbol of modern France, far more potent than Gauloises or Ricard.'

French rail operators have continued to build on that success. The latest high-speed rail link, the Paris to Stuttgart TGV Est, opened in June 2007 with typical French panache: the new TGV carriages are designed by French fashion designer Christian Lacroix and incorporate adjustable tables, reclining seats, electric power outlets, individual reading lights and the kind of lively colour palette you might normally associate with a poolside cocktail. There are also designated cycle spaces, flexible family areas featuring built-in board games, and office areas with wi-fi.

While not quite the fastest train in the world (that honour is currently held by a Japanese magnetic levitation train, or Maglev, which reached 581km/h in 2003), the TGV holds the record as the fastest train on conventional rails, having reached 574.8km/h on a run in April 2007 (though its normal passenger services run at a more leisurely maximum of 320km/h).

According to the French Tourist Board, passenger levels between Paris and eastern France will increase by 65 per cent as a result of these new services, 'with half of this increase expected to come from passengers choosing the train in preference to flying'. In the long term, the train operator expects an estimated 11.5 million passengers to travel on the high-speed line each year.

Go east

One reason for this increase in numbers is the fact that the TGV Est links in with other super-fast services, cutting journey times not just across France but across the whole of Europe. If you want to travel from Paris to Luxembourg it will now take only 125 minutes, from Paris to Frankfurt, 3 hours 50 minutes and from Paris to Zurich 4 hours 35 minutes.

Other improvements in the European rail network include the opening of sections of high-speed line between Brussels and Amsterdam, the opening of a tunnel between Frutigen and Raron in Switzerland, which will cut an hour off the journey between Basel and Milan, new high-speed trains between Moscow and St Petersburg and new routes across the Pyrenees to Barcelona and between Milan and Naples. New high-speed lines have also recently come into service in Germany and Spain.

The launch of Railteam in summer 2007 has also made travelling around the continent much simpler. A collaboration between the main high-speed train companies operating in Europe – German, Austrian, Belgian, Dutch, Swiss and French – it is a similar concept to airline alliances. Ticket rates and services are harmonised, passenger loyalty schemes have been combined and, if you miss your train, it is much easier to get a subsequent one.

Ticket to ride

One great source of information if you want to plan a rail journey is the Seat 61 website, run by rail industry expert Mark Smith, who 'ran away from Oxford to join the circus (or British Rail as it was then called) as soon as he could'. This free-to-use website is a one-stop source of information about how to get from place to place, worldwide, by train and by ship. Smith, who runs the site as a hobby, named it after his favourite, first class, Eurostar seat – one of a pair of individual seats with a table that lines up with the window. In 2006 the website won the Best Personal Contribution category in the First Choice Responsible Tourism Awards and, in 2007, it was voted top travel website by readers of *Wanderlust* magazine.

'Travelling by train from London to Europe is really easy, but finding out about it can be frustratingly difficult,' says Smith. 'Most travel agents only sell flights and packages. Eurostar concentrates on getting you only as far as Paris or Brussels. Even the specialist agencies that sell European train tickets tell you to "contact them for details" and would rather sell you a railpass than get you from A to B. No-one provided basic train times, fares and "how to" information for train journeys from the UK to Italy, Spain, Switzerland, Greece, Russia and so on, let alone how to reach Morocco, Tunisia, Ibiza, Corsica, Crete or Malta by combining train and ship. I thought it was a gap that needed filling, and that I could easily fill it myself.'

Which is exactly what he has done. Whether you want to find out how to get the best deals on a sleeper to Fort William or track down the fastest route from London to Istanbul overland, it's all on the website. The one thing you can't do at Seat 61 is buy the actual tickets, though the website does tell you where you can.

If you're planning on doing a lot of travelling by train it is worth investing in the *Thomas Cook European Rail Timetable* or the *Thomas Cook Overseas Rail Timetable*, which covers the rest of the world. Updated monthly and bi-monthly respectively, they are published by Thomas Cook Publishing and cost £11.50 each.

Ticket agencies for the most popular routes include Rail Europe, for journeys to France, Spain, Italy or Switzerland, German Railways (Deutsche Bahn) for Germany, Austria, Scandinavia and Eastern Europe, Irish Rail for Ireland and Trainseurope for intra-European routes. Further afield, Rail Australia, Amtrak (for the US), Via Rail (for Canada), International Rail (for Australia, North America and Japan) and Tranzscenic (for New Zealand) are useful.

Off the rails

If you want to take your own car but to cover part of the journey by train. From the UK, Eurotunnel lets you put your car on a train to go under the Channel from Dover to Calais. It runs up to four services per hour and standard fares for the 35-minute journey start at £49 each way.

To travel further into Europe, Motorail services currently include: Calais to the South of France; Denderleeuw, near Brussels, to Bologna and Alessandria in Italy; and several routes within Germany and Austria. Weekly Motorail trains also run from Dortmund and Frankfurt in Germany to Rijeka in Croatia.

Tickets for French Motorail services can be booked through Rail Europe, while specialist Motorail agency Rail Savers covers services in most European countries. German-based Optima Tours also sells Motorail train tickets from Villach, in southern Austria, to Bulgaria, Macedonia, Turkey and Greece.

This can be a useful way of covering ground quickly but it is no clean, green option. What you are essentially doing is using a diesel engine to transport a huge train loaded with cars. It would create far fewer emissions if you were to travel on a standard train and hire a car at your destination or, in some cases, even to fly.

Inter-Railing

When Inter-Railing began, 35 years ago, £32 bought a month's unlimited train travel in Europe. If you wanted to do a whistle-stop tour of Europe's great cities, hopping on and off as the urge took you, there was no better way to do it.

TRAINSPOTTING

Mark Smith, the Man in Seat 61, chooses five great rail journeys:

Auckland to Wellington, New Zealand
'This is an epic journey through the country's North Island that will leave you understanding why Peter Jackson, the director of *Lord of the Rings*, chose to set the film in New Zealand. In fact he has said that it was on board an Auckland to Wellington train, as an 18-year-old that he read Tolkien for the first time, and realised how like Tolkien's Middle Earth the New Zealand landscape is. It's also a very historic railway. It was built in 1908 and incorporates some great feats of engineering such as the Raurimu Spiral – actually a couple of hairpin bends, a couple of loops and two tunnels – and the Makatote Viaduct, a huge steel structure 860 feet long and 258 feet high.'
Distance: 601km　**Time:** 12 hours　**Price:** from around £32
Where to book: www.tranzscenic.co.nz

New York – Chicago – San Francisco
'Take the Lake Shore Limited from New York to Chicago and then the California Zephyr from Chicago to San Francisco and you get to enjoy some superb scenery. Highlights for me included going out from New York along the Hudson River, looking out across the Rocky Mountains over breakfast in the dining car and passing through the Sierra Nevada – it's the area where the Donner family, stranded en route to California in late 1846, infamously turned to cannibalism when their food ran out.'
Distance: 5,467km　**Time:** 3 nights　**Price:** from around £75
Where to book: www.amtrak.com

London to Fort William
'The Caledonian Sleeper takes you from rainy central London at night and deposits you in the Highlands the following morning, surrounded by mountains, streams and woods. It's the most civilised, romantic, time-effective and environmentally friendly way to get from central London to the heart of Scotland, and the train feels like a hotel.'
Distance: around 820km　**Time:** 12 hours, 40 minutes　**Price:** from £38
Where to book: call ScotRail (0845 755 0033)

Moscow to Beijing via Mongolia
'This epic, seven-day journey on the Trans-Mongolian and Trans-Siberian railways crosses Siberia, the Gobi desert and mountains in China. It's not as long as the Moscow to Vladivostok Trans-Siberian route but it's more interesting – because of both the people and the scenery. What do you do on a train for seven days? You put your feet up and relax.'
Distance: 7,622km　**Time:** 7 days　**Price:** from around £160
Where to book: www.waytorussia.net

Sydney to Perth on the Indian Pacific
'This is a Cruiseliner train, run by a private company called Great Southern Railway. From Sydney it takes you across the Blue Mountains and the arid country around Broken Hill to Adelaide, then across the hot, dusty, emptiness of the Nullarbor Plain, on the longest stretch of straight railway line in the world. Nullarbor is Latin for "no trees" and it's a place where you really understand what nothing means.'
Distance: 4,343km　**Time:** 4 days　**Price:** from around £290
Where to book: www.gsr.com.au

The rise of budget airlines in Europe and a drop in the price of long-haul fares have done their best to push Inter-Railing off the must-do lists of modern-day gap year students and backpackers. But concerns about the environment and improvements in European rail services are helping to boost the popularity of the concept again. So, too, is a simplification of the system. Gone are the old zones. In their place, passengers can now buy either a single-country pass or a global pass, which covers all participating countries. Passes can be bought from between three days and one month and first-class passes have also been introduced. Prices for a global Flexipass, which gives 5 days travel within a 10-day period, start at £117 for youths (12 to 25s), £182 for adults or £241 for a first-class pass. Half-price passes are available for children from four to eleven.

In the UK, these can be booked through agencies such as Railchoice. These agencies also sell other multi-country passes, including the ScanRail pass, which covers Denmark, Sweden, Norway and Finland, and the Balkan Flexipass, which binds together a Eurovision-like medley of Greece, Bulgaria, Turkey, Serbia, Macedonia and Montenegro. Rail passes for North America, Japan and Australasia are also available.

The important thing to work out before you buy is how many journeys you're planning to take. If you're only planning a couple of journeys it's probably not worth the money, so make sure you have a rough itinerary sketched out first and compare booking individual fares against buying a pass. When you're doing the sums, bear in mind that, even with a rail pass, you may have to pay a supplement to travel on popular high-speed trains.

Testing the water

Despite competition from the likes of Eurotunnel, Eurostar and budget airlines, as well as the loss of duty free revenue, ferries from the UK are still going strong. Statistics from the Passenger Shipping Association showed that 35.9 million journeys were taken between British ports and the Continent, Ireland and British islands in 2006, a rise of 400,000 over the previous year.

That's not a complete surprise. Many companies have simplified their pricing in line with the budget airlines: the earlier you book the better the fare. Ferry tickets have also become simpler to understand and more flexible. Luggage restrictions are fairly loose and check-in is a lot less hassle than at airports.

BAGGING THE CHEAP SEATS

How to get a good deal on rail travel no matter where you're going, according to Mark Smith, the Man in Seat 61:

1. **Generally it's better to buy online than over the phone.** If you call up you'll be charged a booking fee.

2. **Try to buy directly from the relevant train company,** so from www.renfe.es for journeys in Spain or from www.voyages-sncf.com for journeys in France, Spain or Italy. Rail agencies have no incentive to sell you the cheapest ticket, so you may get flogged more expensive fares. Having said that, there are all sorts of quirks; if you're buying through www.voyages-sncf.com, read the instructions at www.seat61.com before you buy to avoid some of the common pitfalls.

3. **Break the journey down into two parts.** If you search for the best fares on journeys between London and Rome you can be quoted some crazy prices if you type it in as one trip through www.voyages-sncf.com. Instead book London to Paris with www.eurostar.co.uk and then Paris to Italy with www.voyages-sncf.com. Another reason why this makes sense is that it allows you to be much more in control of your journey. If you want to, you can travel 2nd class on Eurostar and 1st class on the second leg. It also means that you can stop off in Paris between trains.

4. **If you book in advance you can get some amazing deals,** such as Paris to Madrid or Barcelona for €67 in a four-bed sleeper, or Paris to Rome, Florence or Venice for €35 in a six-bunk couchette. Booking normally opens 90 days before departure and fares go up the closer it gets to the departure date. You don't have to be paranoid about buying tickets literally as soon as booking opens, though. Most companies operate a binary system where fares are cheap until 14 days before departure and then suddenly jump up.

5. **Don't be put off by what might seem to be higher train fares compared to budget flights.** Be realistic about the costs of air travel – counting in taxes, getting to and from the airport and possibly having to book a hotel in order to catch an early morning flight – and trains might seem more reasonable than you thought. After all, you can get from London to Paris for £59 and from Paris to Madrid by sleeper for £48.

On board ship, meanwhile, investment has seen standards improve. Many ferries are now more like cruise ships than sea-buses, with airport-style executive lounges, extensive shops, surprisingly good restaurants and lavish entertainment facilities. Stormy weather aside, they're also one of the most relaxing ways to travel. Book yourself a cabin on a long crossing and you can lull yourself to sleep with the waves or go for a stroll out on deck when you feel the need for some air. The fact that mobile phone reception can be sketchy – or prohibitively expensive – means it's also easier to switch off onboard ship.

But how green are ferries? According to the offsetting website, co2Balance.com, one person's Newcastle–Amsterdam return flight emits 0.36 tonnes of carbon dioxide, whereas an entire Newcastle–Ijmuiden ferry crossing is responsible for only 51kg (0.5 tonnes) of CO_2.

Making waves

From the UK, boats will take you to: Bergen, Haugesund and Stavanger in Norway; Esbjerg in Denmark; Ijmuiden, Hook of Holland and Rotterdam in Holland; Zeebrugge and Ostende in Belgium; Dunkerque, Calais, Boulogne, Dieppe, Le Havre, Caen, Cherbourg, St Malo and Roscoff in France; Bilbao and Santander in Spain; Dublin, Dun Laoghaire, Rosslare and Cork in Ireland and, via the Shetlands, to Iceland (a list of which company goes where is included in the Little Green Book section).

Once you're on the Continent a whole new world of ferry, jet-boat and hydrofoil-hopping opens up. From Norway you can get to Sweden, Denmark and on to Germany, Finland and Estonia. From Spain ferries operate to Italy, the Balearics, Morocco and the Canaries. From Italy, you can get to a dizzying number of destinations by boat, including Tunisia, Spain, France, Sicily, Greece, Croatia. Albania and Malta. Passenger ferries from Morocco to the Canary Islands have also recently launched, while Greek island-hopping is as popular as ever – the *Guide to Greek Island Hopping* by Frewin Poffley is a good place to start working out where to go.

While most of the relevant ferry companies offer direct booking services, it's also possible to buy tickets through specialist agencies such as A Ferry To, Ferry Savers, Cheap4Ferries, All Ferries and Ferry Booker. Try to cross-check fares before going ahead to avoid paying over the odds.

If you're planning to travel as a foot passenger by rail and ferry, combination tickets may be cheaper than booking the train and boat parts of the journey separately. Companies offering these kinds of packages include Sail Rail, which offers all-in passenger fares on various UK–Irish crossings, and Dutch Flyer, which does the same for UK–Holland trips.

Taking the slow boat

Sometimes buses and trains will only get you so far. To cross the Atlantic, or any other large ocean, without flying, you'll need to either join a cruise or go by cargo ship. Neither can compete with air travel in terms of journey time. And, although both normally include food and comfortable cabins as part of the package, neither is cheap. A six-night transatlantic trip on the Queen Mary 2 starts at £899, while cargo ship passengers will pay around £70 per day for a crossing of at least 10 days. Double those fares if you want to travel home the same way.

Cruising is growing in popularity. The UK is the second largest cruise market outside the States, and the Passenger Shipping Association calculates that 1.2 million Britons holidayed on cruise ships in 2006, a 12 per cent rise on 2005. As a means of trans-continental transport, however, the routes covered by cruise ships are limited. Neither is the prospect of Love Boat-style entertainment and dinner at the Captain's table for everyone.

Cargo ships are always going to be a niche form of transport, although, according to specialist booking agencies – which include the Cruise People, Freighter Travel and Strand Travel – increasing numbers of independent travellers are choosing to travel this way.

One appeal is the isolation – Alex Haley (the author of *Roots*) and actor Rupert Everett have both used cargo ships as a form of writers' retreat. However, an increasingly popular reason for travelling by cargo ship is the belief that it offers a green alternative to flying (leaving aside the fact that the length of the journey means that most cargo passengers only go by ship one way, opting to fly on the other leg). As cargo ships are travelling anyway, the thinking goes, the few passengers which each one carries can 'free ride' on the ship's emissions rather than directly contributing to them.

While this argument stands up to a point, shipping is certainly not a guilt-free way to travel. Recent research from BP and the Institute for Physics and Atmosphere in Germany suggests that annual CO_2 emissions from shipping contribute 5 per cent of the global total. This compares to a figure of 2–3 per cent for aviation. Despite the existence of MARPOL, an international convention established in 1983 to help minimise the environmental impact of vessels, ships still produce some 'traditional' pollution from the heavy fuel oil most of them use – including nitrates and sulphates – and contaminate the oceans by pumping out oil-contaminated bilge water, rubbish and sewage.

American environmental group the Bluewater Network claims that a typical cruise ship on a week-long voyage generates 'more than 50 tons of garbage, one million gallons of greywater (waste water from sinks, showers, galleys and laundry facilities), 210,000 gallons of sewage, and 35,000 gallons of oil-contaminated water' – which less-conscientious operators dump straight into the sea.

While ships are starting to address these concerns – partly because the environmental laws that govern them are getting tighter – cruising sometimes gets a bad press for other reasons. One concern is that cruise-goers fail to have a positive impact on the ports of call they visit. Those who stay longer in a destination and travel independently have more time to eat in local restaurants, use local guides and pay for rooms in local hotels whereas those on short, pre-booked, excursions tend to pump money back into the pockets of the tour operator rather than into the local economy.

Two wheels good

Cycling has the lowest impact of any form of transport other than walking. It also gives you the freedom to go wherever the spirit takes you. And you get a free workout while you're en route.

While packing a fold-up bike, or using services such as the European Bike Express, can help you cover serious ground, you don't have to pedal long-distance to enjoy a bike ride. As well as many standard rental outlets, city bike tours are a great, alternative way of seeing the sights in European cities – and beyond.

Bike tour operators currently include City Bike in Tallinn, Two Wheels Tours in Stockholm, the London Bicycle Tour Company, Urban Biking in Buenos Aires and Laid Back Bikes in Edinburgh, specialising in recumbent bikes. And, while not as environmentally friendly as cycling or walking, getting around the city by battery-powered Segway is at least a better alternative to using buses, cars and taxis. A list of Segway tours in cities ranging from Budapest to Sydney can be found on the Segway Guided Tours website.

PAY AS YOU PEDAL

Probably the most practical way for travellers to swap four wheels for two is to use a city bike-sharing scheme. These are normally cheaper, more easily sourced and more flexible than ordinary bicycle rentals. Some of the most popular ones are outlined below, but there are many others.

Vélib – Paris

Launched in July 2007, this scheme offers twenty thousand bikes for use on the streets and 370km of cycle paths around the French capital. The pale grey bikes have adjustable seats, big baskets and lights which come on as soon as you pedal. Available round the clock, they can be picked up from stations set around 300m apart. Rentable with a credit card, the first half-hour of each journey is free, then it's €1 for every half hour. Longer rentals cost €5 for a week or €29 for a year.

Bicing – Barcelona

Also recently launched (this time in March 2007), this scheme is run by Barcelona City Council, which aims to eventually have 3,000 red-and-white bikes for rent from 250 points around the city. The service is free for the first 30 minutes and €1 per subsequent half hour. A credit card subscription

costs €24 per year, or €1 per week, and includes a swipe card to unlock bikes. For subscribers, the first 30 minutes are free, with subsequent half hours charged at €0.30 (two hours is the maximum rental).

Call a Bike – Berlin, Cologne, Frankfurt, Stuttgart and Munich

In typical German style, this is one of the most high-tech bike-sharing schemes. Run by Deutsche Bahn, Germany's national rail service, each bike comes with an electronic lock. If the lock has a blinking green light, the bike is available and you can call the number displayed on the lock. This gives you a code which you enter to open the lock. When you've finished, you lock it up (to any fixed object near a main crossroads) and call the company to let them know you've returned it. The fees cost €0.07 per minute, up to €15 for 24 hours (you register first and the cost is then charged to your credit or debit card).

OYBike – London

Like its German counterpart, OYBike uses electronic locks that work with a phone registration system. The difference with this scheme is that you have to return the canary yellow bikes to OYBike docking stations rather than leaving them in any old bike park. There are plenty of them, though, and most are set close to tube stations, public buildings, key transport interchanges and car parks. The service is free for the first half hour, then £2 for the next half hour, up to a maximum charge of £8 for 24 hours.

City Bikes – Copenhagen

A bit like taking a security-equipped supermarket trolley, to rent a City Bike you put a DKK20 coin in a slot, use the bike for as long as you like, and then get your money refunded when you return the bike to one of 110 racks. The service only runs from May to November and the bikes are less high-tech than those offered by some of the other schemes, but then this is also one of the oldest, in operation since 1995.

Vélo'v – Lyon

To use Lyon's Vélo'v service, you insert a credit card into one of 150 special bike racks around the city. This releases one of its shiny red bikes (like most other schemes, your card is charged if you run off with the bike). A microchip in the bike registers when each bike is taken from a rack, and when it's returned. Cleverly, every time a bike is parked in a rack, its tyre pressure, lights, brakes and gears are also tested. Those with problems are blocked from rental. The first half hour is free, then prices start from €0.50 per hour.

CHAPTER TWO
STAYING THERE

Checking in

How you get to your destination is the most environmentally significant factor of any trip, because of the impact it can have on carbon emissions. But there's more to being a responsible traveller than choosing the right transport. Where you stay when you get there is also important.

Most of us don't change our sheets or towels every day at home, yet we often expect those services when we stay at a hotel. This has a knock-on effect on resources. So, too, does using hotel TVs, DVD players, minibars, swimming pools, gyms and other amenities. There are also more general environmental running costs to be taken into consideration. Our determination to get value for money means we are often more generous with lighting, heating and water use when we travel than we are at home.

The ecological cost of a hotel or resort's building work should also be taken into account, especially if the local area is of special environmental importance. In St Lucia, for example, much controversy was caused when Hilton built the Jalousie Resort and Spa between the island's famous Piton peaks in the early 1990s. An environmental impact study had recommended against the construction of the development and campaigners (including poet and playwright Derek Walcott) had hoped the area would be established as a national park.

And, while the developers behind Palm Jumeirah, a palm-shaped cluster of artificial islands off the coast of Dubai, insist that their development is attracting new marine life, environmentalists have expressed concern that the islands have buried coral reefs, disrupted the natural habitats of fish and sea turtles and, by re-routing currents, are contributing to the erosion of Dubai's beaches.

In an article in the *Salt Lake Tribune* in 2005, Frederic Launay, the director of WWF's Abu Dhabi office, summed the problem up when he stated: 'If you build stretches of five-star hotels with landscaped gardens, you're transforming a wild environment into an urban environment. There will be different species. It's an artificial system.'

Human rights

But choosing a responsible hotel isn't just about birds and bees. People matter too. Tourism Concern, a British-based charity which fights exploitation in tourism, is currently running a campaign called 'Sun, Sand, Sea and Sweatshops' which highlights the issue of poor working conditions in the tourist industry.

'While we relax in the sunshine around the world, life is far from paradise for the waiters, cleaners, cooks, porters, drivers, receptionists and other staff working to make our holidays happy and carefree. Working conditions in the tourism industry are notoriously exploitative,' the organisation states.

Holidays From Hell, a 2004 study by Guyonne James, programme manager at Tourism Concern, compared conditions at five popular holiday destinations – Bali, Mexico, the Dominican Republic, Egypt and the Canary Islands – and found exploitative labour conditions at all of them. These included 'over-dependency on tips, long working hours, unpaid overtime, stress, lack of secure contracts, poor training and almost no promotion opportunity for locally employed people.'

The report also picks up on other ways in which the hotel industry can affect people's lives in tourist areas – principally, that visitor demand for constant running water often leads to the depletion of local water supplies and that land dispossession in the name of tourist development is rife.

While land dispossession occurs throughout the world, it is particularly common in India and parts of Africa where villages may be displaced to create conservation areas, as well as hotels. Minority Rights Group International reports that 'well over 50 per cent of indigenous communities in Kenya have experienced some form of land dispossession in the name of ecotourism or other development initiatives (this reaches 60–70 per cent in Northern Kenya). Affected communities, to name a few, include the Maasai and the Ogiek in the Southern rangelands; the Pokot, Endorois, Ilchamus, Sabaot, Sengwer and Turkana in the Rift Valley; the Borana, Rendille, Somali and the Ghabra in Northern Kenya; and the Orma in the wetlands of the Kenyan Coast.' Even on a smaller scale, displacement can be an issue. Although beaches in most countries are public, some resorts try to ban local people from the sand in an attempt to give guests exclusive use. These problems are particularly relevant to all-inclusive hotels and resorts (see Chapter Three), but they are also worth bearing in mind if you're travelling independently.

Green hotels

A good green hotel or resort should have confronted these issues. No longer does eco-friendly accommodation mean camping in the field of an organic farm, or checking into a tie-dye strewn B&B. Whether you want to kick back, shabby chic style, in a groovy woodland yurt or stay in a sophisticated urban hotel, today it's relatively easy to do either without paying the heavy environmental price of more resource-greedy hotels.

This doesn't mean the hotel just does the odd bit of recycling, has switched to low energy light bulbs, bans disposable plates and cutlery and offers paperless billing.

Many of the more environmentally aware hotels have also invested in long-term strategies for saving energy, recycling water and minimising waste.

The Orchard Garden Hotel in San Francisco, for example, was built using recycled ash, with a lobby lined with panelling made from recycled particle board and key card systems in bedrooms to turn lights off automatically when a guest leaves. In addition, the curtains, bedspreads and sheets all contain recycled content. Furniture is made from sustainably grown maple. There are also low-energy light bulbs, in-room recycling bins, recycled toilet paper, low-flow showers and toilets and organic toiletries. Cleaning is done with organic and natural products.

You can expect more of the same when New York's first green boutique hotel, Greenhouse 26, opens in 2008. Currently under construction, plans for the 19-storey building include a geothermal heating and cooling system, a 500-square-foot roof garden, an organic bar and café, and organic soaps and linen.

In a more low-key way, a firm environmental stance is already being taken at Mocking Bird Hill in Jamaica. Set away from the island's heavily developed beach resorts, on a lush, forested hillside outside Port Antonio, this small 10-room hotel leads the way in sustainable tourism and has oodles of character. Responsible policies here include: using as much home-grown, seasonal produce as possible; minimising, re-using and recycling; avoiding the use of harmful chemicals, relying on natural breezes rather than air-conditioning; and installing solar panels and rainwater tanks. It also encourages guests to engage with the local countryside and community. Unusually, Mocking Bird Hill's website also includes both a clear environmental and social mission statement and updates on the hotel's self-imposed environmental assessments.

How Green is your Valet?

Even so-called 'responsible hotels' come in different shades of green. To find out how ethical your accommodation is, ask as many questions as you can before you book. Here's how some of the best-known green hotels stack up.

L'Ayalga Posada Ecológica, Spain
What is it? A vision of rustic Spanish chic, this Asturian farmhouse, two hours west of Santander, has been carefully refurbished using mostly green materials to create an environmentally sensitive B&B

How green is it? Its five bedrooms get their hot water with the help of solar panels and all grey water is recycled. All the cleaning is done with biodegradable products

How socially responsible is it? Breakfast is locally sourced and organic

How much is it? From around £16 per person per night

Green gauge: 7/10

Torri Superiore, Italy

What is it? A picturesque medieval stone village, near Ventimiglia on the Italian Riviera, Torri Superiore was gradually abandoned. Then, in the early 1990s, an NGO took it over and set about restoring it

How green is it? The project includes a solar-powered guesthouse for visitors

How socially responsible is it? The restaurant serves mostly local and organic produce and courses are offered on communal living and sustainability

How much is it? From around £25 per person per night

Green gauge: 8/10

Milia Mountain Retreat, Crete

What is it? Another restored hamlet (this one was used as a hideout by World War Two resistance fighters before being abandoned), the thirteen guest rooms here look out over olive, pear and carob trees

How green is it? Stream water is piped in, solar panels provide power and everything possible is recycled (fruit and vegetable peelings help feed the local livestock)

How socially responsible is it? The fact that it's locally owned means there's a subtle emphasis on Cretan traditions

How much is it? From around £20 per person per night

Green gauge: 7/10

Kapawi Ecolodge and Reserve, Ecuador

What is it? A remote lodge set on a tributary of the Amazon. Though you have to forsake your credentials to fly in (or hike for ten days to get there), there's a high level of eco-consciousness when you arrive

How green is it? Kapawi's twenty thatched cabanas were built on stilts to minimise disturbance to vegetation. Most of the power and hot water is solar generated, soap is biodegradable and sewage is disposed of through a natural processing system on site

How socially responsible is it? It's currently run as a partnership between a tour operator and the indigenous Achuar people, but the reserve will be handed over to the Achuars in 2011

How much is it? From around £170 per person, for three nights

Green gauge: 8/10

Apani Dhani, India

What is it? A Rajasthani 'eco lodge', comprising a cluster of eight traditional huts in a rural village. Built with mud and thatch and decorated with local craftwork, it's stylish as well as sustainable

How green is it? Electricity and hot water are solar powered

How socially responsible is it? One of the ideas behind the lodge was to prevent the disappearance of the local heritage. Five per cent of Apani Dhani's income goes towards local community projects and guests are encouraged to take cooking and craft lessons, and to visit outlying cultural attractions

How much is it? From around R400 per person per night

Green gauge: 9/10

Lapa Rios, Costa Rica

What is it? Set in a private nature reserve of over a thousand acres of lowland tropical rainforest, the teak and palm bungalows that make up this resort have no need for air-con as they're set up high to make the most of tropical breezes

How green is it? No live trees were cut for the construction. There's solar-heated water, and waste, sewage, recycling, chemicals and water use are all sustainably managed. Access to the interior of the reserve is only possible with a professional guide

How socially responsible is it? The resort employs only local staff, providing direct income to more than 45 families. It educates guests, employees and local communities about conservation and encourages guests to explore the local culture

How much is it? From around £105 per person per night

Green gauge: 10/10

Daintree Ecolodge, Australia

What is it? A cluster of 15 villas set in the Greater Daintree Rainforest, on the northeast coast of Australia. The rainforest contains 430 species of birdlife, as well as myriad other wildlife species and it is this proximity to nature (along with the luxury accommodation and organic spa) which draws in most visitors

How green is it? All the resort's water comes from a nearby waterfall and strict sustainable guidelines are followed on energy and waste management. It also carries out energy management assessments

How socially responsible is it? Aboriginal cultural tourism is another major component of the lodge. Daintree employs the indigenous Kuku Yalanji as guides and, with their help, offers guests cultural rainforest walks, introductions to bushtucker and aboriginal art and craft workshops. The resort has strict guidelines, also, on issues such as intellectual property rights, cultural heritage preservation, cultural understanding, racial sensitivities, guest and staff education and maintaining a working relationship with the Kuku Yalanji

How much is it? From around £230 per person per night

Green gauge: 7/10

Casa Camper, Spain

What is it? One of several diversifications by the Camper shoe company, this 25-room hotel in Barcelona is as sensitive to the environment as it is stylish

How green is it? Green details include refillable soap dispensers (filled with natural olive oil products), a rooftop vegetable garden, in-house recycling facilities, composting, water recycling, hot water from a solar heating system on the roof and organic snacks. To explore further afield, guests can rent wooden Camper bikes

How socially responsible is it? Local employees are chosen as far as possible

How much is it? From around £70 per person per night

Green gauge: 8/10

Adrère Amellal Oasis, Egypt

What is it? Set within the Saharan oasis of Siwa, nine hours from Cairo, Adrère Amellal's 39 rooms have been built by local tradesmen in the traditional way – using rock salt, straw and clay – and decorated in Bedouin style

How green is it? The idea of Cairo-based environmentalist, Mounir Neamatallah, there is no electricity, much of the food is sourced from the hotel's organic garden, an infinity pool is fed by an underground spring and, in the evenings, light is provided by oil lamps, candles and the moon. Water is heated by the sun and all waste and water is recycled. The one downside? You need to travel by 4×4 to get there

How socially responsible is it? Local guides are used to take guests on trips into the surrounding area

How much is it? From around £100 per person per night

Green gauge: 7/10

Jungle Bay, Dominica

What is it? A resort of 35 treehouse-like cottages set on a leafy hillside on Dominica's south coast. Surrounded by cedar trees and fed by a natural spring, the resort is Dominican owned and was designed to 'provide jobs and economic advancement opportunities for local Caribbean residents while preserving the heritage and quality of life of the host community'

How green is it? Constructed from reclaimed volcanic stone and wood, Jungle Bay's environmental initiatives include a policy of re-using and reducing (though not recycling – except for composting food waste) and building cottages for maximum air-flow to avoid installing air-conditioning. The property's goal is to be entirely off the grid by 2009

How socially responsible is it? The resort employs forty Dominicans, almost all from local villages. Some are former banana plantation workers now employed as guides and handymen. The resort also buys some of its produce from local fishermen and organic gardeners

How much is it? From around £50 per person per night

Green gauge: 7/10

Chumbe Island, Zanzibar

What is it? A collection of seven 'eco bungalows' set within the Chumbe Island Coral Park, a privately managed nature reserve and a protected breeding ground for fish and corals

How green is it? Each bungalow gets its water supply through a special rainwater capturing and filtering process. Heated showers are solar-powered, toilets are composting, lights are powered by photovoltaic panels, there is no air-conditioning and waste is minimised

How socially responsible is it? Organic guest soaps are bought from a local women's co-operative and former fishermen from adjacent villages are employed as park rangers and guides

How much is it? From $150 per person per night

Green gauge: 9/10

Kasbah du Toubkal, Morocco

What is it? Set, 60km from Marrakech, at the foot of the highest peak in North Africa, this property describes itself as a 'Berber hospitality centre' rather than a hotel. Run in partnership with the surrounding community, a 5 per cent levy on guests' bills is ploughed back into the local village

How green is it? Rebuilt from a ruin using traditional local methods, the Kasbah's sustainable policies include supplying filtered spring water in an attempt to discourage the use of plastic water bottles. Funding has supported improved waste management facilities in the surrounding area

How socially responsible is it? Run by a local husband-and-wife team, the Kasbah consciously tries to offer a local rather than expat experience. So, meals are strong on Berber flavours, and swimming pools, where people might sunbathe in offensively skimpy clothing, are out (there is a plunge pool in the Kasbah's hammam)

How much is it? From €75 per person per night

Green gauge: 8/10

Eco chic

The Bahamas is usually seen as a place to knock yourself out on rum punches and fight your economic destiny against battalions of one-armed bandits. But Tiamo resort, on South Andros island, is far removed from the heavily commercial side of this small Caribbean country.

Though it's only two hundred miles from the hedonistic thrills of Miami and even closer to Nassau's sky-scraping resort hotels, the surrounding landscape is an almost untouched jumble of jagged shores, glassy creeks and tropical forest. Here, the resort's owners, Mike and Petagay Hartman, have built eleven chic, wooden cottages, set back from the water for minimal impact.

With no air conditioning, the buildings are kept naturally cool with open-sided walls, which encourage a breeze. Powerful showers are fed by solar-heated rainwater. Sunloungers are built from leftover wood from the construction of the cottages and guests are encouraged to take anything that can't be recycled locally home with them. Even the compost toilets are more stylish than your average two-scoops-of-bark-and-a-splosh-of-water job; with their porcelain pans and designer flush buttons, they're sophisticated rather than scary.

At the resort's Kon Tiki-style central lodge, diners are fed on surf-fresh mahi mahi bought from the local fishermen. You won't find conch or grouper on the menu, though, because of fears of over-fishing. Instead of 50-channel TVs and free Wi-Fi, entertainment involves going out with the resort's resident naturalist to paddle through mangroves, snorkel over deep blue holes and search for the island's gigantic indigenous iguanas.

Tiamo insists that responsible travel can be tailored to fit people who like to wear dressy frocks as well as those who'd rather don a hair shirt. Stay here and not only do you have a good time, but you're left knowing more about your own impact on the world. Not by being preached at but because of the Hartmans' belief that their visitors will be more easily persuaded by the ethical philosophy if they are having a good time.

It is a similar ethos at Blancaneaux Lodge, in Belize. A clutch of villas, set on stilts in the Mountain Pine Ridge Forest Reserve, the oldest national park in the country, it is one of three properties in Central America owned by film director Francis Ford Coppola. While environmentally friendly measures include generating its own hydro-electricity – its casitas come without TVs, telephones or air-conditioning to make sure the supply isn't overstretched – and growing its own organic vegetables, it's also glitzy enough to appeal to the likes of Claudia Schiffer and Keanu Reeves.

As these hotels show, you don't have to suffer for your green beliefs. Just as recycled stationery has gone from having the consistency of dry compost to being butter smooth, many environmentally aware hotels have gone seriously upmarket.

The development of such luxurious hotels, albeit with eco-design and eco-services, can be controversial, however. Among more right-on travellers there is an inverse snobbery which goes that the more you 'rough it', the more authentic an experience you will have, and by implication, the less impact. But, if responsible travel is to make a difference, it has to become mainstream, and it's never going to do that if it only caters to one sector of the market. There is also an argument that green hotels aimed at the more worthy backpackers are essentially preaching to the converted. Instead, by gently persuading the private jet-flying, yacht-sailing, bling-wearing minority that they can have their cake and eat it with a less resource-heavy icing, so much the better. Luxury and environmental awareness are not mutually exclusive.

SWEET GREEN DREAMS: HOW TO FIND A HOTEL THAT'S HIGH ON STYLE BUT LOW ON IMPACT

1. **Search the listings on I Escape's website.** This UK-based website lists – and can book – 'exciting and unusual places to stay in some of the world's most beautiful and fascinating locations'. That's quite a claim but the company lives up to its promise, covering the kind of properties you're torn between telling all your friends about or keeping to yourself.

   Most are small, locally owned properties and are culturally and environmentally aware. Importantly, the company also has a clear responsible tourism policy and takes a pro-active approach to its beliefs, questioning hotel owners about their eco and social policies, reporting these in its reviews and promoting the concept if it is absent.

   One of I Escape's most popular properties is Hotelito Desconocido, on Mexico's Pacific coast. The 29 thatched palafitos here are built on stilts to minimise disruption to the surrounding estuary habitat and the resort runs on solar power during the day (at night it's lit by candles). Vegetables are supplied by the resort's organic garden and toiletries in all the bathrooms are biodegradable.

2. **Boutique and luxury hotel guide, *Mr & Mrs Smith*,** also cover some retreats for 'those sybarites who want to stay somewhere that cares as much about the environment as it does for its guests'.

   Its current recommendations include Vigilius Mountain Resort in Italy's South Tyrol region, a modernist Alpine lodge designed by local architect, Matteo Thun. Engineered around the principles of sustainability, access is by cable-car rather than road. It is built from sustainably sourced wood, incorporates ultra-modern insulation, is powered by a biomass plant and aims to be CO_2 neutral. The food served is mostly organic and locally sourced and the pools in the spa are spring-fed.

3. **Look through the Environmentally Friendly Hotels website.** This American site brings together over two thousand green hotels, B&Bs and villas and rates them on everything from whether they have a grey water recycling programme to whether they promote green issues. Its two search facilities – basic or advanced – don't always work very well, and it's not always clear how green individual listings are, but it's a step in the right direction. And, while the website caters for all comfort factors, it does include some luxury options.

   The Al-Maha resort in Dubai, for instance, is set within the Dubai Desert Conservation Reserve. Owned by the Emirates airline, its forty tented suites (partly run on solar power and featuring water recycling facilities) are extravagant enough to appeal to the likes of George Clooney (though this means that they also include eco-unfriendly air-con and private plunge pools) but also help fund the reserve, now home to Arabian oryx, eagle owls, gazelles and sand foxes.

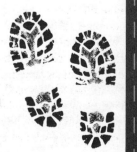

4. **Get a copy of Alastair Sawday's _Green Places To Stay_.** Edited by Richard Hammond and first published in 2006, it's an inspiring guide to over 160 responsible hotels, guesthouses and lodges in 50 countries (you can also search online by map or name on the Sawdays website).

   While most of its entries are in the low- to mid-range category, there are some more decadent options. One of these is Tiger Mountain Pokhara Lodge in Nepal. The perfect place to unwind after a trek in the Annapurnas, its comfortable stone bungalows look out over a medley of icing sugar peaks – including Machhapuchhare, the region's iconic 'fishtail' mountain. In addition to in-house energy and resource conservation measures, the lodge also supports local schools, community forest management projects and wildlife charities.

5. **Search the lodgings section of Sustainable Tourism International's 'eco directory'.** At the posher end of its recommendations are the two El Nido resorts in the Philippines. Not only do these sister resorts feature smart cottages, restaurants and spa services but they also work with the local community to prevent illegal fishing, promote coastal clean-ups and monitor snorkelling and dive sites. Employment and training opportunities are given to the local community, fruit and vegetables are grown organically and waste is managed with ecological sensitivity.

6. **Log onto the Eco Club website** and search its listings of eco-lodges by country. One of the most indulgent is Ulaa, a collection of cosy cabins and spa set on the edge of a lake in Patagonia. The latest in a series of small resorts owned by the EcoTulum company (the others are in Mexico), Ulaa minimises waste and water use, recycles as much as possible and uses 'ecological' engines for its boats. Guests are also encouraged to learn about local wildlife and to engage with the local community, some of whom are also employed by the resort.

The chain gang

It isn't just independent hotels that are attempting to be more responsible. Many of the large hotel chains have now also jumped on the green bandwagon. One of the first was Fairmont. The company formed a Green Partnership in 1990 and publishes an industry handbook on sustainability, _The Green Partnership Guide_. In addition its hotels must adhere to an environmental policy whereby they must attempt to reduce waste, conserve natural resources and 'value the natural and cultural heritage of our properties, allowing us to give our guests an authentically local experience'.

The Inter-Continental group also commissioned an environmental manual for its hotels in 1990. It went on to initiate the establishment of the International Hotels and Environment Initiative, which later broadened its remit beyond hotels to become the International Tourism Partnership.

The Partnership puts together guides on sustainable hotel siting and design and the environmental management of hotels. It also publishes the *Green Hotelier* magazine and has recently launched a *Going Green* document to help hotels implement good practice. This covers staff training and awareness; environmental management; purchasing; people and communities; and destination protection. Many of the big hotel chains are members, including Hilton, Four Seasons, Marriott, Hyatt, City Inn, Rezidor, Six Senses, Starwood, Taj and Scandic.

Inter-Continental won plaudits for the seawater-based eco-friendly air-conditioning system it installed at its Bora Bora resort in 2006. Scandic has refurbished over ten thousand rooms with almost one hundred per cent recyclable materials. Rezidor's Radisson SAS hotel at Oslo airport has two 'ecological' rooms where guests can read and measure their energy consumption (the rooms have low energy lighting, low water use showers, bulk soap dispensers, low flush toilets and recycling bins). And, Marriott recently stated that it was on schedule to fulfil its aim of reducing its greenhouse gas emissions by nearly a fifth between 2000 and 2010.

The smaller chains are getting in on the green act, too. Jumeirah – whose properties include the iconic sail-shaped Burj Al Arab hotel in Dubai – is looking at rewarding environmentally conscious guests with loyalty points. And the fast-expanding Banyan Tree group, which owns eight resorts in Asia but is set to open over twenty  more worldwide by 2010, follows guidelines on corporate social responsibility and environmental conservation. It aims to minimise damage to the environment during resort construction, opt for environmentally friendly operations, support local businesses, employ local staff and engage in community development. So far these initiatives have included the introduction of biological treatment systems to allow waste water to be used for irrigation; the setting up of a school funded through the sale of traditional cushions in Thailand; and the implementation of turtle conservation and coral regeneration programmes in the Maldives.

Critics argue that these chains are not becoming more responsible simply out of principle. Because accommodation is such a competitive area, hotels fall over themselves to offer something different to help them lure in clients. Forget having a bath butler, free wi-fi or a lavish spa: in a world of increasingly competitive marketing, being green is the latest way for hotels to stand out from the crowd.

Such positive green spin can also help protect a hotel's interests for the future. Minimising any impact on the surrounding environment is especially important for coastal hotels where guests might be attracted specifically by nature-based activities such as diving and snorkelling. If neighbouring reefs are damaged by careless hotel management practices, those guests won't be there in ten years' time.

Being environmentally aware can also generate substantial economic savings. Not providing TVs, phones or fridges not only reduces energy use, it also helps cut costs. Likewise the installation of low-energy light bulbs and key card energy control systems; since 2006, when the Fairmont Sonoma Mission Inn & Spa, in California, replaced 4,440 incandescent bulbs with energy-efficient lighting, the hotel claims to be saving $61,000 a year.

The motivation for these changes doesn't really matter so long as businesses are honest about their green initiatives (see 'greenwashing' below). If customers and hotels continue to benefit from this new-found eco-consciousness, it's a win-win situation. There is also an argument that large hotel chains have the finances to implement new technology, and to do it on such a large scale that it becomes cheaper and more easily available across the board, allowing smaller hotels to follow suit.

Green to the core

One sign that green hotels are more than just a fad is that whole hotel chains are being planned around green values (as opposed to hotel chains which also happen to be green). The first property in one such chain planned for California, the Gaia Napa Valley hotel, made headlines in early 2007 when it was announced that guests would find a copy of Al Gore's *An Inconvenient Truth* by their bedside, as well as the more traditional take on a Good Book.

While Gaia's nondescript rooms aren't going to walk off with any style awards, they do win points for environmental commitment. Its green measures include: the use of sustainably sourced wood, recycled supplies and low VOC (volatile organic compound) materials in the building's construction; the provision of low flow toilets and showers; adding Solatube skylights and solar panels to help reduce electricity use; and using environmentally friendly cleaning products. On the other hand, in an example of how blurred the eco-vision has become, rooms also come with fridges and microwaves.

Similar businesses in the pipeline include the new 'earth conscious' brand 1 Hotels and Residences (its first hotel, described as 'responsible luxury', is scheduled to open in Seattle in 2009) and Alt hotels, a new budget chain from trendy Canadian hotel company, Groupe Germain. Recently opened in Montreal, the first Alt hotel features geothermal heating and cooling systems, water recycling systems, energy-efficient lighting, geothermal hot water and heated flooring, sensors in stairwells to reduce lighting use when unoccupied, and a system of direct digital controls for ventilation, cooling and heating.

ASK THE ECO-CONCIERGE:

Ten ways to experience the Big Green Apple, according to the 'eco-concierge' at New York's 70 Park Avenue Hotel:

Slice 'A slick little Upper East Side eatery serving all-natural, organic pizzas in every imaginable variety' (1413 2nd Avenue; www.sliceperfect.com)

BabyCakes NYC 'Time for a sweet, organic break and modern spin on Grandma's homemade treats' (248 Broome Street; www.babycakesnyc.com)

Counter 'Unwind over a sustainably infused vodka cocktail made from one hundred percent organic white corn, one of the delicious indulgences at this organic wine and martini bar' (105 1st Avenue; www.counternyc.com)

Josie's East 'The natural, organic menu here features free-range meats, poultry and eggs, eco-friendly seafood and other green options. Josie's also offers cooking classes for those wishing to try their hand behind the scenes' (565 3rd Avenue; www.josiesnyc.com)

Gominyc 'Drop into this East Village eco-boutique for must-have earrings, a dress made from organic cotton, or other eco-savvy designer products' (443 E 6th Street; www.gominyc.com)

ABC Carpet & Home 'Much of this shop's furnishings are recycled or reclaimed and come from indigenous communities. Other eco-friendly elements include products made from hemp, organic linen, wood, jute and silk' (888 & 881 Broadway; www.abchome.com)

Q Collection 'The philosophy at Q is to create fabrics, furniture and home accessories that have zero impact on the environment – with upscale elegance and cutting edge design' (915 Broadway; www.qcollection.com)

Pritti Organic Spa 'Non-toxic nail polish and organic facials; our favourite is the Organic Orange Ginger Scrub for feet' (35 E 1st Street; www.prittiorganicspa.com)

Great Jones Spa 'Unwind from the city with holistic pampering in this sun-drenched solarium' (29 Great Jones Street; www.greatjonesspa.com)

Union Square Green Market 'Stop by the city's best green market, for goods from local, organic purveyors and a chance to mingle with others of a green persuasion' (Broadway at 17th Street)

What's in a name?

According to research analysts, Mintel, 'ecotourism' is growing by 20–34 per cent each year. Yet, while this 'green rush' progresses, the word ecotourism itself is becoming increasingly unfashionable.

Why? Firstly there is the problem of confidence in the product. Some 'ecotourism' trips involve travelling by plane and visiting sensitive wildlife habitats, neither of which are good for the environment. There has also been more serious misuse of the term. The strength of the green pound means that many hotels, tour companies and other sectors of the travel industry see ecotourism as a marketing opportunity rather than a principle.

This explains why, if you do an online search for ecotourism, you will find everything from adverts offering you the chance to 'speed across virgin snow on a snowmobile through miles of unspoilt winter wilderness' to 'eco' hotels which come with heli-pads and golf courses. In his book, *Final Call*, Leo Hickman even refers to one tourist project in Thailand which was promoted as 'the new ecotourism site of the Asia-Pacific region' while serving up giraffe, elephant, tiger and lion meat on its menu.

But another concern is what actually constitutes ecotourism. While mountain biking along a forest trail may bring you closer to nature, for example, is it really good for the environment? The Planeta website, a South American ecotourism forum, quotes John Noble, editor of Lonely Planet's Mexico guidebook, on this issue: 'What you call "ecotourism" in Latin America, in Europe we call a "walk in the country".'

The Mexican conservationist Héctor Ceballos-Lascuráin is generally credited with coining the term ecotourism in 1983, when he defined the concept as 'tourism that involves travelling to relatively undisturbed natural areas with the specific object of studying, admiring and enjoying the scenery and its wild plants and animals, as well as any existing cultural aspects (both past and present) found in these areas.'

Ceballos-Lascuráin concluded that ecotourism 'implies a scientific, aesthetic or philosophical approach, although the "ecotourist" is not required to be a professional scientist, artist or philosopher. The main point is that the person who practises ecotourism has the opportunity of immersing him or herself in nature in a way that most people cannot enjoy in their routine, urban existences. This person will eventually acquire an awareness and knowledge of the natural environment, together with its cultural aspects, that will convert him into somebody keenly involved in conservation issues.'

Over the past twenty years, however, most people's understanding of what ecotourism means has changed. What was once seen as a niche, nature-based activity has become a wider, more mainstream concept to do with travelling in a way that doesn't harm the environment. As writer Richard Hammond says: 'People used to think going on an eco holiday meant going dry-stone walling in Devon, or on a three-month conservation expedition in Africa. But being green isn't about taking a particular type of holiday. Any holiday can be a greener holiday if you can tread more lightly.'

These days it isn't enough to be green on holiday. Being socially responsible and encouraging a more sustainable approach to tourism go hand-in-hand with environmental awareness. The two are connected; if people are struggling to make a living this can have a detrimental effect on the environment, since they will have to exploit whatever resources they can to survive.

The International Ecotourism Society's (TIES) definition of ecotourism reflects this shift in attitudes: 'Responsible travel to natural areas that conserves the environment and improves the well-being of local people.'

So, too, does Ceballos-Lascuráin's revision of his original definition of ecotourism. His new, 1993, version adds more weight to the social impact of travel: 'Ecotourism is environmentally responsible travel and visitation to relatively undisturbed natural areas, in order to enjoy, study and appreciate nature (and any accompanying cultural features – both past and present), that promotes conservation, has low negative visitor impact, and provides for beneficially active socio-economic involvement of local populations.'

For many people, however, these shifting boundaries merely add to the confusion. Having clear international standards for ecotourism might help avoid these issues but there is currently no single internationally accepted standard. In an article in the *Guardian* in March 2007, Hammond wrote that 'holidaymakers have to grapple with over 350 independent eco-labels, most of which are designed as a checklist for the industry, rather than as a searchable tool for travellers. Many assess only on environmental credentials so they don't provide any guarantee of quality, and none are held to account by one internationally accepted accreditation body so you can't compare like with like.'

In the meantime, for many, the 'eco' label still suggests an environmental rather than social perspective. As do 'green' and 'earth-friendly' even though both concepts have evolved to encompass all areas of sustainability and corporate social responsibility. 'Ethical' covers more of the necessary territory, but I prefer 'responsible'. At the end of the day, the label doesn't really matter, though. Ultimately, it's how you travel that counts.

Greenwashing

Green hotel developments are exciting but, unfortunately, making responsible choices about accommodation isn't always as straightforward as it might be. Don't believe the eco hype without checking facts first. If you're serious about reducing the impact of your stay on the environment, you need to be wary of 'greenwashing', the practice of putting an environmental spin on services or activities that might not be as green as they seem – or which focus attention away from less sustainable activities elsewhere in a business.

An article in *Condé Nast Traveler*, for instance, recently criticised the Six Senses hotel group for promoting suites at Soneva Fushi, in the Maldives, as being staunchly green (they're aiming to be carbon neutral by 2010) while simultaneously building a Thai resort which can only be reached by private plane. Greenwashing often happens on a much smaller scale, too, though. Some hotels claim to be eco-friendly yet supply guests' drinking water in plastic bottles, even where the tap water is drinkable.

This confusion isn't always intentional. Making responsible choices can be confusing. Even when you think you have the facts, balancing environmental, social and economic issues can be difficult. Take the construction of the Hilton Jalousie on St Lucia, which conservationists campaigned against in an effort to protect local wildlife. Dispite these concerns, the resort gained significant local support, with some seeing the development as an economic opportunity.

Even hanging up your towels to show that you're happy to re-use them rather than demanding fresh linen every day isn't always a straightforward choice. This might be a genuine attempt to help save water and not just a money-saving ruse on the part of an otherwise environmentally profligate hotel. But, if you're staying somewhere which employs people to do the washing by hand, by re-using your linen you might be doing local people out of a job.

Travelling is fraught with these sorts of dilemmas and, when choosing accommodation, there are no hard and fast rules. It usually comes down to using your judgement and making choices based on individual merit rather than broad assumptions.

As green travel expert Richard Hammond puts it: 'I like to talk about being *more* responsible. It's not a black and white area, where you're being either responsible or you're not. Nothing we do is one hundred per cent green, and the very nature of travelling means that you have a footprint. Responsible travel is about trying to lessen that footprint.'

Sorting the (green) wheat from the chaff

Some things can be done to help you make the right choices, however. Seeking out specialist websites and guidebooks (such as those mentioned in the Sweet Green Dreams box on page 55) can help, though you need to read between the lines here, too. I recently ordered a guide to cool 'ecological' hotels expecting to be inspired by stylish hotels with responsible management practices. Instead the book listed only hotels constructed with natural materials. It offered no information on the properties' environmental footprints.

Asking the experts is an alternative way to source unbiased, up-to-date information. Judith De Witt, for example, is a director of Rainbow Tours, a specialist tour operator to southern and eastern Africa and the Indian Ocean islands (see Chapter Three). Asked to name a genuinely responsible place to stay, De Witt recommended the Anjajavy hotel in Madagascar.

'It's the best lodge in the country but it also offers direct and indirect employment to four of the most remote villages on the planet,' she told me. 'Over ninety per cent of its employees are local and the hotel contributes to a health clinic where women can give birth in safety and people can be treated for things like burst appendixes, both of which would have caused deaths before the clinic existed.

'The hotel also contributes to a school and has implemented a project to reduce food miles by growing their own produce. They have also planted a tree nursery, not to offset emissions but as a way of protecting the forest for the future.'

Name checking

Sourcing accommodation listed under a recognised certification scheme is another way of verifying a hotel's green credentials, but with so many such schemes in operation, this can be bewildering. One of the best-known schemes is Green Globe, established in 1993 by the World Travel and Tourism Council (WTTC). This includes many genuinely green accommodation providers, it is not without its critics.

A report commissioned by WWF in 2000 found that the Green Globe system promotes confusion by awarding different – but misleadingly similar – logos to those companies that commit to undertaking its certification system, and to those that have actually achieved certification. Since the first part of that process is carried out by the applicant themselves (businesses are only independently inspected at the certification stage), there is plenty of room for greenwashing.

In an attempt to fill the gap for a well-recognised global ecotourism certification scheme, an eighteen-month feasibility study was launched in 2001 by a number of groups, including the Rainforest Alliance and the International Ecotourism Society, to determine the need for such an institution and work out how it might be implemented. It concluded that a Sustainable Tourism Stewardship Council (STSC) should be formed which could grant powers of certification to a network of regional certifying organisations.

The only such network established so far is the Sustainable Tourism Certification Network of the Americas, which launched in 2003. A lack of demand from tourists for recognisable certification is said to be one of the reasons for the slow implementation of the scheme elsewhere. In the meantime, some of the more successful independent certification schemes and labels include Ecotourism Australia and, in Europe, the Voluntary Initiative for Sustainability in Tourism. This brings together certification schemes and eco-labels in various European countries, including The Green Key (covering properties in Denmark, Estonia, France, Greenland, Lithuania and Sweden), OE Plus in Switzerland, Legambiente in Italy and The Green Tourism Business Scheme in the UK (see Chapter Four).

The European Ecolabel has also been reasonably successful in establishing accreditation for environmentally aware accommodation. Hotels, mountain huts, B&Bs, farmhouses and campsites are all eligible to apply for certification. Successful operators can then display the scheme's distinctive flower logo.

Fairtrade holidays

Not all accreditation systems take the economic and social benefits of tourism into account, as well as environmental issues. In an effort to address this, Tourism Concern, which initiated the International Network on Fair Trade in Tourism, has spent several years working with the Fair Trade Labelling Organisation and other NGOs investigating whether the Fairtrade label might be applied to tourism.

The report's recommendations for businesses included: establishing Fairtrade partnerships between tourism and hospitality investors and local communities; transparent and accountable business operations through environmental and social audits; employment of local residents (including managerial positions); anti-corruption practices; a fair price negotiated with local suppliers; fair distribution of tourism revenues; use of local products and materials where appropriate and ecologically sustainable; fair and sustainable use of natural resources and fair wages and working conditions.

The Fair Trade in Tourism South Africa (FTTSA) system has taken this idea even further, setting up a scheme which assesses hotels, tour operators and other tourism businesses on criteria such as whether they provide fitting wages and working conditions for their staff. However, aside from a very broad nod in the direction of sustainability, it doesn't take ecological concerns into account.

One of the projects certified by this scheme is Bulungula Lodge, in the Eastern Cape province. It is 40 per cent owned by the Nqileni village and guests are encouraged to explore the local culture.

Community tourism

The idea of tourism which benefits people is not a new thing. Often such projects are labelled community tourism. There are many examples of accommodation which aims to follow this ethos. Some of the best of these are outlined below.

- **Shinta Mani, in Cambodia**, operates both as a luxury hotel (there's a pool and a spa) and as a training school for disadvantaged locals who want to work in the hospitality industry. Each year the hotel trains twenty young people.

- **Nihiwatu**, a luxury island hideaway in Indonesia, features fourteen luxury villas and bungalows. The owners of the resort have founded a non-profit organisation that fosters educational projects, health-care services and economic growth in the local communities.

- **The Green Hotel, in Mysore, India**, was originally built as a summer palace for the Wadeyar princesses. Now run as a hotel, local builders helped to renovate the building, all proceeds go to local causes and it gives training and employment to slum-dwellers and widows.

- **Chalalán Ecolodge, in Bolivia**, is set within the Madidi national park and entirely managed by the indigenous Quechua-Tacana community. Highlights of staying here include being able to explore the wildlife with the help of knowledgeable insider guides.

- **Guludo Beach Lodge, in northern Mozambique**,
  is a small British-owned operation run on Fairtrade
  principles. The idea is that by offering guest
  accommodation in nine tented bandas (bungalows),
  funds will be generated to alleviate poverty, protect the
  local environment and give work to the local people. Guests are encouraged to meet local people and 5 per cent of the revenue goes towards building a school and water points, and running a research project on humpback whales.

Safari so good

Ecotourism and community-based tourism projects are all deeply worthwhile but many are foreign-owned or run. There is often good reason for this. But it is particularly satisfying to come across projects that are both owned and run by local communities, as well as merely funding them.

Despite the rampant land displacement in eastern Africa highlighted by Minority Rights Group International, safari lodges are an increasingly common example of businesses operated by local people. Once an almost exclusively colonial business, slowly tourists have started to realise the value that comes from having the traditional custodians of the land in which a lodge is set contribute to the tourist industry.

Il Ngwesi, on Kenya's Laikipia plateau, for example, is both owned and staffed by the Maasai. Overlooking a vast forested plateau, its six stilted bandas are the epitome of rustic chic. They also help fund schools and mobile clinics and help protect wildlife. Nearby is Tassia, which is run by the Mukogodo Maasai, of the Lekurruki Community Conservation Group Ranch.

And, in South Africa, the Madikwe game reserve is home to two ultra-sophisticated community-owned lodges; Buffalo Ridge, owned by the Balete Ba Lekgophung community, was the first 100 per cent community-owned safari camp in South Africa (the community owns a 45-year lease to operate the lodge with traversing rights across the reserve) while Thakadu River Camp is owned and run by the local Molatedi community.

Village people

It isn't just safari lodges that are embracing local cultures. Three other pioneering African community-owned initiatives are Kawaza in Zambia, Nhoma in Namibia and Kahawa Shamba, in Tanzania.

Kawaza, in Zambia's Luangwa Valley is set within a popular safari destination, but it is not a safari lodge (though add-on safaris can be arranged). Instead, it is a 'cultural tourism' project, offering visitors the chance to experience daily life as guests of the local Kunda people in Kawaza, a typical farming village. Guests can either visit for the day or stay overnight, trying out a range of activities from fishing in dugout canoes and learning to cook Kunda-style to trekking into the forests to help collect wild honey. Income from these visits helps fund community development and offers an alternative to poaching.

In Namibia, interested visitors can arrange to stay at Nhoma, a tented camp beside the Ju/'hoan village of //Nhoq'ma. Owned by the villagers but operated by the proprietors of nearby Tsumkwe Lodge, it provides a much-needed source of income for the villagers and has helped fund community development initiatives, including a school. Guests are invited to join the villagers, San bushmen, in tracking down food and medicine in the bush or learning about other aspects of daily Ju/'hoan life.

Kahawa Shamba means 'coffee farm' in Swahili and was established in conjunction with the tour operator Tribes Travel, Cafédirect, the charity Twin and the UK's Department for International Development. It aims to bring extra income to small-scale coffee farmers through tourism, with local families hosting guests in traditionally built huts (albeit with iron beds and Western-style bathrooms). Now owned by the local Chagga tribe, Kahawa Shamba brings both income to the host families and funding for wider community development projects.

The project is included in Tourism Concern's *Ethical Travel Guide*, written by Polly Pattullo and Orely Minelli. A useful directory of socially responsible tour operators and accommodation providers in over sixty countries, each one is listed geographically. It covers many small, community-run projects.

HOME FROM HOME: FIVE RESPONSIBLE HOLIDAY RENTALS

Aqualogis, France
A peaceful, floating chalet outside the village of St Firmin, in Burgundy (around ninety minutes from Paris by TGV), this property was designed to make as little impact on the local ecology as possible. It sleeps up to eight.

Cerro da Fontinha, Portugal
This small terrace of six self-catering cottages (from studios to two-bedrooms) was made from locally sourced, natural materials and offers good access to the local countryside, including one of the biggest coastal reserves in Europe. Guests can order in baskets of organic fruit and vegetables.

Ionian Eco Villagers, Greece
This clutch of seven, privately owned self-catering properties on the island of Zakynthos (Zante) is mostly solar-powered. Bookings help fund local conservation projects – the area is home to endangered sea turtles, monk seals and other wildlife. Properties sleep between two to five people.

Boda farmhouse, Sweden
Built in 1830 and set in rolling countryside around an hour from Gothenburg, this picturesque old farmhouse sleeps eight. Outside there's a large sunny lawn, rolling pasture and forest to explore. If you're lucky, the genial owners will take you for a walk up the neighbouring hill to pick blueberries.

Can Marti Agroturismo, Ibiza
Very different from the hedonistic side of Ibiza, the four colourfully decorated apartments on this organic farm are all about avoiding the use of excess resources. You won't find air-conditioning, TV or a swimming pool but you will find plenty of character. Apartments sleep two to four.

Home-stays

Home-stays take the community tourism concept even further by offering accommodation in the homes of local families, an approach that is similar in some ways to B&B accommodation. Villagers gain income and tourists get an insight into local life. While many of these services can be arranged through relevant tourist boards, some companies specialise in home-stays (also sometimes known as 'paying guesthouses').

Himalayan Homestays is one such project. The company offers simple accommodation with families in the Ladakh, Sikkim and Himachal Pradesh regions of northern India. As these are traditional homes and not specifically designed with Western tourists in mind, accommodation is welcoming but basic (expect toilets of the long-drop, compost variety and little or no electricity). It's also cheap.

How to be a more responsible guest

- Choose a locally owned hotel where possible

- Be a generous tipper

- Don't eat all your meals – or do all your shopping – at the hotel. Spread your money around instead

- Conserve energy by switching off the TV, lights and any other electrical appliances when you leave your hotel room (many hotels now have key cards that do this automatically) and by avoiding the use of air-conditioning and heating where possible

- If you do use air-con or heating, don't crank them up too high. Keep windows and doors closed and remember to turn them off when you leave your room

- Conserve water by keeping showers short, avoid baths and don't do unnecessary laundry, especially in arid locations

- Avoid unnecessary waste by refilling water bottles and avoiding plastic bags when you shop

- Use recycling facilities if they are provided

- Ask your hotel whether it has a responsible tourism policy. Is it committed to reducing waste and water use? Does it try to minimise damage to wildlife? Does it employ local staff and pay them a fair wage? Does it try to source local produce? Does it provide re-fillable soaps and use low-energy lighting? Does it use green cleaning products?

Because this type of accommodation is so directly linked to local people, it is crucial that tourists are sensitive to local customs during their stay. There have been reports of less scrupulous home-stay guests causing offence or, worse, disrupting local culture by dressing inappropriately or by ostentatiously drinking or taking drugs. Even minor actions can cause offence: a behavioural code drawn up by the Ladakhi women from Himalayan Homestays includes not interfering with the cooking – a literal case of too many cooks spoiling the broth.

Closer to home, you've more chance of avoiding faux pas, but the home-stay concept is an equally good way to explore local culture. Take Italy's Agriturismo scheme, a network of farmhouses that offer bed and breakfast or self-catering accommodation. If you know which region of Italy you're aiming for, you can search through the Agroturismo website (in English) for contact details of members and then book in for a slice of rustic luxury.

Slow travel

Some people talk about 'slow travel' as being a responsible way to travel. A sister concept to the Slow Food movement, this is all about escaping the kind of travel where you run around a city in 48 hours having ticked off all the sights but gained few real insights. Although more a happy side effect than a stated intention, it's also quite an environmentally and socially sensitive way to travel.

If you believe that the best way to really appreciate a place is to travel less but stay longer in each destination, you don't have to travel overland to Mongolia to test the philosophy. Even on a two-week holiday, you can still follow the slow travel principles, by renting a house or apartment and getting to know the surrounding area in depth rather than hopping from hotel to hotel. Or, try living even more like a local by swapping houses with someone. The ultimate slow travel choice, you live among the local community, do your shopping locally, don't put extra pressure on resources and don't create demand for yet more hotels and resorts. Home-swapping agencies include Holswap, Homebase Hols, Homelink, Geenee and Intervac.

Camping

Provided you're staying in a tent – and not in an enormous holiday park or a caravan, both of which are significantly less environmentally sensitive – this is as close to nature as accommodation gets. With little necessary equipment besides a tent, sleeping bag and a camping stove, it's also a cheap and low-impact way to sleep.

HAPPY CAMPERS: EIGHT COOL CAMPSITES

You don't have to rough it to sleep under canvas these days. The ultimate low-impact style of accommodation has had a luxury make-over. If you feel the urge to loiter within (a stylish) tent, here are some of the best sites to try 'glamping' as it's known in the trade.

Mary Jane's Farm, USA
This Idaho farm offers either tented B&B or organic farm apprenticeships. These intensive one week courses include meals, accommodation and training in cooking, gardening, composting, knitting, sewing and starting your own B&B.

Hoopoe Yurt Hotel, Spain
The four comfortable yurts here are set amid three scenic hectares of olive groves and cork oak forest beneath Andalucía's Grazalema Mountains. Showers are solar-heated, there's a chlorine-free swimming pool and reflexology, yoga or massage can be arranged. It's also within spitting distance of Jerez's sherry bodegas.

Canvas Chic, France
The twelve stylishly furnished yurts here are set above a river gorge in a scenic corner of the Ardeche, in southern France. The whole place has been designed to give the feel of wild camping while providing all the facilities – but not the crowds – of traditional campsites. Facilities include proper beds, luxury bed linen and a small table d'hôte-style restaurant.

Chhatra Sagar, India
Two hours drive from Jodhpur, in India, this spectacular camp consists of eleven luxury tents pitched on top of a century-old dam. Elaborately decorated, with hand-painted henna floors, each open-sided tent has a private porch that looks out over a bird-filled lake. Excursions into rural Rajasthan can also be arranged.

Treebones, USA
Set on California's spectacular Big Sur coastline, this collection of sixteen low-impact yurts is located in a picturesque spot overlooking the Pacific Ocean. If the view isn't relaxing enough, in-yurt Shiatsu massages can also be booked. When the yurts are fully booked, you can bring your own tent.

Patagonia EcoCamp, Chile
The brightly painted domes here are smart and comfortable, and are connected by wooden boardwalks to two larger communal domes, where meals are served. Designed to mimic the huts of the indigenous Kawesqar people, each also has a window in the ceiling for stargazing.

Islas Secas, Panama
'Boutique' camping is the order of the day at this tropical island hideaway. Accommodation is in seven luxury yurts, each situated on a small cove, and days are spent swimming, snorkelling, fishing, whale watching or snoozing. There are no phones, televisions or radios.

Paperbark Camp, Australia
Set in the New South Wales bush, this tented resort aims to make as little impact on the environment as possible: the site was cleared by hand to avoid damaging eco-systems, lighting is solar, waste-water is pumped off-site to avoid polluting the local creek and the twelve tents are built on raised wooden platforms.

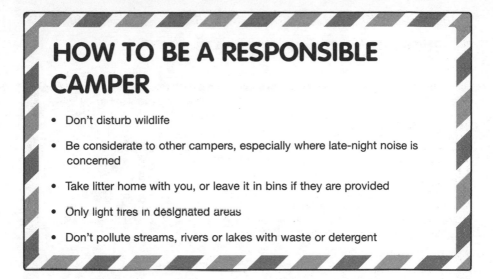

HOW TO BE A RESPONSIBLE CAMPER

- Don't disturb wildlife

- Be considerate to other campers, especially where late-night noise is concerned

- Take litter home with you, or leave it in bins if they are provided

- Only light fires in designated areas

- Don't pollute streams, rivers or lakes with waste or detergent

If you're looking for ideas on where to pitch a tent and other canvas-minded matters, several guides have come out on the subject in the past couple of years. *Britain's Camping and Caravan Parks* by Visit Britain and *Caravan and Camping Britain and Ireland* by the AA both give clear information, though Punk Publishing's *Cool Camping* guides to England, Scotland and Wales are more specifically designed for travellers with tents rather than caravans. The Camping and Caravanning Club, *Camping Magazine*, Camping UK and UK Campsite also provide lots of useful information.

For wild camping, extra care is needed. As well as the more general points outlined in the box below, try to keep groups small, don't damage vegetation by camping on an obviously over-used site, or staying in the same place for longer than a few nights, and avoid lighting fires. Try to cover your tracks, too. Don't leave food scraps and don't go to the toilet within thirty metres of a water source. Excrement should be buried but not tampons or sanitary towels, which animals can dig up.

BOUTIQUE CAMPING

Cool camping these days doesn't mean putting up with damp sleeping bags or wind-whipped tents. If you want to sleep outside but you want to do so in comfort, many 'boutique' campsites now offer ready-assembled tents or yurts, often with proper beds and sometimes even en-suite bathrooms.

Some of the best-known UK boutique campsites include: Eco Retreats in Powys, Cornish Tipi Holidays near St Kew, Vintage Vacations on the Isle of Wight, La Rosa outside Whitby, Northumbrian Wigwams, Belle Tents camping on the edge of Bodmin Moor and Tented Lodges in Wales. Feather Down Farm also provides posh, ready-equipped tents at nine working farms throughout the UK. All come with flush toilets and a traditional wood-fired oven, as well as access to a henhouse where guests can help themselves to eggs. Companies such as Tangerine Fields, Boutique Camping and Camp Kerala now provide similar services at many music and book festivals.

For an atmospheric rather than strictly practical take on camping, Laura James' *Cool Camping* (Collins) and Tess Carr and Kat Heyes' *Happy Campers* (Bloomsbury) are both entertaining reads.

CHAPTER THREE
PACKAGE HOLIDAYS

All wrapped up

Whether you're looking for a couple of weeks by the sea or a month trekking between remote mountain villages, sometimes it can be easier, quicker and cheaper to buy a package than to travel independently. But there are also strong arguments against travelling in this way. The displacement of traditional communities to make way for resorts, and poor working conditions, as discussed in the previous chapter, are widespread within the package holiday industry. And many traditional package holidays contribute to the erosion of local landscapes and culture.

In 2005, around nineteen million people from the UK took a package holiday, many of them to the Mediterranean. As in other parts of the world, the resorts that cater specifically to package tourists are sometimes badly planned and cheaply built, with little regard for the local environment or traditional architectural styles.

Supporting these developments can also contribute to a vicious cycle whereby a picturesque spot is discovered, then a few backpackers arrive, word spreads, the developers move in and soon, as Joni Mitchell sang, paradise gets paved over and turned into parking lots, hotels and all the other flotsam and jetsam of the mass tourism infrastructure. Once a place turns into a tarmac'd eyesore, the tourists stop coming and, unless the resort can be reinvented, the whole cycle begins again somewhere else.

But large resorts can also have a more immediate impact on a destination. Building bars, restaurants and other facilities that cater for foreign rather than local tastes can have a corrosive effect on local traditions. Without adequate disposal facilities, sewage and other waste is sometimes just dumped. And such a high density of visitors created by many package holidays – all of whom demand water for swimming pools and showers and power for satellite TVs and air-conditioning – can put intense pressure on local resources, sometimes diverting them away from local communities.

Deal or no deal

More generally, the worst offenders in terms of package holidays tend to be all-inclusive deals. Because tourists on this type of holiday pay for their transport, accommodation, food, drink and entertainment up front, there is little incentive for them to venture outside their resort. Trapped in what are essentially gated communities, many all-inclusive holidaymakers don't interact with the local culture beyond watching a staged 'traditional' dance show or bumping into local staff.

Compared to independent travellers, tourists on this type of trip don't usually spend much money at local shops, restaurants and other businesses, either. According to the UN Environment Programme (UNEP), 'in most all-inclusive package tours, about eighty per cent of travellers' expenditures go to the airlines, hotels and other international companies (who often have their headquarters in the travellers' home countries), and not to local businesses or workers.'

UNEP quotes a survey of Jamaica's tourist industry carried out by the Organization of American States (OAS), which found that 'all-inclusive hotels generate the largest amount of revenue but their impact on the economy is smaller per dollar of revenue than other accommodation subsectors.'

This siphoning off of revenue created through tourism from destination countries to the ones where the package companies are based – known as 'leakage' – is widespread. It can be an issue even when the hotels featured in all-inclusive deals are not owned by large multinational companies. In 2004 the UK sustainable tourism charity, the Travel Foundation, commissioned a report on the economic impact of the all-inclusive hotel sector in Tobago. It noted that 'significant proportions of funds do not reach Tobagonians and otherwise do not remain on the island for very long. Two main reasons for this assertion are that all payments are made abroad and, while most [all-inclusive] hotels are owned by Trinidadians, only one is Tobagonian-owned.'

Taxing times

Various damage limitation exercises have been carried out in package holiday destinations over the past few years, some with more success than others. In 2002, Spain's Balearic Islands attempted to undo some of the damage caused by decades of mass tourism by introducing an 'eco tax' on tourists; each visitor paid €1 per night of their stay and the money was used to make environmental improvements.

The tax was unpopular within the industry, however. Hoteliers and tour operators worried that visitor numbers would drop because of it and there was resentment because the levy didn't apply to those staying in private apartments. The following year the electorate voted out the tax.

The Gambia successfully follows a similar but much simpler scheme, whereby the tourist board collects £5 from each visitor, either on arrival or included in the cost of a package holiday. This then goes towards improving the country's tourist infrastructure. The government had previously attempted to tackle the problems caused by all-inclusive holidays by banning them. It was hoped that this would encourage visitors to go out and spend money with local businesses. But protests – largely from tour operators – meant the policy was abandoned.

Other original ideas for lessening the impact of all-inclusive package tourism, especially at very fragile sites, include a suggestion made by the British think tank, the Centre for Future Studies, that future ecotourists should enter a lottery to win the right to visit some of the world's most popular ecotourism destinations, rather than allowing unlimited access to large groups. Others argue that carefully managed ecotourism is one of the best incentives for ensuring the environmental protection of a site.

GREEN GONGS

Eco hotels, responsible tour operators and other ethical travel businesses have been springing up as quickly as branches of Starbucks over the past few years, and keeping up with the latest developments can sometimes seem overwhelming. But the number of green tourism award schemes has grown in tandem with the businesses they are designed to reward. Celebrating good practice within the industry, they can be a useful source of information. The following are some of the best known:

Virgin Responsible Tourism Awards
Launched by Responsible Travel in 2004 and now sponsored by Virgin Holidays (along with *The Times*, World Travel Market and *Geographical* magazine) these awards aim to 'find tourism ventures all over the world that make a positive contribution to conservation and the economies of local communities while minimizing any negative impacts of tourism'. There are currently thirteen different categories.

Tourism for Tomorrow Awards
Designed to reward best practice in responsible tourism across four categories – destination, conservation, investor in people and global tourism business – these awards were originally set up in 1989 by the Federation of Tour Operators, were later taken over by British Airways and are now presented by the World Travel and Tourism Council.

The Green List
Not an award scheme as such, but an annual list published in the American version of *Condé Nast Traveler* magazine. Now into its thirteenth year, the categories range from hotels, lodges and resorts to tour operators, skiing companies and destinations. 'Winners' are chosen by an independent panel of judges.

Reading between the lines

While package holidays are never likely to be the most responsible way of travelling, not every all-inclusive is exploitative, not every wildlife holiday is intrusive and not every winter sports trip is damaging (see Chapter Four). If you're considering buying a package deal, booking with a responsible tour operator is one good way to start minimising your impact.

Most reputable tour operators now have written responsible travel policies, which lay out how your trip will maximise the benefits to the destination and minimise the negatives. Some of these shout louder than others but most now cover the basics: offering locally led excursions; reducing pressure on local resources; protecting local landscapes and culture and providing local goods and employment.

This doesn't mean opting for an expensive tailor-made trip. The 'big two' tour operators in the UK (TUI Travel and the Thomas Cook Group) both have responsible travel policies. These companies are also signed up to the Federation of Tour Operators (FTO), whose members represent over 60 per cent of package holiday operators. In addition, the FTO has its own responsible tourism committee and has recently introduced 'Travelife' gold, silver and bronze sustainable tourism logos for the holiday, hotel and tourist businesses its members cover.

The Travel Foundation, which works with the UK travel industry (and is supported by it), has also helped improve the situation in some of the most popular tourist destinations. In Cyprus, for example, it is helping to regenerate mountain villages, in Sri Lanka it is assisting communities to rebuild their livelihoods after the 2004 tsunami and, in Tobago, it has established an 'Adopt a Farmer' scheme to forge links between the agriculture and tourism industries and, eventually, decrease dependency on imported produce.

In June 2007 the Foundation launched a new project, targeting 10,000 hotels in Mediterranean holiday resorts in a campaign to encourage them to be more sustainable. Properties in Spain, Turkey and Greece were offered information on how to save energy, source local produce and better manage their waste. The Foundation's chief executive, Sue Hurdle, said that it was keen to 'demonstrate that small changes by tourism businesses can make a really big difference to their bottom line – and locally to destinations.' Some of the big tour operators also offer their customers the chance to make an opt-out donation of a few pence per person to the Travel Foundation when they book a holiday.

Off the beaten track

The demand for traditional sun, sea and sand holidays may be slowly declining but, while DIY travel is the real growth area, business is also good for independent tour operators. Because they tend to be experts in a particular area, they can often make suggestions that travellers might not otherwise have considered, and cover less well-trodden ground.

Many independent tour operators launched responsible tourism policies long before their mainstream counterparts, but the Association of Independent Tour Operators (AITO), which represents over 150 such companies, also provides its own responsible tourism guidelines. In order to become a member of the organisation, operators must each appoint a member of their staff as a responsible tourism representative and formally accept AITO's responsible tourism guidelines. Companies can then work towards the organisation's in-house classification scheme. Companies that have achieved AITO's three-star grade (their highest grading) are listed on their website.

The charity Tourism Concern has also set up an Ethical Tour Operators Group. This collection of small and medium-sized independent tour operators currently includes: Adventure Alternative, Baobab Travel, Cazenove & Loyd, Expert Africa, Explore Worldwide, Gane & Marshall, Hands Up Holidays, Into Africa, Nepal Trekking, Rainbow Tours, Simply Tanzania and Tribes Travel.

Then there are the specialist online travel agents. The best known of these in the UK are Responsible Travel and Travel Roots. The former is a kind of ethical travel supermarket, selling 2,500 trips from 200 companies, while the latter has a more 'boutique' collection of around 40 packages.

WHAT TO ASK YOUR TOUR OPERATOR BEFORE YOU BOOK

- Does it have a responsible travel policy?

- Is it committed to reducing waste and water use?

- What advice does it give about minimising disturbance to wildlife and marine environments?

- How does it support the local economy?

- Does it use local staff and guides, pay them a fair wage and encourage its suppliers to do the same?

- Does it encourage its suppliers to buy locally sourced produce?

- How big will a tour's group size be (several smaller groups will have less impact than one huge one)?

Going local

The companies mentioned above are largely UK-based. For locally run tours at your destination, the Ethical Escape, Eco Friendly Tourist and Eco Tour Directory websites all contain listings for responsible local tour companies, as well as accommodation.

In the UK, Responsible Travel also features trips by some local tour operators (member companies are listed in alphabetical order on the site) as well as British-based companies. And Tourism Concern's *Ethical Travel Guide*, by Polly Pattullo and Orely Minelli, includes extensive listings for locally run tour companies worldwide.

CHAPTER FOUR

ACTIVITY HOLIDAYS

Nature vs nurture

As travel has become cheaper and easier, our expectations have grown. While there will always be those who want to spend two weeks lounging by a beach, others are increasingly choosing to travel to more remote, more 'exotic' locations; the latest destinations among ultra wealthy 'champagne tourists' are the Arctic, the Antarctic and space. We might not all be descending on – or ascending to – those destinations but, in our search for the next big thrill, we are increasingly travelling to areas known for their unique wildlife. Yet, although tourist revenues may help protect an area's ecology, nature-based holidays can also contribute to its destruction.

The first problem is that money isn't always spent where it is most needed. For example, according to the Travel Operators for Tigers (TOFT) campaign, tiger tourism brings in hundreds of millions of pounds for India's travel operators and accommodation providers yet only a tiny proportion of that is reinvested in the parks and reserves tourists visit. 'Average park entry fees are around 200 rupees per visit, raising a mere £2.79 per overseas visitor,' it states. 'Often only a small part of this gets back to the park itself as it is lost to regional or central government funds.'

Added to that are the environmental implications of flying, which is often part of the deal. And the opening up of an 'unspoilt' destination to tourists guarantees that it won't remain so for long. Accommodation is built, restaurants open up, traffic is increased, water and energy supplies are provided and, inevitably, these have an effect on local wildlife. Destinations can literally become victims of their own success.

In an article in *New Scientist* in 2004, entitled 'Beware the ecotourist', Anil Ananthaswamy warned that 'evidence is growing that many animals do not react well to tourists in their backyard. The immediate effects can be subtle – changes to an animal's heart rate, physiology, stress hormone levels and social behaviour, for example – but in the long term the impact tourists are having could endanger the survival of the very wildlife they want to see.'

This won't come as a complete surprise to anyone who has witnessed herds of minibuses descending on a lone cheetah while on safari, or a whirlwind of boats crowding around stingrays in the Caribbean. But nature tourism can also have an impact where contact is less obviously intrusive.

A 2002 study on the impact of dolphin-watching boats on bottlenose dolphins in the Sado estuary of Portugal monitored the respiration and behaviour of dolphins during the peak season for dolphin watching. It found that 'in the presence of boats, the dolphins spent significantly less time at the surface, made fewer exhalant blows, had shorter inter-blow intervals and made longer dives. Using behavioural parameters, the increase in tailslaps, alteration of activity, changes of orientation and changes within the group were also significant in the presence of boats. Inter-blow interval, dive duration and tailslapping were all significantly correlated with the number of boats.' The report concluded that the dolphins were showing avoidance behaviour towards boats.

Habituation is another possible side-effect of nature tourism. According to Arthur Pedersen, who wrote a 2002 manual titled *Managing Tourism at World Heritage Sites* for UNESCO, 'habituation is often mistakenly seen as positive because it brings visitors closer to the wildlife. Tour operators sometimes put food out to attract animals to places where visitors can see them.' This might not always produce the result the tour operators are hoping for, however. 'Habituated wildlife may become aggressive while begging for food, and can injure and even kill the unwary visitor,' says Pedersen.

Galapagos grief

Ever since Charles Darwin first set foot on the Galapagos Islands in 1835, leading him to develop his theory of natural selection, the Ecuadorian archipelago has enjoyed a reputation as a naturalist's dream. So much so that tourism increased in the Galapagos from 40,000 in 1991 to over 120,000 in 2006, leading to a rise in invasive species and a severe threat to natural biodiversity. According to the Charles Darwin Foundation, there are now 748 species of introduced plants in the Galapagos compared to 500 species of native plants.

This mass tourism is deemed so great a problem for the islands that, in June 2007, UNESCO's heritage committee added them to its list of world heritage sites in danger. The World Heritage List consists of 848 properties of special cultural or natural value, only 30 of which are currently on the 'in danger' list. The fact that the Ecuadorian archipelago is now one of them is particularly significant since it was the first area to be declared a world heritage site when UNESCO began the scheme in the 1970s. It is hoped that the move might lead to a restriction in visitor numbers.

THE BIG BLUE

The impact of diving holidays

Dive holidays are a growing sector of the package holiday market; in 2004 the diving portion of the market was estimated to be worth over £75 million a year. As with other types of holiday, there is a growing demand for trips to increasingly exotic locations; Cape Verde and the Philippines are now popular alternatives to traditional dive destinations such as the Caribbean and the Red Sea.

Yet reefs are notoriously fragile ecosystems. According to the WWF, 27 per cent of the world's reefs have already been destroyed, a figure which is likely to rise to 60 per cent in the next 30 years if current trends continue. Disease, hurricanes, the warming of the oceans and over-fishing are all factors in this vanishing act, but poorly managed tourism can also have an effect. If coral is caught with a finger, a carelessly placed fin or a dropped anchor, it can be irreparably damaged. Sun tan oil may pollute the water in areas where lots of divers or snorkelers congregate. And sewage from boats or coastal hotels can encourage the growth of reef-suffocating algae. The sale of souvenirs made from coral or conch shells is also a problem in some areas, as is the practice of fish feeding.

One way to reduce the impact of your diving trip is to sign up for one of the special environmentally inclined courses run by the Professional Association of Diving Instructors, or PADI. These include a Peak Performance Buoyancy course, a Coral Reef Conservation course and a Project AWARE course (this is linked to a spin-off charity which was set up to stress divers' roles in conserving underwater environments). It is also worth making sure that any company you book with has a written environmental responsibility policy. Like many other operators, Dive Worldwide clearly states on its website that it endeavours to use only diving operators who are environmentally responsible. It also advises anyone booking a dive holiday to:

- Dive carefully in fragile aquatic ecosystems
- Be aware of your body and equipment placement when diving
- Keep your diving skills sharp with continuing education
- Consider your effect on aquatic life
- Understand and respect underwater life
- Resist the urge to collect souvenirs
- Obey all fish and game laws
- Report environmental disturbances or destruction of dive sites
- Be a role model for other divers
- Get involved in local environmental activities and issues

On the wild side

Being sensitive to your surroundings is especially important when you are on a nature holiday. On a typical package tour, your impact will be swallowed up to a certain extent by the sheer volume of people around you. In an 'untouched' location your footprint will be much more obvious. This is especially the case with animal-watching trips.

Choose tours led by a qualified naturalist guide and think about contacting a relevant charity so that you can educate yourself before you go and make a donation when you get back. Arthur Pedersen, who wrote the UNESCO tourism management manual, has more straightforward advice: 'Many experts say simply that if visitors elicit a negative response from wildlife they are too close.'

ANIMAL MAGIC: RESPONSIBLE WILDLIFE SPECIALISTS

Wildlife Worldwide
Set up in 1992, this company specialises in tailor-made wildlife-viewing holidays.
Where does it cover? Worldwide, from cruises in Antarctica to birding holidays in Trinidad and Tobago.
How responsible is it? The company works with several conservation organisations, including the Galapagos Conservation Trust, the Raincoast Conservation society and the David Shepherd Wildlife Foundation. It was highly commended in the 2006 First Choice Responsible Tourism Awards (now Virgin Responsible Tourism Awards) after raising over £50,000 for conservation.

Discovery Initiatives
A specialist wildlife package operator, the company runs both group and tailor-made trips.
Where does it cover? Worldwide, but especially good on India and central and southern Africa.
How responsible is it? The company has a clearly stated responsible tourism policy and its mission is to use wildlife tourism to fund conservation. Its website has extensive contact details for the conservation charities it funds and it runs educational as well as recreational trips – its Ranger Safari trips in India include instruction on animals, plants, ecology, conservation and community issues in India's parks.

Out of the Blue Holidays

Running since 1999, this is the travel side of the Whale and Dolphin Conservation Society (WDCS).

Where does it cover? Worldwide, from whale watching in Alaska to dolphin spotting in Wales.

How responsible is it? The company has a written responsible travel policy and offsets its customers' carbon emissions. It's a non-profit organisation, so all the proceeds from its trips go back into funding the society's conservation projects.

The Travelling Naturalist

The company has been running small group naturalist trips for over twenty years and is particularly strong on birdwatching holidays.

Where does it cover? Worldwide, including plenty of interesting European destinations.

How responsible is it? The company asks customers not to disturb wildlife, forbids the collecting of specimens and believes that ecotourism can promote conservation. It therefore runs tours to 'several countries with a dubious environmental record, believing that by working with conservation-minded local agents and organisations within those countries, we can help to strengthen their hand.' It also supports various charities.

Naturetrek

Operating since 1986, this Hampshire-based company has branched out from running birdwatching and botanical holidays to offer a wide range of wildlife trips.

Where does it cover? Worldwide, from bear watching in Canada to family wildlife holidays in India.

How responsible is it? As well as having one of the most detailed responsible tourism policies of any wildlife company, Naturetrek also runs tours on behalf of several conservation organisations, donating 10 per cent of the income from these to conservation causes. It has helped BirdLife to promote the conservation of Madagascar's Mahavavy Delta Wetlands, home to the critically endangered Sakalava Rail.

World Primate Safaris

This is a new, Brighton-based company specialising in primate safaris.

Where does it cover? Uganda, Rwanda, Tanzania, Gabon, Madagascar, Borneo and Sumatra.

How responsible is it? The company makes a contribution from each safari sold to the conservation and preservation of primates in the relevant destination, including funding for local community projects. It also has a detailed responsible tourism policy which outlines its environmentally friendly and socially responsible approach, and encourages its clients to follow suit. It also gives clients strict instructions on minimising disturbance to animals – not visiting them if ill, not touching them and not taking flash photographs.

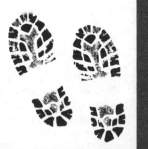

Not so green greens

Diving and nature holidays aren't the only activity-based trips that can cause problems for the responsible traveller. For golf resorts, pressure on water supplies is a particular problem, especially in arid regions. Although there are already over 32,000 golf courses in the world, according to the WWF around 5,000 hectares are being cleared for golf courses annually, some of them consuming more than 2 million litres of water every day – as much as some towns. In the 1990s the number of golf courses in Europe alone increased by 80 per cent.

In parts of Spain this is contributing to an already-acute water shortage – and one which is likely to get worse as global warming progresses. Spain saw its worst drought on record in 2005. Yet the number of golf courses along the country's southern coastline had more than doubled between 1989 and 2003, from 91 to 250, and developers are planning around 21 new courses per year over the next decade.

Nor are water shortages the only environmental problem golf resorts pose. Many greens are kept groomed with the help of pesticides and, although some courses are built on brown-field sites, or reclaimed land, others threaten biodiversity through the introduction of non-native plants. In some areas they can also impede the movement of migrating animals.

Fairer ways

Fortunately for golfers, the fairway isn't completely out of bounds. Choosing to play on an established course in a cool, wet climate, where water sources are less likely to be overstretched, is one way to start. More imaginative designers are also coming up with organic courses that don't need to be mowed as often, require less irrigation and fertilisation and are pesticide-free. Many also actively encourage wildlife, with nesting boxes put up around the course and planned migration corridors built, where appropriate.

Some existing courses have also signed up to Golf Environment Europe's Eco Management Programme (formerly called Committed to Green). This Scottish-based organisation aims to promote sustainable golfing by ensuring that accredited clubs and courses submit an environmental policy statement, establish an environmental working group, undertake a full environmental audit and develop an environmental management plan.

The Scottish Golf Environment Group also encourages environmental awareness on Scotland's golf courses. It takes inspiration from Colin Montgomerie's quote that 'a golf course which has been sensitively designed and managed in a way which works with nature rather than against it is normally more interesting and challenging.'

A slippery slope

In many of the developed world's mountainous regions it is noticeable how much damage has been inflicted on the landscape in the name of skiing holidays. The cutting of pistes has caused deforestation and soil erosion and the construction of ugly concrete hotels and apartments and a tangle of ski lifts and other winter sports infrastructure has marked the landscape.

There has been a marked disturbance to wildlife, too. When people ski over very light or patchy snow, the vegetation below it can be trampled. A 2007 study into the impact of high-altitude ski-runs on alpine grassland bird communities, published in the *Journal of Applied Ecology*, found that 'not a single bird was spotted in one third of the ski runs, and in areas adjacent to ski runs, bird numbers were lower than in undisturbed areas.' Heli-skiing is thought to be especially damaging since it takes skiers to otherwise undisturbed areas and, along with scenic flights, creates a lot of noise. It has been banned in France since 1992.

Yet you only have to open the property pages of a national newspaper to see that the construction industry is booming around the Alpine resorts. As global warming increases and snowfall becomes less reliable on lower slopes, the building work is creeping ever higher, causing fresh damage. More immediate methods of tackling this lack of snow have also had an effect on the environment. In the most extreme cases, there have been reports of snow being flown in to uncovered pistes by helicopter. More commonly, resorts rely on artificial snowmakers, which work by forcing compressed air and water through a nozzle when temperatures are below freezing; as the mix falls it freezes.

Little is known about the environmental effect of the additives thrown into this mix to help speed up the process, but we do know that snow guns require vast amounts of energy and water; WWF Italy recently reported that, in Bolzano, where artificial snow is used on two thirds of slopes, water consumption has doubled within five years because of the use of these machines.

Indoor ski centres, or snowdomes, rely on similar techniques to create snowy slopes, often in extremely arid regions. Probably the most famous of these is

Ski Dubai. A 25-storey indoor snowdome selling itself as an 'unforgettable snow experience', it's also a disorientating one, hurtling visitors straight from 40°C heat and desert culture into a frosty landscape which comes complete with a café serving crêpes and fondue beside a 'crackling fireplace'.

The attraction is at least attempting to diminish its footprint – a heat exchanger uses Ski Dubai's chilly air to cool the neighbouring shopping mall and the snow collected at the bottom of its slopes is scooped up and recycled. Snowdomes also potentially reduce the number of flights taken to real ski resorts. But, despite these considerations, it would be difficult to argue that indoor ski centres are an eco-friendly phenomenon. With six thousand tonnes of snow on its slopes, Ski Dubai consumes a titanic amount of energy and water.

SKIDOO OR SKI-DON'T?

The pressure group Mountain Wilderness is currently campaigning against noise pollution caused by the recreational use of snowmobiles, which it believes should be better regulated. 'In the mountain one can be amused without motorised means, in silence and without polluting,' it states.

The California-based environmental organisation the Bluewater Network has published a paper on snowmobile use. This notes that snowmobiles are one of the fastest growing markets of the motorised recreation industry, but warns that they are also 'multiple impact machines that damage air and water quality, area wildlife, natural peace and quiet, public health, and visitor safety.'

Though some newer machines now run on biodiesel, Bluewater Network's paper states that snowmobiles equipped with two-stroke engines 'discharge up to one-third of their fuel unburned into the environment and are one of the largest unchecked sources of hydrocarbon pollution nationwide [in the US]. The concern with this discharge is threefold: the effect of toxic emissions on air quality, the discharge of raw fuel, and the effect of both on water quality.'

The paper also cautions against the impact snowmobiles have on wildlife and noise. 'At Voyageurs National Park, noise from a single snowmobile could be detected from a distance of 400–600 feet depending on the terrain, and from five snowmobiles noise could be detected at 800–1000 feet. Based on noise characteristics alone, snowmobiles are incompatible with other forms of winter recreation such as snowshoeing, cross-country skiing, wildlife observation, and hiking to enjoy natural sounds.'

Let it snow

While winter sports holidays are never likely to be 'deep green', a lot can be done to reduce their impact. Cross-country skiing, snow-shoeing and other activities all have less impact on the mountains than downhill skiing. Booking with an AITO-registered company is also a good idea, since they will have a general commitment to responsible tourism.

Specific green skiing initiatives exist, too. In America, the National Ski Areas Association set up a 'Sustainable Slopes' environmental charter for ski areas in 2000 to improve environmental performance within the industry. Many resorts are signed up, including Vail, which is now one 100 per cent wind powered and contributes to local conservation projects. The hitch? Realistically, most visitors have to fly to get there. In Europe the winds of change are slowly blowing, too. In 1991, Germany, Austria, France, Monaco, Italy, Liechtenstein, Switzerland and Slovenia all signed the Alpine Convention, an agreement designed to protect the sustainable development of the Alps.

One way of finding out whether it is working on the ground is to visit the Ski Club of Great Britain's Respect the Mountain campaign website. This links through to the club's Green Resort Guide which outlines the environmental measures being taken, or not taken, at various resorts in six areas: recycling, green power, traffic reduction, sewage management, climate policy and green building policies.

Austria stands out from the pack here, with six resorts that fulfil each criterion. It also has some of the strictest planning laws in Europe. France is starting to catch up, however. The world's largest ski area, the Three Valleys, is now run entirely on hydroelectric power. Other initiatives include the use of biodegradable diesel in all its company vehicles, creating new meadow pasture to help preserve the indigenous black grouse and organised rubbish collection from the pistes. The Ski Club also publishes a seven-step code outlining what individual skiers and snowboarders can do to help:

1. **Be aware of your environmental impact as skiers and boarders.** Educate yourself about your environmental impact on the mountains, and what you can do to minimise it.

2. **Do not leave litter on the slopes.** When the snow melts, the litter will still be there. Bin it or take it home. Orange peel takes up to two years to break down, and cigarette butts up to five years. If you find litter on the slopes, do the right thing – pick it up.

3. **Respect the natural habitat of mountain animals and plants.** If you ski through trees, you can damage them by knocking off branches and killing young shoots under the snow. Take care. Many areas are out of bounds to protect the natural habitat of animals and plants – not just for safety reasons.

4. **Choose a resort which uses environmentally friendly practices.** Many resorts now use bio-diesel fuel in piste-bashers, solar panels for heating, hydro-electricity/wind energy for power and a host of other initiatives. Some resorts use the International Organization of Standardization (ISO) 14001 as a mark of their environmental credentials.

5. **Encourage tour operators to adopt green policies.** Find out if your tour operator offers train travel as an alternative to flying, if they use paper from sustainable forests for their brochures, if they use low-wattage lightbulbs in their chalets and biodegradable detergents.

6. **Do your bit to reduce global warming on holiday and at home.** Re-use your towels each day, re-cycle household waste and switch off electrical appliances when not in use.

7. **Reduce CO_2 emissions.** By flying fewer miles, or switching from air to rail, you can help reduce the volume of greenhouse gases that contribute to climate change. When possible, use your bike instead of your car.

OFF THE BEATEN PISTE

In 2004, entrepreneur Sofia de Meyer left behind life as a London solicitor to open Whitepod, a low-impact mountain camp close to where she grew up in the Swiss Alps. Offering a winning mix of style and ecological sensitivity, the camp proves that you don't have to book into a traditional ski resort to have a good time on the slopes.

Whitepod's dome-shaped tents ('pods') are set on wooden platforms around her family's chalet. Designed to have minimal impact on the environment, the camp features a chemical-free filtration system, is heated by wood-burning stoves (the fuel comes from sustainable local sources) and, at the end of the season, the domes are dismantled. Local, organic produce is used as much as possible – often bought directly from the producers – and waste is recycled.

The resort actively promotes alternative winter activities as well as skiing. Best of all, it's deeply peaceful; with no road access, guests arrive by ski or snowshoe.

Voluntourism

Volunteering trips are a growing sector of the package holiday market, one which has developed rapidly since the Asian tsunami. They can vary widely but a typical trip lasts for around two weeks and involves a mix of sightseeing and community work, such as teaching, construction or sports coaching.

Some of the best-known specialist agencies include: Original Volunteers, the Different Travel Company, Gap Year For Grown Ups, Global Vision International, International Voluntary Service, International Volunteering, Hands Up Holidays, i-to-i (which is now owned by First Choice), The Leap, People and Places, VSO, Working Abroad and Worldwide Volunteering. The following also run environmental volunteering projects: Biosphere Expeditions, Earthwatch, Blue Ventures and Coral Cay Conservation.

Despite good intentions, however, a few volunteering trips have come in for criticism. Some don't properly vet prospective volunteers to make sure that they're qualified for the work they're doing. Others fail to ensure that the projects are of real benefit to local communities, and run in tandem with their wishes. There has also been concern that some trips can benefit the volunteer more than the communities involved and that short-term volunteering can do more harm than good by constantly creating and then breaking attachments with vulnerable communities.

According to Kate Simpson, who carried out research into the subject at Newcastle University, volunteering can also risk creating unemployment; why should businesses or organisations pay local people to do a job when they can get a well-meaning Westerner to do it free of charge?

To help tackle some of these issues, Simpson has drawn up an Ethical Volunteering Guide. This can be read, free of charge, on the Ethical Volunteering website. In brief, it suggests asking the following seven questions before signing up:

1. Exactly what work will I be doing? Can the organisation provide a brief job description?

2. Does the organisation work with a local partner organisation?

3. Does the organisation make any financial contribution to its volunteer programmes?

4. Does the organisation have policies on eco and ethical tourism?

5. What time frame is the volunteer programme run on?

6. Can the organisation give me precise contact details for my chosen programme?

7. What support and training will I receive?

The Irish development organisation Comhlámh has also drawn up a volunteer charter, which can be downloaded as a PDF from its website, Volunteering Options.

CHARITY BEGINS ABROAD

Fund-raising package holidays that involve trekking to the top of Kilimanjaro or cycling from 'Andes to Amazon' claim to combine adventure travel with philanthropy. Participants either raise sponsorship for the trip before they go – usually around £1,500 to £3,000 for a two-week trip – or pay the balance themselves. The trips are designed to be fairly challenging, to justify the sponsorship, and profits go to a named charity.

Companies currently offering these tours include Charity Challenge, Classic Tours, Discover Adventure and Skyline Overseas. Most large charities also have details of relevant forthcoming trips on their websites.

If you're sponsoring someone to take part in one of these trips be aware that in some cases your money will effectively be subsidising their holiday. A direct donation to the charity concerned might be more effective. But then no one wants to be a kill-joy.

CHAPTER FIVE

TREADING SOFTLY

Cultural consideration

Travel can be a liberating experience. From deciding to change career, to writing a novel or getting hitched, some of our most inspired ideas occur when we're away from home, immersed in new sights, sounds and cultures. But that sense of freedom can come at a cost if it's enjoyed without respect for the places and people we're visiting.

Common sense suggests that loud, drunken behaviour doesn't go down well in many cultures. Wearing hot pants to visit a temple might not be the most appropriate clothing, or shoving a camera in someone's face the most subtle way to introduce yourself. In 2007, Hollywood actress Cameron Diaz caused offence by strolling around the ancient Peruvian city of Machu Picchu wearing a bag emblazoned with a Chairman Mao slogan: not the most sensitive choice in a country where the Mao-inspired terrorist organisation, the Shining Path, led a campaign of bombings, assassinations and massacres in the 1980s.

Travelling with a Western outlook can also create problems. You may expect transport to run on time, to pay the listed entrance price to an attraction, to queue one by one or to have a seat to yourself on a bus. But that's not how things work everywhere. In a hot climate, with insect bites prickling and a crowd of interested observers, frustration can sometimes boil over into anger. This is usually counter-productive, and disrespectful.

Fading glories

UNESCO director, Francesco Bandarin, has said 'it is an inevitable destiny' that manmade attractions will be threatened. 'The very reasons why a property is chosen for inscription on the World Heritage List are also the reasons why millions of tourists flock to those sites year after year.'

Visitors require infrastructure, which has a knock-on effect in terms of construction and pollution. Soil compaction and erosion, the trampling of vegetation and littering are routine problems that tourist attractions face. Although most visitors are sensitive enough to know not to damage ancient monuments, souvenir-hunting is another problem: Britain's museums are filled with the loot of nineteenth-century tourists, and vandalism still occurs on a much smaller scale at many destinations.

Some of the most threatened sites are highlighted by the World Monuments Fund (WMF). Dedicated to the preservation of architectural and cultural sites around the world, every two years it publishes a list of the one hundred most endangered. Those highlighted in 2007 included Captain Scott's Hut in Antarctica, the nineteenth-century city of Fianarantsoa in Madagascar and the thirteenth-century Epailly Chapel of the Order of the Temple at Courbon in France, as well as several sites in Iraq.

Neglect, vandalism, conflict and global warming are often to blame, but tourism can play a role too. The west bank of the Nile at Luxor, in Egypt, contains some of the most important archaeological sites in the world, including the Valley of the Kings, the Valley of the Queens and more than five thousand nobles' tombs, shrines and temples. According to the WMF, 'dramatic increases in tourism endanger not only the famous monuments in the area, but tourism development plans have also removed thousands of people from their century-old mudbrick homes in the village of old Qurna and demolished traditional buildings and communities.'

TEN WAYS TO CONNECT WITH LOCAL CULTURE

Meet The People Tours
Where? Asia, Africa, Cuba and Chile.
What? Run jointly by fair trade retailers Traidcraft, and the tour operator Saddle Skedaddle, these holidays pave out a route around some of the producers that supply work to Traidcraft. There's also time for sightseeing and relaxing along the way.

Insider Tours
Where? Peru, India and Sri Lanka.
What? A family-run business, based between the UK and Sri Lanka, with local partners in tour destinations. Most trips are based around community projects. While a wide range of accommodation is available, the company's well-researched network of homestays is one of its selling points.

Cucina Firenze
Where? Florence.
What? A cookery course spin-off from owner Mariangela Catalani's 'gourmet' B&B. Set in the city's Santa Croce district, while there's plenty of more traditional instruction, the emphasis is on getting to know the area as much as the food. Part of the fun is getting out of the kitchen and visiting local markets and artisan craft shops.

Equatorial Travel
Where? India, Morocco and Ecuador.
What? A self-styled 'fairtrade' holiday company, based in the UK but running culturally minded tours abroad. Typical trips range from learning the sitar in India to arts, crafts and markets tours in Morocco. All support local guides and businesses.

Muir's Tours
Where? Worldwide.
What? A non-profit organisation which runs wildlife safaris, activity holidays and 'immersion into certain cultures by staying with indigenous people in a variety of remote places'. It tries to benefit all who are involved in, or affected by, its tours and all profits are divided between charities in the relevant country.

Kooljaman
Where? Australia.
What? An Aboriginal-owned wilderness camp at Cape Laveque, on Australia's northwest coast. Guests can stay in a variety of accommodation – from simple camping to swish safari-style tents – and spend their time exploring the local culture and nature with the help of local guides.

Go Differently
Where? Thailand, Cambodia, Laos, India, Bhutan and Bali.
What? A specialist ethical tour company, it offers small group and tailor-made holidays and volunteering trips 'based on the appreciation and respect of the local environment and people'. Many of the trips are community-based and include the chance to visit homestays.

Wind, Sand and Stars
Where? Specialises in Sinai.
What? Takes individuals, as well as students and other groups, into the desert and its communities with the help of Bedouin guides. Or, as the company puts it, it works 'in harmony with the people who have roamed the desert landscapes for thousands of years'.

Green Visions
Where? Bosnia and Herzegovina.
What? Runs locally led 'eco tours' which explore both the traditional culture and natural environment of the region. Trips range from one-day hikes to five-day adventures and are run with the support of local villages.

Village Ways
Where? Northern India.
What? Primarily walking holidays between – and staying in – rural mountain villages, though village stays (without walking) can also be arranged. The aim is to generate sustainable local employment and thereby help halt the migration of young villagers to the cities.

Going by the book

It makes sense that the more you know about a place's culture and history, the more you will get from a trip. Take time to read up on a destination before setting off (and at the very least, learn to say please and thank you in the local language). This shows respect for the places and people you are visiting – and is the only sure-fire way to avoid causing unintended offence.

Mainstream guidebooks can be a useful starting point. Most include background information on the history, culture and politics of a destination and have taken the responsible tourism ethos on board. Bradt guides has a reputation for focusing on responsible tourism and its website includes a well thought-out section on giving something back. The company's founder, Hilary Bradt, believes that travelling sustainably involves far more than carbon emissions as a result of air travel, and that tourists can be a force for change. 'Travelling with the hope of having a positive impact is always going to be more rewarding than staying at home for fear of having a negative one,' she says. 'I think we should stop feeling guilty about travel and rejoice in the positive contribution we can make. Simply being there helps.'

Lonely Planet is also starting to highlight more low-impact experiences. In addition to its destination guides, it publishes some interesting niche books, including *Code Green*, about 'discovering a more authentic travel experience', a *Traveller's Guide to Volunteering* and a series on *Watching Wildlife*. The company also has a section on responsible tourism on its website and established the Lonely Planet Foundation in 2005. This commits 5 per cent of the company's annual profit towards grass-roots charities and has a mission to 'travel widely, tread lightly, give sustainably'.

The Rough Guides series is known for including in-depth background information on destinations, as well as more practical advice. Its *Ethical Travel 25* title is pretty slimline compared to its weightier books on *Climate Change* and *Ethical Living* but Rough Guides founder, Mark Ellingham, has been outspoken on his unease about 'binge flying'.

'The tobacco industry fouled up the world while denying [it] as much as possible for as long as they could,' he has said. 'If the travel industry rosily goes ahead as it is doing, ignoring the effect that carbon emissions from flying are having on climate change, we are putting ourselves in a very similar position to the tobacco industry.' He has urged readers not to fly to destinations within a six hundred-mile radius and, more controversially, stated: 'It is hard to say the positive impact of travelling can ever outweigh the damage done by simply travelling to the destination. Balancing all the positives and negatives, I'm not convinced there is such a thing as a "responsible" or "ethical" holiday.'

For cities, the *Time Out* guides are excellent, partly because they are written by locals. And, while Sawdays guides focus specifically on accommodation rather than destinations, they are worth a mention here because they encourage a responsible attitude to travel by neglecting chain hotels and mass market resorts and, instead, picking out small hotels, inns and B&Bs. The series' founder, Alastair Sawday, has also instilled the company with serious eco credentials. It is carbon neutral, prints on sustainably sourced paper and publishes a guide to *Green Places To Stay*, as well as a sister environmental series, *Fragile Earth*.

For more information on the cultural impact of travel, check out Tourism Concern's *Ethical Travel Guide*, written by Polly Pattullo and Orely Minelli, and *Final Call* by Leo Hickman, which goes behind the scenes of the tourist industry.

How to photograph responsibly

- If possible, always ask before taking pictures of people and/or their property, whether it's a market stall or a home.

- If there is time, build up a rapport with someone first before asking to take a picture – chat about their lives, tell them your name, ask theirs, say where you are from, buy something from their market stall.

- Don't flash camera equipment about. Keep it in an ordinary-looking bag until you need it. As well as being more secure, it may mean that people don't just see you as another tourist on the prowl for pictures.

- When travelling in poorer countries, where few people have cameras, giving someone an instant picture, such as a Polaroid, is a treasured present and a much better 'thank you' for being in a photograph than money. You'll suddenly find that everyone wants their picture taken.

- If people do ask for payment for a picture, fair enough. Negotiate the rate and be clear about whether that fee is per photo.

- Be aware of gender differences. In many cultures you will find it easier to photograph people of the same sex as you.

- When photographing children, ask for parent/guardian consent first if possible, and also ask the children themselves.

- Don't make promises you can't keep. If you say you will send copies of the pictures, do so (otherwise give a Polaroid, or at least show them the screen on a digital camera).

- Show some trust, sharing and fun. Let the people you photograph use your camera to take a picture of you and/or each other.

- Digital photography is more environmentally benign than film, with all its chemical processes, especially

if you take lots of pictures.

- If you take pictures professionally, remember to ask people to sign a model-release form (an agreement that they don't mind their picture being used commercially) if possible. If there are language or literacy difficulties, this may not be feasible. Presenting a form for someone to sign is intimidating if you cannot explain it clearly.

- Try travelling without a camera sometimes. You may find you enjoy your travels even more. There'll be less to carry, less to worry about and more chances for equal interaction. You won't forget it all. Buy postcards, make a scrap book of tickets, keep a journal, make friends and memories.

Advice given by Paul Miles, a professional photographer and writer, specialising in islands and sustainable tourism (www. paulmiles.co.uk)

Insider information

It isn't always possible to employ local guides but, where it is, it makes sense to do so. Whether running through the mating rituals of bonobos, unravelling a new depth of meaning to a Fra Angelico fresco or leading the way through the lesser known streets of a city, having a capable, knowledgeable guide in tow can make the experience both more entertaining and more meaningful.

In 2006, the travel magazine *Wanderlust* launched an award for guides to recognise their value. Named the Paul Morrison Guide Award, in honour of the magazine's late co-founder, the winners are nominated by readers and chosen by a panel of judges. Speaking about the award, *Wanderlust's* co-founder Lyn Hughes said that 'what separates the great guides from the merely good ones is the ability to empathise, to understand when clients are tired or suffering from information overload. A lot of travel companies are simply happy with someone who speaks English.' The inaugural award was won, jointly, by KC Bhuwan, a trekking guide based in the Annapurna region of Nepal, and Manda Chisanga, a safari guide from Zambia.

REALITY CHECK

'Reality' tours offer a different take on the insider experience, leading tourists through squatter settlements – usually in Rio, Cape Town, Johannesburg or Mumbai. The purpose of these trips is to show how life is for those who don't live in those glossy quarters of a city that we normally see as tourists.

The fact that these trips are also described as poverty tourism or 'poorism', however, helps explain why they're not always seen as a good thing. Critics of reality tours have claimed that they are an exercise in voyeurism and an attempt to cash in on the poor. While invasion of privacy is certainly an issue – and one that is relevant in many other areas of tourism – most reality tour operators are sensitive about intrusion. They also claim that the tours are a way of fostering understanding and generating income in areas that wouldn't otherwise benefit from tourism.

One example of these trips is Reality Tours and Travel, which takes tourists into the 432-acre Dharavi squatter settlement in Mumbai. Christopher Way, who runs the company along with business partner Krishna Poojari, has said: 'We're trying to dispel the myth that people there sit around doing nothing, that they're criminals. We show it for what it is – a place where people are working hard, struggling to make a living and doing it in an honest way.'

If you do join a reality tour, don't take photographs without asking and choose one run by a company which has a clear responsible tourism policy.

PORTER PROTECTION

In addition to hiring local guides, using local porters when trekking can be a good idea. In the Himalayas, around Kilimanjaro and on the Inca trail, porters are readily available. By employing them to go with you, it can make the journey easier, and create much-needed employment.

Porters often get a raw deal, however. To save on costs, some tourists cut down on the number of porters they employ, expecting one person to carry huge weights. Porters are also often badly equipped, making their way up mountains in flip-flops and a flimsy jumper. Unsurprisingly, many end up with frostbite, altitude sickness or hypothermia. Tourism Concern reports that, in Nepal, porters are often poor farmers from lowland areas, 'as unused to the high altitudes and harsh conditions as western trekkers'. It also states that Nepalese porters suffer four times more accidents and illnesses than Western trekkers.

To prevent this, choose a tour operator that abides by guidelines on the treatment of porters published by the International Porter Protection Group (Tourism Concern publishes a list of the UK tour operators which do). The guidelines state that:

- Clothing appropriate to season and altitude must be provided to porters for protection from cold, rain and snow.

- Above the tree line porters should have a dedicated shelter, either a room in a lodge or a tent, and a blanket or sleeping bag. They should be provided with food and warm drinks, or cooking equipment and fuel.

- Porters should be provided with the same standard of medical care as you would expect for yourself, and life insurance.

- Porters should not be paid off because of illness/injury without the leader or the trekkers assessing their condition carefully. Sick/injured porters should never be sent down alone, but with someone who speaks their language and understands their problem, along with a letter describing their complaint. Sufficient funds should be provided to cover the cost of rescue and treatment.

- No porter should be asked to carry a load that is too heavy for their physical abilities (maximum: 20 kg on Kilimanjaro, 25 kg in Peru and Pakistan, 30 kg in Nepal).

Oppressive regimes

One of the most difficult decisions to make regarding responsible travel is whether to visit countries with oppressive governments, or those with objectionable human rights records. Many people feel that visiting such countries supports those regimes, either by funding the relevant governments or, more directly, by staying in facilities which might have been built with the use of forced labour.

The Burma Campaign UK, for example, calls for a tourist boycott of Burma (Myanmar) because of the brutal activities of the country's military dictatorship and the detention of democracy leader Aung San Suu Kyi. It publishes a list of so-called 'dirty' companies which it says support the Burmese government. This includes tour operators, such as Abercrombie & Kent, and Lonely Planet, which publishes a guide to the country.

Others, however, claim that small-scale, responsible tourism in Burma can be beneficial. The campaign group, Voices for Burma, states that: 'There is a place for responsible and ethical tourism to the country by individual travellers, in terms of aiding the economic welfare of local communities and raising awareness of the situation in Burma.'

Tourism Concern, however, believes that the idea of responsible travel in Burma is 'a very simplistic and idealistic view of international tourism. It is obvious from witnessing trends in neighbouring Thailand that this is not how the majority of tourists operate. It is not possible to encourage one type of tourist to travel to Burma but ban another inevitable set of travellers.'

Burma isn't the only problematic destination. There have also been calls for a tourist boycott on China, partly because of its poor human rights record and partly due to its activity in Tibet, which it annexed in 1951. In addition to its violent treatment of the Lhasa uprising of 1959, when thousands of Tibetans were killed and the Dalai Lama was forced into exile, China has systematically attempted to erode Tibetan culture, most recently by opening a rail link from Beijing to Lhasa in 2006. The Free Tibet Campaign offers advice for travellers to Tibet on how to maximise the benefit of any trip for Tibetans (rather than Chinese tourism businesses), how to avoid causing offence at religious sites and how to avoid getting Tibetans into dangerous situations with the Chinese authorities.

And, while not calling for an outright boycott, Tourism Concern is also running a campaign to increase awareness of human rights abuses in the Maldives. It states that, under the dictatorship of Maumoon Abdul Gayoom, nearly half the local population live on just over US $1 a day, that much-needed fresh fruit and vegetables are going to tourist islands rather than to local people and that 'the government continues to impose severe restrictions on freedom of expression'. The human rights NGO, Friends of Maldives, is also calling for a boycott of selected resorts, linked to members of the Gayoom regime. Its website includes an updated list.

For the most up-to-date list of concerns surrounding particular countries, try looking at the websites of Human Rights Watch and Amnesty International.

EIGHT SHORTCUTS TO A CITY

Like A Local
Where? Cities worldwide but mainly Amsterdam.
What? A service that connects you to suitable locals, from biking fanatics who will take you on a tour of the quieter corners of a city to cake lovers who will Introduce you to the city's best foodie spots.
How? You book ahead and pay per experience – either sightseeing, eating dinner at someone's home or staying overnight with someone.
Getting in touch: 00 31 20 530 1460; www.like-a-local.com.

Insider Tour
Where? Berlin.
What? A choice of themed walking and bike tours of the city (from 'Third Reich' to 'Beer and Sauerkraut') led by enthusiastic locals rather than professional guides. Most are group tours, so you won't be on your own.
How? You book and pay – usually around €12 – online.
Getting in touch: www.insidertour.com.

Chinatown Alleyway Tours
Where? San Francisco.
What? Not-for-profit two-hour walking tours led by young locals and organised with the help of the Chinatown Community Development Center. Tourists are steered off the main streets, to explore the culture, history and contemporary life of Chinatown. Or, as they put it, 'see the community like the residents see it'.
How? Book online and pay $18 on the day.
Getting in touch: www.chinatownalleywaytours.org.

My Genie In Paris
Where? Paris.
What? A 45-minute chat with a local insider, ending with a personalised itinerary. Your chance to pick their brain about everything from attractions and restaurants to markets, specialist shops and good places for a riverside walk.
How? Book ahead and they'll meet you in your hotel lounge – for €75.
Getting in touch: 00 33 1 43 18 18 46; www. mygenieinparis.com.

CPH Cool
Where? Copenhagen.
What? Private guided walks, in Danish or English, through the city's trendiest neighbourhoods – Vesterbro and City. 'No more monuments and museums – we show you the trendy shops, secret backyards, cool cafés and hot spots of the vibrant city. Experience Copenhagen the way we like it.'
How? Two hour walks cost DKK200.
Getting in touch: 00 45 2980 1040; www.cphcool.dk.

Big Apple Greeter
Where? New York.
What? 'See New York through the eyes of a New Yorker.' Tourists are matched with one of over three hundred volunteer 'greeters' and, for between two to four hours, they're shown the friendlier side of the Big Apple.
How? It's a bookable, free service. There's a no tipping policy but satisfied customers can donate online.
Getting in touch: 00 1 212 669 8159; www.bigapplegreeter.org.

City Sherpa
Where? Helsinki.
What? A seasonal, summer-only service which pairs willing locals with wishful tourists, the aim is to spend a few hours in a local's company being shown an insider's take on the Finnish capital.
How? Contact one of the sherpas through the scheme's blog and they will decide whether or not they want to be your partner in crime. It's a free service.
Getting in touch: http://blogit.hs.fi/citysherpa.

Couchsurfing
Where? Worldwide.
What? This site made its name by pairing up people who needed somewhere to stay for a night with anyone boasting a spare sofa. But its mission is to 'create educational exchanges, raise collective consciousness, spread tolerance and facilitate cultural understanding', which means you can also use it just to meet a friendly face for a coffee.
How? You sign up to become a member and then search online. It's free to use.
Getting in touch: www.couchsurfing.com.

Food for thoughtful travellers

From pizzas in Naples to tom yam soup in Thailand or masala dosas in India, food instils a sense of place better than any travel guide. But eating local isn't only enjoyable, it's also responsible. Forgoing imported food and drink in favour of local (ideally organic) alternatives cuts down on food miles and puts money into local pockets.

The concept can be taken too far, however. Many traditional 'delicacies' are made from, or include, endangered species. In 2007, for example, WWF Hong Kong put out a list of 'five things not to eat during the Chinese New Year'. This included abalone, shark fin soup, sea cucumber, facai moss and health tonics containing endangered species such as wild ginseng, Asian freshwater turtles, seahorses, saiga antelope, pangolins, geckos and tigers. 'All of these species are subject to overexploitation and uncontrolled trade,' the organisation states. The International Fund for Animal Welfare (IFAW) also cautions travellers against eating whale or bush meat.

Many of the world's fish stocks are also becoming endangered. The Toronto-based Endangered Fish Alliance advises against eating swordfish, Chilean seabass, orange roughy and caviar on the grounds that they are being 'overfished, oversold and overeaten', though it is not an exhaustive list.

You might also want to avoid certain foods on ethical grounds. Compassion in World Farming (CIWF), which campaigns against cruelty to farm animals – including the caging of hens and the long-distance transportation of live animals – also protests against the production of 'posh nosh' involving the inhumane treatment of animals. Among its list are frogs legs, which the organisation states often come from Indonesia, where they are sliced up (while still conscious) at local cutting centres. Foie gras is also slated. Produced by force-feeding ducks and geese until their livers expand to an abnormally large size, according to CIWF 'the swollen liver expands the abdomen and can make walking and breathing difficult, as well as causing other health problems. Many of these birds are kept confined in cages throughout the force-feeding period.'

Savvy souvenir hunting

Shopping for souvenirs can help fund local communities and promote traditional crafts and skills. In many areas, for example, traditional textiles and organic skincare products are made by women's co-operatives, generating employment for those with otherwise limited options.

Before you splash out on more exotic mementos, though, be aware that certain articles are best avoided. Rare hard wood products and ancient artefacts are obvious no-nos, as are endangered species, or anything made from them. Over eight hundred species of animals and plants are currently banned from international trade and a further thirty thousand tightly controlled by the Convention on International Trade in Endangered Species (CITES). Yet a recent campaign by the WWF stated that a stool made out of an elephant's foot, a leopard-skin waistcoat and a live scorpion had all been brought into the UK as grisly souvenirs.

IFAW'S LIST OF WHAT NOT TO BUY

Ivory 'Poaching is still rampant in both Africa and Asia to supply the huge demand for ivory products. Ivory is often carved into jewellery, chopsticks, hair slides, ornaments and name seals. Elephant leather and hair products are also commonly for sale.'

Reptile skins 'Skins from crocodiles, alligators, snakes, lizards and other reptiles are often made into bags, shoes, watch straps or belts. It is hard to tell the difference between the skin of an endangered and non-endangered species.'

Tortoiseshell 'The term commonly used for sea turtle shell, which is frequently turned into souvenirs such as sunglasses, hair slides and jewellery. International trade in the products of all marine turtles is illegal. Yet they are still widely available in resorts all over the world.'

Seahorses 'The primary uses for seahorses are traditional medicines, souvenirs and curios (dried trade) and trade as aquarium pets (live trade). The global trade in dried seahorses exceeded 24.5 million individuals in 2000.'

Corals 'Commonly harvested for souvenirs, corals play an essential role in shallow water reef ecosystems by providing food and shelter for thousands of other species. Many species of corals are protected, with trade either regulated or strictly prohibited.'

Seashells 'Harvesting in great quantities has pushed some into the endangered zone – especially large ones such as the queen conch and the giant clam which take many decades to grow.'

Sharks' teeth 'Pendants or mounted jaws are common in many coastal resorts around the world. More than one hundred million sharks are killed each year and the increasing trade in shark souvenirs is pushing threatened species closer to extinction.'

Big cat skins 'Tigers, leopards, cheetahs and lions have long been slaughtered for their beautiful and distinctive furs. Despite falling numbers in the wild and the fact that they are protected from international trade, the market for big cat coats, bags, rugs and other trophies continues.'

Caviar 'Sturgeon eggs are considered by some as a luxury. All 27 species of this fish are threatened or endangered, usually caught before they reach sexual maturity. The beluga sturgeon, the world's largest freshwater fish, is now in danger of extinction after 250 million years on earth.'

Live animals 'About ninety per cent of reptiles and amphibians die before leaving their country of origin, due to inhumane captive and storage conditions. A further ninety per cent die within a year after being taken home.'

Traditional medicines 'While many of these are made from species which are not endangered, some products are made from protected plants and animals such as tigers, rhinos and bears. Tiger bone, organs, genitals and whiskers are all used to treat various ailments. It is estimated that one tiger out of the five thousand wild tigers left is poached each day to supply this trade.'

Other wildlife items 'While not always illegal, it is wise to also steer clear of any products made from furs, claws, teeth, butterflies, insects, birds' eggs or stuffed animals. Many of these products are from endangered or threatened species.'

More common mistakenly bought souvenirs include ivory carvings and jewellery, tortoise and turtle shell accessories, big cat skins, reptile skin handbags, belts and shoes, porcupine quill coasters and lampshades, coral and shells. According to IFAW, 'Many tourists buying souvenirs made from wildlife have no idea that they have done anything wrong, often because these items are sold openly in vacation resorts, airports, shops and markets — masking the bloody truth behind the wildlife trinkets being sold.'

Animal attractions

It isn't just buying wildlife that it pays to be cautious about. From dancing bears to elephant rides, many living animals have been – and are being – exploited in the name of tourism. The RSPCA advises travellers not to patronise bullfights, rodeos or circuses on cruelty grounds. Animal rights campaigners have also criticised less-obviously exploitative animal attractions, such as zoos and aquariums.

According to the Captive Animals Protection Society (CAPS), 'Zoos are a relic of a bygone age – a Victorian concept which, as our knowledge of the animal kingdom grows, becomes even less palatable.' The society 'is totally opposed to the incarceration of animals and believes that zoos misinform rather than educate, and further, divert funds from positive conservation. Animals remain threatened or are even driven to extinction, whilst precious resources are drained away on expensive, high profile breeding projects with no serious hope of success.'

Wildlife charity the Born Free Foundation also runs a 'Zoo Check' campaign, which protests against holding animals captive for entertainment. 'Whether in zoos, circuses, animal shows or marine parks, wild animals suffer physically and mentally from the lack of freedom that captivity imposes', the organisation states.

But others argue that properly managed zoos can be a useful educational tool, championing endangered species and highlighting the importance of conservation. Ticket sales at London Zoo, for example, which is run by the Zoological Society of London, help generate around £10 million each year for conservation programmes.

GENERAL RULES OF THE TRAVELLING ROAD

Avoid using endless plastic water bottles to cut down on non-biodegradable plastic waste. Instead, fill up from taps or filtered/ boiled water dispensers. Try to use returnable glass bottles for soft drinks.

Try not to create unnecessary litter. Waste disposal can be a problem in less developed countries. On a related note, try to avoid take-away food and drinks.

Avoid excessive wrapping and plastic bags – you don't need a plastic shopping bag to carry three postcards back to your hotel. Better still, pack your own re-usable shopping bag.

Use re-chargeable batteries, or use solar or wind-up torches and radios instead.

Conserve water by taking short showers, forgoing baths and not leaving the tap running when you're brushing your teeth.

Switch off unnecessary air-conditioning, heating, lighting and electronic gadgets – especially when you're not in your hotel room.

Hire bicycles for short trips and try to use public transport for longer journeys.

Read up before you go but don't take what you read on the page so literally that you switch off from reality. Veering off into the unknown, diverting from the plan and being open to other views are all part of the experience.

Buy local produce in preference to imported goods and hire local guides.

Be respectful of local norms and dress appropriately.

Be patient and acknowledge that people in different countries have different attitudes – especially where time is concerned.

Haggle with humour and keep a sense of perspective. The 100 rupees you're being asked to pay over the odds for a service won't make a big dent in your budget, but they might make an enormous difference to a person living on a few dollars, or less, a day. Pay what something is worth to you.

Support local conservation or community charities.

Begging the question

How to respond to begging is one of the most common dilemmas facing travellers to developing countries. It is difficult to ignore a plea for help from somebody in a desperate situation, but by handing out money or sweets to children, for example, you might be encouraging them into a dependency on hand-outs from tourists and discouraging them from finding more constructive employment – or, in the short term, from going to school. And there's no guarantee that your money is going to where it's most needed.

There are no right or wrong answers. Janice Booth, who co-wrote Bradt's *Rwanda* guide suggests, 'if you decide to give cash on the spot, then do look the person in the eyes, smile and say an appropriate "good morning"; being given a coin is probably far less of a novelty to him or her than being treated like a human being.'

She also advises learning how to ask a person's name in the appropriate language. 'The effect is astonishing on someone, whether child or adult, who's used to being ignored or pushed aside. Even if you only learn their name, tell them yours and then say goodbye, you've lifted them several rungs up the scale of humanity – and again, that's what they'll remember. Or if you're refusing to give, then use their name politely as you say "no". By using their name you give them dignity, and they respond.'

Making a more substantial donation to a relevant local charity, where your money can be distributed more fairly, is one practical solution. Pens, crayons and notebooks are also normally well received by local schools. Stuff Your Rucksack, a website backed by TV presenter Kate Humble, takes the concept further. You can look up destinations on the site before you go, see what various organisations there need – from books for a school to clothes for an orphanage – and take out supplies with you.

ARE WE NEARLY THERE YET?

Travelling responsibly with children

'We took our boys (then four and eight) to Tanzania two years ago, and they loved it. Going on holiday to somewhere with a very different culture, and approaching it in a sensitive way, can make a really positive impact on your kids. Mine still remember the people they met and the wildlife they saw. They vividly remember going to a Maasai school in a very poor rural region and noticing how different it was for the children there. They now have an appreciation of what these rural Tanzanian school kids have (or have not) in comparison to the facilities they enjoy at school. Also, actually meeting these children, and laughing with them, means that when they now see images of children in Africa on TV, instead of them just being a story, they see them as real people. My eldest also came home with a passion for wildlife, and wanting to care for wildlife. He's into birding now!'
Amanda Marks, Tribes Travel

'Children on holiday with their parents are learning as they go. If their parents are cavorting on the beach, playing golf, treating waiters with contempt, dragging them to nightclubs, swearing at the natives, refusing to speak the language, chasing the English papers for news of the football and heading straight for McDonald's in every town, then cultural messages are being learned.

'We used to stay with farmers (via a book called *Vacances et Weekend a la Ferme* – from which I got the idea to publish my own books) en route to Cahors to stay with my sister. They would always be delightful with the children, and we expected the boys to speak French – of a sort. My sister was deeply rooted in France so being with her felt very "French". Holiday time would involve visiting markets and villages, canoeing down rivers and immersing ourselves in the countryside. I would chat away to everyone I met, irritatingly perhaps, but that must have had some effect. Both boys speak French, are passionate about responsible travel and wouldn't do any of those things I derided in the second sentence – would they?'
Alastair Sawday, Alastair Sawday Publishing

CHAPTER SIX

HOLIDAYING AT HOME

Best of British

In the 1850s a cabinet-maker and temperance worker called Thomas Cook began organising 'grand circular tours' of Europe that included travel, food and accommodation. These were arguably the first overseas package holidays from the UK. A century later, however, a young journalist called Vladimir Raitz created something much closer to what we would describe as a typical package holiday, when he chartered a plane and took a group of paying teachers and students to Corsica on an all-in trip that included transport, tented accommodation, food and wine. This burst of sun – at a price that many people could afford – was just what post-war Brits wanted and the concept rapidly took off. By 2006, over sixteen million of us were holidaying in Spain each year.

But before the rise of cheap package holidays, the majority of the British population had holidayed at home – largely in the seaside resorts which had boomed in the mid-nineteenth century with improvements in transport. Now, with growing concerns about air travel and dramatic improvements in the standard of food and accommodation in the UK, more of us are choosing to holiday at home once more.

Happily for anyone worried about carbon emissions, this is also one of the greenest ways to take a break. Distances covered by transport within the UK are minimal compared to taking a long-haul flight and, with a bit of planning and effort, many journeys can be done by public transport.

Britain also has generally good access to recycling and other managed waste facilities. An increasing number of outlets stock or serve delicious organic, seasonal, locally grown food. And, while not always adhered to, firm legislation on issues such as pollution, working conditions and the treatment of animals means that the UK is also a relatively socially responsible destination.

In many ways it is also easier to travel responsibly in your own country, since you will be better informed of environmental issues such as water restrictions and social challenges than you might be in less familiar destinations. That said some holidays are greener than others. As with choosing a holiday abroad, if you want to make sure you're enjoying a green experience you need to do your research before you leave home.

Boutique style

The rise of the 'boutique' hotel has added to this newfound enthusiasm for Blighty. While B&Bs and even campsites are now getting in on the act, the boutique concept started out as a way of describing hotels that were small-scale and stylish. More recently the term has become a largely meaningless label: if Fawlty Towers were around today, it would probably be decked out with fancy wallpaper and a rash of scented candles and calling itself a boutique hotel. Indisputably, however, the 'boutique' trend has raised standards throughout the industry. These days finding a decent duvet, quality bedlinen, ground coffee and fresh milk in your hotel room isn't unusual.

In the UK, the Malmaison and Hotel du Vin chains carved a niche with characterful urban properties that featured personal service and a realistic price tag – Malmaison's latest opening, in Oxford, is a former prison, while Hotel du Vin's Birmingham branch used to be a hospital. Other trailblazers included 42 The Calls in Leeds and The Eton Collection, which owns five properties in London, Leeds and Edinburgh. Elsewhere, Liverpool's Hope Street Hotel and Nottingham's Lace Market Hotel are model examples of the trend, as are the Townhouse Company's five boutique hotels and serviced apartments in Edinburgh and Glasgow.

Britain's cities don't have a monopoly over stylish small hotels, however. In Cornwall, Olga Polizzi's elegant Tresanton Hotel remains perennially popular. And, out in the sticks a new breed of contemporary country house hotel has developed over the past few years, sticking two sophisticated fingers up at the more staid end of the country retreat experience.

First past the post was Babington House in Somerset, a 28-bedroom mansion which opened in 1998 offering weekending urbanites pared-down, designer bedrooms and a sleek cow-themed spa. Several other contemporary country house hotels have joined the herd since then, many of them catering elaborately for families (see box opposite). Among the most successful are Cowley Manor and Barnsley House in Gloucestershire and Whatley Manor in Wiltshire.

In response to this new competition, many of the more old-school country house hotels have upped their game. In a rush to stand out from the crowd, many now positively promote local food and drink, provide local employment and training, and otherwise boost local economies.

Whether your tastes veer towards ancient or modern, the *Good Hotel Guide* is a useful independent source of information on characterful UK accommodation. The following marketing groups can also be helpful: Chic Retreats, Chic Treats, Design Hotels, Great Hotels of the World, Great Small Hotels, I Escape, Leading Hotels of the World, Mr and Mrs Smith, Pride of Britain Hotels, Small Luxury Hotels of the World, Tablet Hotels, Travel Intelligence, Unusual Hotels of the World and Welsh Rarebits (details for these are included in the directory at the back of the book).

Cross-checking prices on websites such as www.laterooms.com, www.kayak.co.uk, www.traveljungle.co.uk, www.hotels.co.uk, www.lastminute.com, www.needahotel.com, www.priceline.co.uk and www.expedia.co.uk can be a good way of scouting out discount rates at a wide range of hotels. Before you book, check for unbiased reviews on websites like www.hotelchatter.com and www.tripadvisor.co.uk. Another useful website is www.allgohere.com, which rates UK hotels according to how disability-friendly they are.

SILVER SPOONS PROVIDED: FOUR WAYS TO TRACK DOWN A LUXURY FAMILY RETREAT

Baby Friendly Boltholes

An online directory of rental properties which combine 'taste with toddlers', the website currently features eighteen stylish family-friendly places to stay in the UK (as well as some abroad), many of them in Cornwall and Devon.

Luxury Family Hotels

This collection of five decadent hotels – Woolley Grange in Wiltshire, Fowey Hall in Cornwall, the Ickworth in Suffolk, Moonfleet Manor in Dorset and the Elms in Worcestershire – features some of the most elaborate children's facilities and activities in the country. None come cheap though.

Hip Hotels Kids

Due for publication in 2008, this is the next project from Hip Hotels founder Herbert Ypma, a coffee table guide to chic hotels that cater for families.

Take The Family

One of several specialist family travel websites (others include Baby Goes 2 and Family Travel), its current recommendations include several luxury, family-friendly hotels. Calcot Manor, for example, is an elegant country house hotel and spa in the Cotswolds which features an Ofsted-registered crèche, a 'playzone' and specially designed family rooms and suites, while Bedruthan Steps, a large, four-star hotel in Cornwall is big on both the environment (it has a written sustainable tourism policy) and on children. There are several children's clubs, a baby listening service (which is monitored from the reception), indoor and outdoor play areas, children's swimming pools and special meals.

Upmarket B&Bs

While the odd horror still exists, many B&Bs have now gone down the boutique road, offering style and elaborate (often homemade, organic) breakfasts at prices that compare well with hotels. Staying in a B&B is a great way to get a cultural insight into a local area and because they are independent business, many offer locally bought and produced food. Local tourist boards can be a good starting point for finding B&Bs, although the rating systems they apply tend to put more emphasis on properties having individual shaver points and matching crockery, rather than on whether they provide an enjoyable experience.

Some of the UK's best B&Bs are included in Alastair Sawday's *Special Places To Stay*. The website includes a map and word search facility, while the accompanying books offer a little more detail. Other useful sources of information include Distinctly Different, Wolsey Lodges and Farm Stay UK. For properties in London, At Home in London, the Bed and Breakfast Homestay Association and Uptown Reservations are also helpful.

Gastro tourism

For many, the ultimate break involves staying somewhere where the organic and local philosophy is maximised. This is good news for the environment because it cuts down on air miles – and polluting pesticides – but it is also socially responsible. By buying local produce from hotels, restaurants and attractions, tourists generate money and employment for local communities, helping to support rural economies.

The popularity of restaurants – and gastropubs (see box opposite) – with rooms has been one of the big successes in UK tourism over the last decade. Some of the best-known examples include The Star Inn at Harome, in North Yorkshire, which lives up to its name with a Michelin star, and Mr Underhill's in Ludlow, Shropshire, where the food is equally highly rated. Celebrity chef Rick Stein's food and accommodation empire is so all-encompassing in Padstow, Cornwall, that the town has been dubbed 'Padstein'.

Culinary tourism has really come into its own in Scotland and Wales, however. Restaurants with rooms north of the border include Monachyle Mhor and Ardeonaig Hotel in the Trossachs, the Albannach in Lochinver, the Three Chimneys on Skye and the Summer Isles Hotel in Achiltibuie. In Wales, The Drawing Room in Powys, Tyddyn Llan in Denbighshire and Plas Bodegroes in Gwynedd are among Welsh restaurants with rooms making the most of the demand for fresh, local ingredients.

At the top end of the price bracket, some of the most lavish eating and sleeping experiences can be had via Relais & Chateaux, an organisation which promotes small but sophisticated independent hotels and restaurants. Among its UK listings are the Waterside Inn at Bray, Le Manoir Aux Quat' Saisons in Oxfordshire, The Vineyard at Stockcross in Berkshire, Summer Lodge in Dorset and Glenapp Castle in Ayrshire.

It's not unusual to find foodie hotels with their own kitchen gardens, while properties such as Charlton House in Somerset even have their own farms attached (in this case it supplies the hotel with rare breed beef, lamb, venison and organic spelt). If you want to take the organic ethos a step further, Penrhos Court in Herefordshire, a fifteen-room hotel with an award-winning organic restaurant, runs dedicated 'green cuisine' courses.

SIX GASTROPUBS YOU CAN STAY AT

The Victoria at Holkham
Set on the north Norfolk coast this smart bohemian hideaway (its colourful interiors were designed by Miv Watts, mother of actress Naomi) is part of the Holkham estate. Its rooms are decadently comfortable and the fact that it's within pebble-hurling distance of Holkham Beach is a big selling point. So, too, is a menu that draws on local produce such as crabs from Cromer, mussels from Brancaster and venison, beef, game and eel from the Holkham estate.

The Sun Inn
Once a standard village pub, this Essex establishment – in Dedham, close to the Suffolk border – has been restyled by gastropub king Piers Baker and transformed into an altogether more cosseting experience. Modern Mediterranean cooking includes locally sourced produce from individual fruit and vegetable growers, a farmer who naturally rears rare breed meat, fish from day boats and herbs from the inn's garden.

The Village Pub
Tucked away in Barnsley, the Gloucestershire village that's home to the Barnsley House boutique hotel (in fact they're under the same ownership), this stays just on the right side of twee. With its mismatched wooden furniture, botanical prints and chintzy curtains, it's a lesson in cosy country style, without being too Disneyfied.

The Bell at Skenfrith
Just inside the Welsh border, in Monmouthshire, this ancient inn was named Michelin's Pub of the Year 2007. Bedrooms are luxurious but understated while good, modern cooking is helped by an adherence to 'unfussy, seasonal menus with locally sourced food from responsible and trustworthy establishments'.

The Punchbowl Inn
Sister establishment to the Drunken Duck in Ambleside, this Cumbrian hideaway is a no-nonsense retreat. Big on stone walls, slate floors and wellies, it features a hearty country menu (think mini cottage pies and fillet of Galloway beef with garlic mash and wild mushrooms) and access to spectacular views.

The CB Inn
Named after Charles Bathurst, lord of the local manor when it was built in the eighteenth century, this Swaledale bolthole is characterful as well as chic. Beams, ancient flagstones and simple white linen give a no-nonsense feel in the restaurant, while bedrooms are equally smart but unpretentious. If you're going for a hike, picnics can also be supplied.

Other good organic accommodation can be found through the *Organic Places To Stay* website and accompanying book, which lists a wide range of hand-picked small hotels, B&Bs and self-catering facilities in the UK.

Cottage escapes

Cottage holidays offer the chance to get to know an area well and, particularly in the countryside, to boost the local economy. One of the more responsibly minded operators is Under The Thatch, a small holiday rental company based in Ceredigion, west Wales, run by Greg Stevenson, an architecture lecturer and consultant.

The idea behind the company is that some of the problems associated with conventional cottage rentals – properties sitting empty for long periods and locals forced out by rising house prices – can be alleviated by confronting the issues head on. It never buys houses that were previously occupied by local people but instead renovates derelict, architecturally significant buildings using traditional methods and materials. Some cheaper structures, including gypsy caravans and converted railway carriages, are let out to help subsidise the renovation of more traditional properties.

This is no hair shirt experience though. The fifteen properties run by the company have been given four or five star gradings by the Welsh tourist board. It's also environmentally sound. Lime is used instead of cement, limewash instead of acrylic emulsions, and wool insulation rather than fibreglass. The company tries to ensure that its cottages are full by dropping its prices substantially in winter, in order to generate year-round custom for local shops and businesses.

Other specialist rental agencies and marketing organisations include Classic Cottages, Ecosse Unique, the Good Cottage Guide, Helpful Holidays, Hoseasons, Special Escapes and Rural Retreats, while English Heritage, the Landmark Trust, the National Trust, the National Trust for Scotland and the Vivat Trust all feature properties with historic and architectural character.

The website Next 6 Weeks specialises in short-notice lets. For larger, or grander, holiday lets, Celtic Castles, Large Holiday Houses, the Big Domain and Stately Holiday Homes are all worth contacting. And, if you want an all-frills service, the Great Escape Holiday Company features properties in Norfolk and London where private chefs, childminders and other services can all be arranged.

FIVE GREEN PLACES TO STAY IN THE UK

Loch Ossian Youth Hostel, Scotland
Thanks to a £130,000 'green-over' in 2003 the hostel now features an ecologically sound water and waste-disposal system, dry toilets which require no flushing and produce composted material, and a grey water system which processes used water through sand, gravel and a natural reed bed. Food waste is composted, power is provided by a wind turbine and a multi-fuel stove provides heat and hot water. Windows have been created using recycled floated glass, and 'bat-friendly' paints have been used.

Strattons Hotel, Norfolk
As well as re-writing its environmental policy every year, this small, family-run hotel buys local produce, avoids unnecessary packaging, recycles waste, provides toiletries in refillable dispensers rather than miniature plastic bottles, uses mainly low energy lightbulbs and has installed water-saving 'hippos' in toilet cisterns. 'This shows that being green doesn't mean you have to skimp on style,' says Richard.

Eco Cabin, Shropshire
Set in an 'Area of Outstanding Natural Beauty', the cabin's purpose-built design is constructed with local Douglas Fir, native larch boarding and British sheep's wool insulation. Internal walls are lined with reed board and lime plastered. The floor has been finished in native ash, and environmentally friendly paints and wood finishes have been used throughout. Most of the furnishings are recycled or reclaimed, hot water is provided by solar energy – and heating from a wood pellet stove – while electricity is supplied by Good Energy. It also offers guests a 'buy local' shopping service, bicycle hire and a cotton nappy hire and laundering service.

Higher Lank Farm, Cornwall
'Just because you have a young family doesn't mean you can't be green. This place shows you how,' says Richard. A small farmhouse B&B with two self-catering cottages, it caters specifically to young families. Green initiatives include nappy buckets and a nappy laundry service and the owners are planning to start a wormery, so that compostable disposable nappies can be used. The farm also provides recycling bins for newspapers, plastics, bottles and cardboard and refillable pump dispensers for hand and body washes. The cottages (barn conversions) have high levels of insulation, wood-burning stoves and underfloor heating to save on oil consumption and 'A' rated electrical appliances.

Lundy Island campsite, Devon
Set just off the Devonshire coast, this island is managed by the Landmark Trust, which lets out various properties as holiday rentals. It also has a campsite – a large grassy field sheltered by a granite wall. Close to the centre of the village, near the Tavern and shop, an adjacent building provides hot and cold water, three showers and six toilets. 'Camping is low impact and, because the island is only accessible by boat, it's perfect for a green mini adventure,' says Richard.

As chosen by Richard Hammond editor of the Green Traveller website and the author of Green Places To Stay *(Alastair Sawday Publishing)*

Green breaks

While the UK is full of 'light green' opportunities for holidaying, there are some darker green options. As discussed in Chapter Two, many of the big hotel chains have implemented green initiatives such as key cards which automatically turn off lights and electrical appliances when guests leave a room. Some individual hotels in the UK have gone further. The Zetter, in London, for example, features an air-conditioning system which runs on water pumped from a borehole 1,500 feet below the building (post-filtration, the water is also supplied in the guest rooms) and is decorated with eco-paints and recycled timbers.

Further north, the five-star Gleneagles hotel is aiming to go carbon neutral – partly by installing a woodchip boiler – while, at the cheaper end of the scale, in 2006 the Lockton and Langdon Beck hostels were the first in the UK to be awarded the European Ecolabel because of their responsible approaches to energy efficiency, water use and staff training.

Green B&Bs, meanwhile, include the Old Chapel Forge near Chichester – where water is solar-heated, 'sun pipes' take the place of lights and there's a water-harvesting system – and Cumbria House, in Keswick, where energy-saving initiatives are paired with discounts for guests who arrive by foot, bike or public transport. In Snowdonia, the owners of Bryn Elltyd B&B have installed solar heating, solid fuel stoves supplied by their own trees and renewably sourced electricity. Food is also mostly organic and locally sourced.

There are now several UK 'eco' cottages, too. Some of the best-known include the cottages at Trelowarren, in Cornwall, which have been decorated with organic paints and feature showers and baths fed with recycled rainwater, and the Aislabeck eco lodges outside Richmond in Yorkshire. These are made from sustainable materials, feature woodchip boilers, evergreen roof gardens, a reed-bed sewage system and renewably sourced electricity and get their water from a natural spring.

To find more green places to stay, the Green Tourism Business Scheme recognises over a thousand sustainable businesses in England and Scotland. It rates them according to around 120 criteria, and then certifies them bronze, silver or gold. Members include many hotels, guesthouses and cottages, all of which can be searched for via maps on its website. The one catch is that businesses can only apply for membership if their properties are members of other quality assurance schemes, such as the AA or Visit Britain.

Similar initiatives on a more local scale include Discover Devon Naturally, a council-run scheme which lists green accommodation and attractions on its website, while the Considerate Hoteliers Association is a nationwide scheme which aims to 'encourage, assist, cajole and motivate fellow hoteliers to adopt sound and sustainable environmentally friendly and socially responsible practices'. Its website lists member hotels.

THE HAPPY CAMPERS' TOP FIVE UK CAMPSITES

Shell Island, Gwynedd
'This is a firm favourite as we both started camping here as kids. This tent-only site has some three hundred acres of land allocated to camping so you can really have your own little piece of wilderness. A must for enthusiastic beachcombers, it has three beautiful beaches which hold a treasure trove of shells – up to two hundred different varieties – and it has one golden rule: campers may not pitch within twenty yards of another tent in the same field unless prior agreement is reached with adjoining campers. A very popular rule.'

Tresseck Campsite, Hereford
'Fancy drifting down a slow river? Then pack your tent for a holiday at Tresseck campsite in Hereford. Perfect for a bit of peace and tranquillity, you can launch your canoe directly from the campsite and explore the picturesque River Wye. After all that strenuous activity what better than an evening around the campfire – a treat positively encouraged here.'

Fisherground Campsite, Cumbria
'We love this campsite as it's great for both big and small kids. It's brilliant for families, with plenty of adventure activities to keep even the most energetic children happy. There are rafts on the pond, a tree house, a zip wire, Tarzan ropes and an adventure course. The campsite is at Eskdale – well positioned for family walks and trips to the lakes.'

Glyn Y Mul Farm, West Glamorgan
'Go back to nature when you stay at this small family-run campsite on a working farm. It promises peace and quiet camping with all the treats of the Welsh countryside – magnificent scenery, clear water swimming holes and rushing rivers. As well as the more traditional campsite it also offers woodland camping with absolutely no facilities (by arrangement) – so if you've ever yearned for a real getaway this one is for you.'

Ewelease Farm, Dorset
'Every August the farm is open for tent camping. The campsite is stunning, in an area of outstanding natural beauty with its own beach. It has amazing views, is never too crowded and campfires are allowed on the beach so you can sometimes catch your supper if you're lucky. The only problem is that it's only open for 28 days a year.'

Campsites chosen by Tess Carr and Kat Heyes, authors of The Happy Campers *(Bloomsbury)*

Getting around

For a low-impact UK holiday, the best thing you can do is ditch the car, or at least make sure you're sharing the ride. It isn't always possible to reach the most remote destinations without your own wheels but, if you're concerned about carbon emissions, bus, train and ferry services will get you to most places between Orkney and the Scillies with a little effort (forward planning is even more important if you're taking a bike with you). The Traveline website is great for working out routes on public transport.

Better still, cycle. According to sustainable transport charity Sustrans, nearly half the UK population lives within a mile of the National Cycle Network. This now covers ten thousand miles, including long-distance routes such as the Sea to Sea (from Cumbria to the North Sea), Hadrian's Cycleway (from Glannaventa to Tynemouth), the Cornish Cycleway (from Land's End to Bude) and Belfast to Ballyshannon in Northern Ireland. Sustrans publishes maps and guides to these routes, as well as more general guides to the network. The Bike Events, Bike Week, Cyclists' Touring Club and Company of Cyclists websites are also useful sources of information.

If you're not confident enough to go it alone, various specialist tour operators arrange cycling holidays in the UK. Some are guided, some self-guided, and often luggage carrying services are part of the deal. These include Bicycle Beano Holidays, Byways Breaks, Country Lanes, Galloway Cycling, Cycle Breaks and Saddle Skedaddle. And, if you're not in peak shape, Natural Discovery rents out electric bikes in the Surrey Hills for day trips or longer breaks. These come with a small motor attached and can deliver power if and when you need it.

The lie of the land

With over 80 per cent of the UK population now living in urban areas, having access to nature has never been so important. Being active outdoors can relieve stress and increase our health. Yet many natural environments are under pressure from development, so making the most of the countryside isn't just personally beneficial, it can also be a responsible way of ensuring the natural world is vauled by society. It can foster understanding of rural lifestyles and generate interest in the preservation of natural landscapes. Simply using National Parks, nature reserves, Areas of Outstanding Natural Beauty, Sites of Scientific Interest and other green spaces can help to ensure that they aren't lost.

MOUNTAIN BIKING WITH CARE

Done with consideration, mountain biking is one of the most responsible ways to get out into the countryside. In the early days of the sport cyclists often used hiking trails, causing conflict with walkers and leading to erosion of footpaths, especially when used in wet conditions.

In response to such concerns, however, a number of specialist off-road mountain biking centres have been built in the UK, many of them run by the Forestry Commission in sustainably managed forests. Some of the most popular include Coed-y-Brenin and Afan Argoed in Wales and the 7 Stanes in Scotland. The International Mountain Biking Association (IMBA) provides information, guides and maps of these centres, as well as long-distance routes such as the Trans-Cambrian Way, a hundred-mile, three-day trip from Knighton in Powys to Dovey Junction near Machynlleth.

The association also actively promotes environmentally sound and socially responsible mountain biking. It advises cyclists to: ride on legal trails only; leave no trace; control their bike; always give way; never scare animals; and plan ahead.

If you haven't tried mountain biking before, several companies run beginners courses. Tyred Out, for example, organises year-round trips in Snowdonia National Park that take advantage of purpose-built tracks and scenic forest trails. Coaching in gear changing, braking techniques, route selection, basic navigation and general bike handling is given and the company also offers surprisingly chic accommodation.

Countryside tourism isn't just about nature, however. In many rural areas traditional industries such as agriculture, fishing and mining have declined and tourism has become a crucial factor in local economies. Of course, tourism has its downsides. Road congestion, house prices pushed up by second-home owners and conflict over land use can all cause problems in rural areas. But the benefits generally outweigh the negatives.

Tourism doesn't just help those who work directly in hotels and restaurants or at attractions. Visitors to the countryside use post offices, banks and grocers – especially outside the main holiday seasons when other tourist-focused restaurants and other services are more likely to be closed – which helps ensure the continued existence of those services. Supporting local artists and craft producers and visiting local festivals can also help enrich communities and promote traditional skills.

LOW-IMPACT COUNTRYSIDE TRIPS

Learn to surf

If you haven't surfed before, or you feel in need of some instruction, the British Surfing Association (BSA) is a good place to start. It runs courses at the National Surfing Centre in Newquay and recommends other surf schools on its website. It has also established a code of conduct for surfers, which covers safety, being considerate to others and reducing your environmental footprint.

On safari in Perthshire

Set near the eastern end of Loch Tay, outside the unpromisingly named Dull village, Highland Adventure Safaris takes visitors out to spot deer, eagles, mountain hare, ptarmigan, wheatears, meadow pipits and grouse, before serving up shortbread and whisky-laced afternoon teas. The company has a gold award from the Green Tourism scheme.

Go with the flow

The Outdoor Swimming Society encourages swimmers to go beyond chlorinated indoor pools and embrace chilly water, fresh air and freedom by taking a dip in clean lakes, rivers and lidos in the UK. River and lake swimming can be dangerous, however, so to avoid problems, heed the advice of the River and Lake Swimming Association, whose website gives information on various issues to be aware of when swimming outdoors. Alternatively, go with the professionals and join a swimming holiday in the Scillies with Swimtrek. The company's strapline is 'Ferries are for wimps, let's swim' – which gives you a good idea of what to expect.

On the wild side in Gower

If you fancy being a bit more self-sufficient, but don't know where to start, Dryad's Family Bushcraft Camp courses are an excellent first step. Taking place at Parc-le-Breos valley, in the centre of the Gower peninsula, during these outdoor weekends families can try a range of activities, including nature walks, coastal foraging, shelter building, fire lighting, wilderness cookery, willow craft and tracking. The Bushcraft UK website lists other companies offering similar trips.

Free range holidays

Shacklabank is a family farm in Cumbria that also offers 'free range' walking holidays. Guests are pampered with delicious homemade food, cosy accommodation and personal guiding from farmer-turned-walking guide Alison O'Neill. For other good walking trips, contact the Ramblers Association. Britain's biggest walking charity, its website has information on everything from specialist guides and maps and walking festivals to local walking groups and UK walking holiday companies.

Far out fun

An excellent way to introduce your family to the outdoors in a safe environment, Cape Adventure's 'family week' holidays take place every August, in Sutherland, in the far northwest of Scotland. Suitable for children of eight and up, and their parents, activities include hiking, survival skills, sea kayaking, beach walks, land yachting and surfing and cater for both first-timers and more experienced visitors. It's also as cosy as outdoor activity centres come, with comfy beds, proper hot showers, wood-burning stoves and lashings of home-cooked food.

Go solar

Traditional diesel-powered boats can disturb wildlife and pollute waterways. Solar-powered boats offer a more environmentally sensitive sailing experience. Four operators in the UK currently run passenger trips on solar boats: Bluebird Boats on the Serpentine in London, Chichester Harbour Conservancy in West Sussex, Coniston Ferry Services in the Lake District and the Norfolk Broads Authority. The Electric Boat Association also provides lots of information on low-impact boating.

On the water

Lough Erne has long been a popular destination among fishing and boating fans. But, building on Northern Ireland's newfound stability, the local tourist board is now trying to net a wider catch of visitors – including canoeists. One of the initiatives it has put in place is the Lough Erne Canoe Trail, which runs for over 50km of scenic, watery terrain, from Belturbet in the southeast to Belleek in the northwest. Along its length is a string of waterside attractions. Most have jetties which canoeists can paddle up to and park their equipment alongside while they explore on land. There's also a range of lough-side self-catering cottages, hotels and campsites. For guiding and equipment, contact the Outsiders' canoe club or visit the Lough Erne Canoe Trail website.

Argey bargey

The Caledonian Canal in Scotland connects up with lochs to link the North Sea to the North Atlantic between Inverness and Fort William via the Great Glen. Fingal of Caledonia is a hotel barge which cruises Loch Ness and the Caledonian Canal, stopping off at regular intervals for sightseeing, walking, cycling, canoeing and sailing. A schedule of different trips operates throughout the year, from themed wildlife cruises to Walk the Great Glen Way trips, where you hike along during the day and sleep in the barge at night. The Waterscape website contains plenty of ideas and information on other trips around Britain's waterways.

Country matters

Bearing the Countryside Code in mind can minimise the impact of your trip. The code applies to all parts of the countryside in England and Wales (the Scottish Outdoor Access Code offers similar advice north of the border) and, in brief, advises visitors to the countryside to:

- Be safe, plan ahead and follow any signs

- Leave gates and property as you find them

- Protect plants and animals and take your litter home

- Keep dogs under close control

- Consider other people

The Countryside Code and Countryside Recreation websites also include detailed listings of countryside charities, organisations, activity providers and rural businesses. Some of the largest organisations include the Association of National Park Authorities, Countryside Council for Wales, Forestry Commission, Natural England, Northern Ireland Countryside Access and Activities Network (CAAN) and Scottish Natural Heritage.

Many natural environments are managed by charities and rely on both volunteer workers (see below) and financial donations. If you use a particular area of the countryside regularly, you might want to contribute to its preservation. The National Trust for Scotland, for example, recently introduced an outdoors membership scheme where those who sign up enjoy all the benefits of standard NTS membership but whose money directly funds the organisation's outdoor work.

While there are many small charities dedicated to specific elements, or parts, of the British countryside, some of the larger countryside charities include the Campaign to Protect Rural England, the National Trust, the Royal Society for the Protection of Birds (RSPB), the 47 regional Wildlife Trusts and the Woodland Trust.

Other organisations are successfully campaigning to clean up Britain's coastline. Blue Flag, for example, is an international organisation that runs a scheme to award beaches and marinas with good water quality and properly managed sewage treatment, while ENCAMS, which runs the Keep Britain Tidy campaign, oversees the Quality Coast Awards in England (a separate Clean Coast Project covers Wales and Ireland).

The Marine Conservation Society publishes an annual Good Beach Guide, which rates 1,200 beaches in the UK and Ireland according to water quality. It has also established a Seaside Code to promote responsible behaviour at the beach.

THE MARINE CONSERVATION SOCIETY'S SEASIDE CODE

- **Check the public notice boards** for information on water quality, currents and emergency phones

- **Follow any advice from lifeguards** and understand the system of safety flags

- **Never leave young children unsupervised**

- **Do not swim when the sea is rough,** or where there are known currents or riptides

- **Do not use inflatable beds or toys** – currents can easily take you out of sight

- **Swim parallel to the shore rather than out to sea**

- **Do not swim immediately after a meal** and never after drinking alcohol

- **If you've been ill after bathing report the illness** to Surfers Against Sewage

- **If you see someone in trouble, alert the lifeguards,** or contact the coastguard – do not attempt to rescue them yourself, unless you are qualified and have help

- **Take rubbish home,** or place it in a bin

- **Join in with the MCS beach litter campaigns,** Beachwatch and Adopt-a-Beach, at your local beach

- **Keep your dog from fouling the beach**

- **Bag it and bin it** – don't flush it

- **Report canisters, drums or pollution** to the Environment Agency, or the Scottish Environment Protection Agency. Do not touch

Down on the farm

With sales of organic food increasing and a growing popularity for box delivery schemes, local markets and farm shops, some small-scale British food producers are doing well. Conventional agriculture, however, is in decline, defeated by low supermarket-driven prices as well as health scares such as BSE and Foot and Mouth disease. In response, many UK farmers have diversified into tourism. This has made the countryside more accessible for visitors and helped rural communities become more sustainable.

Farm Stay UK lists a wide range of B&Bs, cottages, caravans, campsites and bunkhouses on farms. You can search for these by map on the website or order the organisation's free annual guide. The website also carries links to regional farm-stay websites. There are also specialist rental agencies. Cartwheel, for example, covers farm-based self-catering cottages and B&Bs in Cornwall, Devon, Somerset and Dorset.

For days out at a farm, the 'Visit A Farm' page on the National Farm Attractions Network's website gives contact details for farms by region, and includes several pick-your-own fruit farms. The network also runs an annual awards scheme for farm attractions. Recent winners include Farmer Palmer's Farm Park in Dorset, which has a straw 'mountain', a play barn, an animal barn, daily cow milking demonstrations and outdoor adventure facilities. The Soil Association website also lists organic farms and farm attractions that are open to the public.

Farmer 4 A Day, in Cheshire, offers half day and full day farm experiences showing what life is really like on a modern dairy farm. These cover milking, feeding and mucking, and the full day package includes lunch at the local pub and a take-home pack of local cheeses. A less hands-on experience is on offer at Garroch Glen, in Dumfries and Galloway. This traditional farming estate puts together guided nature walks, fishing trips, horse and carriage rides and alfresco picnics for tourists, as well as operating informative and enthusiastic farm tours.

City farms also provide welcome green space and are often run in collaboration with local communities. The Federation of City Farms and Community Gardens represents 59 city farms in the UK as well as community gardens and allotments. Many of these are open to the public.

Architectural attractions

The threat of development also looms over much of our man-made heritage. For many castles, churches, follies and other architecturally or historically significant attractions, tourism provides an economic rationale for their continuing existence. As the cliché goes, it's often a case of using it, or losing it.

In addition to the National Trusts, the main heritage bodies in the UK include English Heritage, Historic Scotland, Cadw and the Environment and Heritage Service in Northern Ireland. The Civic Trust also works to improve the quality of the built environment and its impact on people. Its website contains a useful directory of other heritage organisations, including the local Heritage Initiative, Save Britain's Heritage, the Garden History Society, the Georgian Group and the Society for the Protection of Ancient Buildings.

The Civic Trust runs annual Heritage Open Days each September, in conjunction with English Heritage. Designed to celebrate England's architecture and culture, the event offers free access to properties that are usually closed to the public or normally charge for admission over four days. These range from castles and temples to factories and follies. Other similar events include Doors Open Days in Scotland and Open House London.

Volunteering

Many people are now choosing to spend part of their holidays in a more hands-on style, volunteering with local groups on a range of projects. The National Centre for Volunteering website is a good one-stop shop for finding general information and advice on volunteering in England and beyond. It includes contact details for volunteering organisations by area of interest, such as animal welfare, arts and heritage, environmental and conservation, and health and social care. The website also contains links to UK volunteering organisations such as Do It, Timebank and REACH.

Many of these organisations cover regular part-time volunteering or long-term placements, however. For volunteering holidays, the British Trust for Conservation Volunteers (BTCV), the National Trust, National Trust for Scotland and World Wide Opportunities on Organic Farms (WWOOF) are all good starting points.

The first three organisations mainly cover conservation and environmental work, from dry-stone walling to beach cleaning, while WWOOF can put volunteers in contact with organic farms, gardens or smallholdings around the world.

FIVE BIG GREEN DAYS OUT

Centre for Alternative Technology, Powys
Focusing on how twenty-first century daily life can be made more sustainable, this attraction looks at practical ways of dealing with climate change, pollution and resource waste. Displays cover renewable energy, environmental building, energy efficiency, organic growing and alternative sewage systems. The centre also runs a range of residential courses.

Whisby Natural World Centre, Lincolnshire
There's a café, Fairtrade gift shop and six miles of nature trails to explore here but the main attraction is the 'Our Changing World' exhibition. Designed with children in mind, this runs through topics such as climate change and eco-friendly technology in a lively, informative style.

Ecos Millennium Environmental Centre, Antrim
With interactive displays covering both environmental issues and nature conservation, this centre is set in a developing country park, so there's a particular focus on wildlife. It's also built and run sustainably, using solar panels and wind power. Coppiced willow is grown on site and electric bikes can be hired to explore the park.

The Genesis Centre, Somerset
An open demonstration of sustainable building, this is part of the Somerset College of Arts and Technology. Besides being a showcase for natural materials and green architecture, what makes it particularly interesting is that sections of the building have been cut away to clearly show the processes behind its construction. There's also a shop on site, selling books, ecopaints and green cleaning materials. Guided tours are available for pre-booked groups.

Craigencalt Ecology Centre, Fife
Surrounded by woodlands, wildflower meadows, a herb garden and ponds, the main attraction at this Scottish centre is the UK's first 'earthship', a building made from earth-filled tyres and aluminium cans that is designed to naturally store the sun's heat. It's very visitor-friendly, with a regular programme of events and workshops.

Green attractions

Many modern tourist attractions have successfully incorporated green design elements and responsible practices into their businesses. The Eden Project in Cornwall, for example, is a disused quarry turned botanical attraction that features recycling facilities, solar panels and wind power. It also offers discounts for those arriving by public transport or by bike.

If you want to take the green theme a step further, there are a growing number of specialist environmental attractions in the UK. Local tourist boards provide information on green attractions and events, as do the websites Where Can We Go and What's On When. More specifically, the 'Centres of Inspiration' guide published by *Green Futures* magazine covers more than 20 green attractions in the UK, from wind turbine tours to wildflower trails. The guide can also be downloaded as a PDF from the Green Futures website. Eco Escape, a handy guide to 'responsible escapism' in the UK also gives lots of ideas on green attractions, green places to stay and eat and green festivals.

THE BIG CHILL

Spa breaks may be associated with personal wellbeing but they haven't traditionally been especially pampering for the planet. Spas often come with swimming pools, saunas and steam rooms, which use a lot of water and electricity and, in many cases, generous supplies of chlorine. The washing and drying of fluffy towels and bathrobes also leaves a heavy carbon footprint. And spa treatments often involve heavy use of polluting, non-biodegradable products.

Happily, however, a new breed of eco spa has sprung up in recent times. Built from sustainable natural materials, making use of natural amenities such as hot springs and switching to organic, biodegradable products, these are much more forgiving on the environment. While the trend is only just starting to catch on in the UK, here are five spas that are at least heading in the right direction.

Titanic Mill, Huddersfield
An 'eco' spa set in a former textile factory, it boasts a chlorine-free pool, borehole-supplied water, electricity from photovoltaic roof tiles and heating from a biomass generator that burns chippings from industrial waste.

Thermae Bath Spa, Bath

While not as green as it could be, this spa complex does win some points for utilising the only hot springs in the country to warm its two natural thermal baths (famously used by the locals since Roman times). It also uses earth-friendly Pevonia Botanica products in its beauty treatments.

The Hay Barn, Gloucestershire

Daylesford Organics is better known for its organic food store but the company also runs an eco-friendly spa, the Hay Barn. The building is designed to make efficient use of natural light and ventilation and features low-energy lighting and heating. It also uses mostly organic products.

Senspa, Hampshire

This New Forest spa may not be as green as some of the others on this list but it does offer incentives for car-free guests, source its energy from a green supplier and use organic, biodynamic, sustainably sourced products.

Monty's Spa, Somerset

Part of Charlton Hotel, which is run by the founders of the Mulberry company, this spa is as organic in philosophy as the rest of the business (which also includes the Sharpham Park organic farm). The spa is generally as environmentally profligate as the next one but it does use 100 per cent natural products, including some tailored around the farm's spelt crop.

Budock Vean, Cornwall

Along with the hotel it is set within, this spa holds a gold award from the UK's Green Tourism Scheme. While not an 'eco' spa as such, it does use local organic beauty products in its treatments and recycles waste water from the spa to water the hotel's 65-acre organic garden.

CHAPTER SEVEN

THE FINAL COUNTDOWN

Wanted on board?

So you've decided to travel more responsibly? Probably the first thing scribbled on your holiday to-do list is how to get to a destination and find a place to stay without betraying your environmental ideals. But how you prepare for a trip is as important as what you do when you're there.

Packing up

Unless you travel with only the clothes you stand up in, sooner or later you'll need to confront the issue of luggage. Trouble is, baggage tends to come with a lot of baggage.

Before a product has even reached the factory stage, its material may have been bleached with chlorine, coloured using heavy metal dyes or treated with substances such as formaldehyde to prevent creasing. Yet the International Agency for Research on Cancer (IARC) has suggested a causal relationship between exposure to formaldehyde and nasopharyngeal cancer (cancer of the back of the mouth and nose). And prolonged contact with heavy metal dyes can cause cancer, as well as nausea, vomiting, diarrhoea, headaches and an impairment in cognitive, motor and language skills (the phrase 'mad as a hatter' is thought to come from the prevalence of mercury poisoning among eighteenth- and nineteenth-century milliners in France, who regularly handled mercury-soaked fabrics).

'Natural' fibres are not always good either. If your snazzy new holdall is made from cotton,

PACKING LIKE A PRO
Five things the travel experts always take with them. Do they get it right? You decide...

The Entrepreneur
Justin Francis is co-founder of online travel agency www.responsibletravel.com

1. **Polaroid camera**
'Just for the joy of giving people pictures (rather than taking them) and watching their faces as they develop in front of them.'

2. **Phrase book**
'Travelling with a little respect earns you respect.'

3. **Kikoy**
'These East African cotton wraps are the most useful multi-purpose garment on the planet. Use them as a scarf, a sarong – whatever you want!'

4. **Good book**
'Based in the destination, or written by a local person.'

5. **Water bottle**
'To fill up with tap water, so there's no need to buy plastic bottles.'

the likelihood is that the raw material it was shaped from was grown with the use of pesticides. According to the Environmental Justice Foundation, cotton accounts for 16 per cent of global insecticide use, more than any other crop, and has been found to cause vomiting, paralysis, incontinence, coma, seizures and death among people in the developing world who are routinely exposed to such chemicals.

There are social as well as environmental considerations, too. The production of some high street goods notoriously involves the use of sweatshop labour. According to the campaign group No Sweat, 'from the small, backstreet sweatshop to some of the biggest corporations in the world, child labour, forced overtime, poverty wages, unsafe conditions, harassment of women workers and intimidation of trade unionists are commonplace.'

It can be difficult to figure out just how socially and environmentally responsible a company's products are. The Ethiscore website is a good starting point. This gives ethical ratings for a wide range of products and companies based on twenty issues, covering both corporate social responsibility and product sustainability, and is run by the people behind *Ethical Consumer* magazine. It rarely makes reassuring reading, though; a report by the magazine in June 2006 found 'systemic abuse of workers' rights and lack of environmental accountability in the production of nature-orientated holiday equipment'. The report's author, Katy Brown, found that 'traditionally, tents, sleeping bags and rucksacks would be the key purchases for more ethically-based holidaymaking, so the fact that a great deal of manufacturing is spreading to the Far East to companies who employ child labour may come as a shock to many campers with a conscience.'

Only 4 of the 34 companies included in the report had an established code of conduct for workers at supply companies and many factories were not independently monitored. Neither did they have environmental reports, with the exception of the German company Vaude, which was also the only firm in the list to feature products with Oeko Tex certification (the Oeko Tex Confidence in Textiles label shows that products are free from harmful ingredients such as pesticides and carcinogenic dyes).

Aside from Ethiscore, the best way of discovering how responsible a company is, is to find out whether it has an established ethical code of conduct. For example, the Pentland Group (which includes travel gear brands such as Berghaus and Brasher) and Rohan are signed up to the Ethical Trading Initiative, an organisation that encourages companies to assume responsibility for the labour and human rights practices within its supply chain. The Fair Labor Association in the United States has similar goals.

If you want to ensure your money is supporting companies who treat their workers fairly, look for products certified by the Fairtrade Foundation, or those which have been approved by the International Fair Trade Organisation or British Association for Fair Trade Shops. These organisations try to ensure that disadvantaged manufacturers in the developing world are paid a fair price for their goods and that workers receive a decent standard of pay and conditions. Though Fairtrade certification is often associated with food and drink, it also covers cotton.

How luggage adds up

15.7: average number of bags lost, per thousand passengers flown, by airlines represented by the Association of European Airlines

20kg: recommended weight of luggage economy class passengers should be able to check in for a flight

30%: increase in a car's fuel consumption caused by travelling with a fully loaded roof rack

40kg: recommended weight of luggage first-class passengers should be able to check in for a flight

90kg: rough amount of fuel saved per hour on a flight carrying 300 passengers if everyone were to check in 10kg of luggage rather than 20kg

Sources: International Air Transport Association (IATA); the Society of Motor Manufacturers and Traders (SMMT); IATA; IATA; AEA

Old gold

Let's face it, much of today's travel gear is simply fashion accessory masquerading as specialist equipment. While it is undoubtedly exciting to own a matching set of monogrammed Louis Vuitton leather hold-alls, or a daypack made from material so hi-tech it has been trialled by NASA, are they *really* necessary for that two-week stay at a Moroccan riad?

Think shabby chic instead. Could you reuse granddad's old suitcase or that canvas backpack last used on a school camping trip? Failing that, there are plenty of luggage suppliers turning old into new. Don't panic if you're not into tie-dye bum bags and patchwork didgeridoo cases: a lot of today's recycled luggage is surprisingly chic.

Among the best are the reconfigured sail bags sold through Ecocentric. From laptop bags to daypacks, each one is made from the decommissioned sail of a yacht or boat; the bag's label tells you what type of sail it has been made from, what type of boat it was taken from and which seas it has seen. The catch? They don't come cheap. Those on a budget should check out Planet Silverchilli's recycled rubber range instead. Though more suitable for daytrippers than those setting off on longer journeys, its recycled rubber tote bags, transformed from old car tyres by two Mexican-run charities, are seriously stylish as well as bargain-priced. Or try Earthpak's sporty-looking Smosho daypacks, which are sold in the UK through Natural Collection and feature a single strap for a jaunty over-the-shoulder look. These are made from recycled plastic drinks bottles and dyed in an environmentally friendly way.

You can still make sure your luggage stands out from the crowd if you're recycling your own gear, with a cheap and colourful luggage tag from Green Green Home. Made from re-used juice packs, by a women's co-operative in the Philippines, these include bright purple 'Elephant Juice' and orange 'Lion Jungle Juice' designs. The packaging also comprises non-biodegradable foil and plastic that would otherwise go into landfill sites or incinerators.

New tricks

Sometimes making do and mending just won't do. If you need to buy new kit, look for organic natural materials such as cotton or hemp. The self-styled 'environmentally trendy' range of organic hemp- and cotton-mix rucksacks from Pure Sativa, for example, is well-priced, sturdy and a model in utility chic, while its wheeler holdalls are just the thing to make getting around easy from Milan to Miami. Other sources of hemp luggage include Spirit of Nature and The Hemp Store.

For more specialist outdoor equipment, try sportswear company Patagonia. Its environmental credentials include running a garment recycling programme, a commitment to 'environmentally friendlier' fibres, such as recycled polyester, organic cotton, hemp, organic wool and chlorine-free wool and donating 1 per cent of sales to environmental organisations. It also does a nice line in backpacks; its Lightwire daypack comes with a laptop sleeve and 'ample room for rock shoes, chalk bag and a session-ending pale ale'.

British outdoor gear specialist Millets has also recently launched a green camping collection by Eurohike and a green clothing line from Peter Storm. Collectively called One Earth, the range features sleeping bags made from recycled bottles, organic cotton tents, wind-up torches, solar radios and tops made with sweetcorn, which can be composted once you've worn them out.

Power to your backpack

There is one alternative way of minimising the environmental impact of your luggage: make it work for a living. Several companies now produce solar-powered backpacks, which offset some of the energy used in their manufacture by generating power for gadgets when you're on the go.

The first to hit the market was the Voltaic™ backpack, which comes with three lightweight, waterproof solar panels embedded in its back and a battery pack to store energy until you need it. Its four watts of power are never going to challenge the national grid but it will charge phones, cameras, two-way radios, iPods and other small electronic gadgets (it's stocked by Electronic Zone). Similarly powerful but more clumsy-looking is Reware's Juice Bags, available from ESC Outdoor, which are fitted with flexible solar panels and can be worn either as a backpack or shoulder bag.

TAKING A HIDING

Should you get in a lather about leather? While the material wins points for its longevity, this is outweighed by the environmental and animal welfare issues associated with its manufacture. Leather production essentially subsidises the meat industry – which turns over vast swathes of land to grow animal feed and promotes the large-scale consumption of meat. It also contributes significantly to global warming. Flatulent farm animals account for 10 per cent of the world's greenhouse gas emissions. Where animals are intensively reared, animal welfare issues must also be considered.

Nor is leather always as natural as it might seem. Carcinogenic substances such as chromium are often used in the tanning process and, because environmental regulations have been tightened up in the West, much of the dirty work is now done in the developing world, where the health of workers is often directly affected. While leather substitutes are now being widely manufactured, the fact that they are done so using polyurethane and other plastics may put some responsible travellers off buying them. Other alternatives include buying second-hand leather or searching out companies such as Entermodal, which produces vegetable-tanned leather items.

Travelling light

Now you've got the right luggage, the question is what to put in it. When the journalist William Boot, the anti-hero of Evelyn Waugh's comic masterpiece *Scoop*, is sent to cover a war, his boss, Lord Copper, advises him to 'travel light and be prepared'. Instead Boot ends up with an 'over-furnished tent, three months' rations, a collapsible canoe, a jointed flagstaff and Union Jack, a hand pump and sterilising plant, an astrolabe, six suits of tropical linen and a sou'wester, a camp operating table and set of surgical instruments, a portable humidor, a Christmas hamper complete with Santa Claus costume and a tripod mistletoe stand, and a cane for whacking snakes.'

If you're the type who gets excited by Gore Tex and gadgets, you may find it easy to empathise with Boot's over-provisioning. Head into any outdoors shop and only the most strong-willed will escape without some shiny new piece of kit. But, given that most of us can navigate the route from beach bar to guesthouse without the use of SatNav equipment and night-vision goggles, your best course of action is to resist the urge to be overly prepared and pack light instead.

PACKING LIKE A PRO
The Explorer
Author and filmmaker Benedict Allen has made many expeditions to remote corners of the globe, without any 'backup'.

1. **Survival kit**
   'This would vary with the terrain but it must be small, so that you are not tempted to leave it behind in camp.'

2. **Compass**
   'I stick with a basic Silva model.'

3. **Bivvi bag**
   'Nothing like knowing you can camp out wherever.'

4. **Pork scratchings**
   'Or mint cake. Chocolate melts in the tropics, but these and nuts are good energy raisers and also morale boosters.'

5. **Knife**
   'Mine was made by a crocodile hunter and given me in the forests in PNG. It has a sheath made of lizard skin, a pig tooth carved handle, and the blade is sharp enough to pierce a crocodile through the eye in an emergency.'

In environmental terms, the less weight you carry with you, the more fuel-efficient your travels will be and the less CO_2 your trip will produce. But there are social implications of travelling light, too, not least that you can more easily use public transport, or your feet, to get around when you reach your destination, which will help narrow the gap between you and the people you are visiting.

Apart from some business trips and specialist sports holidays, you should be able to fit everything you need into one bag, case or rucksack. With clothing, as with luggage, making do with what you have is better than buying a whole new wardrobe every time you pick up your passport. So, too, is trying not to pack things 'just in case': even the most obscure items are becoming easier to pick up en route and, if you find you need to buy something at your destination, putting money into local pockets will be appreciated.

Scrubbing up

Take particular care over your wash bag. In the UK we spend over £6 billion each year on cosmetics. This isn't a sign that we're a particularly grubby nation but that marketing works. Gone are the days when all you needed to remember to pack was your toothbrush. Travelling now is more likely to involve wrestling the average toilet bag shut, so bulging is it with 'must-have' specialist holiday products. From self-tanning creams and exfoliating shower gels to sun lotions, cooling gels and insect repellents, every opportunity to brush up is catered for – and heavily pushed by advertising campaigns.

All this grooming comes at a cost. You don't have to be a vegan to feel that testing cosmetics on animals is wrong, yet many holiday skincare products have been tested on animals. A 2003 report by *Ethical Consumer* magazine, for example, found that the companies behind some of the most popular brands of sunscreen in the UK – the Ambre Solaire, Coppertone, Píz Buin and Soltan brands – had all used animal testing. This might sound surprising, given that a UK ban on animal testing for cosmetics products and ingredients has been in place since November 1998 (an EU-wide ban is planned to come into effect in two stages, in 2009 and 2013). But, without a global ban, cosmetics sold in the UK, and the ingredients that go into them, are often either tested on animals elsewhere, or companies pay third parties to carry out tests for them.

Confusingly, you can't always trust the advice on a product's label. 'We don't test our products on animals' could mean a product's ingredients, rather than the finished item, have been tested on animals, while 'we don't test our products or ingredients on animals' doesn't mean that a company hasn't commissioned someone else to do animal testing for them.

EXCESS BAGGAGE

'One of the best things about travelling is that you can free yourself of the clutter that haunts you at home, and not to be a slave to the latest gadgets, all the things we're constantly being told we need, which we don't.

'The way to be truly liberated when you travel is to travel light. But to do that you need to be relaxed enough to realise that whatever you need you'll find at your destination. That's why I love boats – you have to travel light on boats. When you think of the great adventurers, the best ones all had naval backgrounds. I think it gives you a confidence in being able to strip back your kit to the basics and then improvise when you need to.

'Packing is also about creating psychological ballast. Often when we pack for a trip we're nervous, and packing lots of stuff from home gives us reassurance, but actually all those things just weigh you down. Simplicity is better. People tend to overdo it and take far too much, especially with clothes. If you've got a river for water and a tree for hanging things, you can do washing wherever you are.

'Invariably what the locals use is the best, and the more extreme the environment is, the more that is the case. When I was in Alaska I took some fantastic kit with me but I gradually developed a different kit, plugging various gaps as they appeared.

'I found I went back in time to find my materials. Wooden kit was better than metal because, when it breaks, you can repair it or re-use it, whereas broken metal is just useless. Wool was also good. I had some great merino long johns. And I was still wearing my thick canvas trousers long after the fancy wax trousers I had taken with me were ripped to shreds.

'As it began to get cold, I found that the winter boots I had taken with me from Britain weren't working. Instead, I got some canvas mukluks, with moose-hide soles and thick felt liners. They let my feet move and kept me warm, even when it got down to minus 80, yet they were made locally for about $20.'

Guy Grieve spent a year surviving in the Alaskan wilderness with only basic equipment. He wrote about the experience in his book, The Call of the Wild *(Hodder & Stoughton).*

Toxic shocks

The European Cosmetic Toiletry and Perfumery Association reckons that the average person uses at least six cosmetic products – soap, shampoo, conditioner, deodorant, toothpaste and moisturising cream – each morning. That doesn't sound too shocking, until you realise that these products may contain over one hundred different chemicals, and together form a potentially harmful toxic cocktail.

In an article in *The Ecologist* in June 2005, the magazine's health editor, Pat Thomas, warned that many of the industrial chemicals that go into things like shampoos and hand creams may be absorbed into the body, stored in fatty tissue or vital organs and cause harm.

'Medical research is proving that fragrances can trigger asthma and that the detergents in shampoos can damage delicate eye tissue,' it reads. 'Epidemiological data links hair-dye ingredients with bladder cancer and lymphoma.'

Fly in the ointment

Worryingly for travellers, sunscreen and insect repellent contain some of the biggest toxic offenders. Most conventional insect repellents include the pesticide DEET (also commonly listed as N, N-Diethyl-m-toluamide or N, N-Diethyl-3-Methyl-benzamide). While this is a highly effective insect repellent, research carried out at Duke University, in North Carolina, found that heavy exposure to DEET and other insecticides may cause memory loss, headache, weakness, fatigue, muscle and joint pain, tremors and shortness of breath in some people.

Another reason to go easy on the bug spray? There have been anecdotal reports of DEET melting plastic dashboards and shrivelling watch straps.

Chemical cover-up

There are two basic types of sun lotion: sunscreens, which absorb and reflect the sun's rays, and creams containing zinc oxide or titanium dioxide which physically block out rays. While skin cancer is a serious health risk, wearing sunscreen as a preventative measure may cause problems of its own.

Ironically, some sunblocks contain suspected carcinogens. The chemical diethanolamine (DEA), for instance, is used in many lotions as an emollient. According to the International Agency for Research on Cancer (IARC), while not in itself harmful, when DEA is combined with other ingredients in cosmetics it can form nitrosodiethanolamine (NDEA), which has been linked with stomach, oesophagus, liver and bladder cancers. There have also been suggestions that titanium dioxide may be carcinogenic if absorbed by humans, although this has not been conclusively proved.

Most sunscreens also contain preservatives known as parabens, which are thought to be oestrogen mimics, and have been found in high concentrations in breast tissue taken from women with breast cancer. A 2001 study at the University of Zurich also showed oestrogenic activity in lab tests after exposure to benzophenone, homosalate, and octyl-methoxycinnamate (octinoxate), chemicals commonly found in commercial sunscreens. Parfum and phthalates are also thought to be endocrine disrupters.

Washed up

The real issue for travellers is that, by being slap-happy with these products, we are not just threatening our own health but that of others. According to the UN's Water for Life campaign, about 90 per cent of sewage in developing countries is discharged straight into water courses without treatment. While many of the ensuing health problems are caused by contamination with bacteria from untreated human waste (more than 2.2 million people, mostly in developing countries, die each year from diseases associated with poor water and sanitary conditions), those who drink water from sources which are contaminated with chemicals have been found to suffer skin lesions, cardiac problems and cancers.

While not on the scale of an oil spill from a tanker, the relatively small amounts of pollution caused by the careless discarding of travellers' cosmetics do matter. Rinse off a chemically laden shampoo in a shower in a developing country, and there's a good chance that the run-off will be flushed, untreated, straight into the local water supply, affecting the health of anyone who drinks from or washes in it.

Damage to the environment is another concern. Campaigners believe that some of the toxic chemicals present in commonly available cosmetics don't break down easily and can form dangerous compounds when they degrade. These may then accumulate in soils, rivers, animals and plants – worrying enough at home but an issue of even greater concern in countries where adequate waste services and recycling facilities are not always available.

In 2005, scientists at the University of California Riverside reported that two-thirds of the male turbot and sole collected near a sewage discharge point, three miles off the state's Huntington Beach, were growing ovary tissue in their testes. The research found that the only pollutant which could be exclusively identified as playing a contributory role in this phenomenon was oxybenzone, an ultraviolet light (UVA) absorbing ingredient of many suntan lotions.

Mountains of rubbish

Problems are also caused by the packaging that many products come wrapped up in. In countries with no official recycling initiatives, most discarded plastic bottles and other rubbish ends up in landfill. There they contribute to the production of methane, a greenhouse gas, and leach toxic chemicals into the soil or water sources. That's if they reach the local tip. Often, waste is simply dumped in someone else's backyard. In China, where two billion plastic bags are thrown away each day, the ensuing tumbleweed of discarded bags, disposable food trays and polystyrene cups is so noticeable that there is a term for it: white pollution.

One of the most publicised cases of littering by tourists has been the degradation of the world's highest peak. With over two thousand people having reached the summit of Everest since Sir Edmund Hilary and Tensing Norgay first climbed the mountain back in 1953 – and many thousands more trekking to Base Camp – the dumping of rubbish in the area has got so bad that the mountain is now jokingly referred to as 'the world's highest junkyard'. Recent clear-up efforts have had some effect – the Nepalese government makes expeditions pay a deposit, which is only returnable if they bring their rubbish back down, and offers financial incentives for porters to fill empty bags with litter along trekking trails – but dropping litter in the first place shows a basic lack of respect for the people and places you are visiting.

Elsewhere, rubbish is often flushed out to sea. According to the Marine Conservation Society, over the past ten years beach litter has increased by 80 per cent. This not only makes our shorelines less attractive but it is also a serious threat to wildlife. The Society estimates that, globally, over a million birds and one hundred thousand marine mammals and turtles die every year from entanglement, or ingestion of litter.

GREASY PALMS

How demand for cosmetics is fuelling deforestation

A vast amount of fuel and water are used up in the creation of cosmetics, and their packaging, as are an increasing number of plant ingredients. Palm oil is one of the most obvious examples. Obtained from the fruit of the palm oil tree, it is used as a bulking agent and preservative in an estimated one in ten supermarket products, from biscuits and chocolate to soap and shampoo.

Its cheapness and versatility mean that palm oil plantations now cover an area of eleven million hectares in Malaysia and Indonesia, the countries in which 90 per cent of the world's palm oil is produced. This has supplied a much-needed source of local income but, according to the WWF, the industry's growth has come at a high social and ecological price.

Not only is the demand for palm oil plantations fuelling the rapid clearing of the most biodiverse tropical forests in the world – 80 per cent of the orang-utan's habitat is estimated to have been lost in the past twenty years – but forest fires to clear land for plantations are a regular source of haze in Southeast Asia, posing health problems. And the planting of oil palms is squeezing out food crops, potentially pushing up prices for basic staples such as corn and rice.

Throwing in the towel

Around 45 billion sanitary pads and tampons are bought each year, most made from bleached cotton and plastics. The majority of these are incinerated or thrown into landfill sites but others are flushed directly into sewage systems, along with condoms, cotton buds and other 'sewage-related debris'.

In the UK filtering manages to trap most, though not all, of this material before it flows directly into rivers and seas. In developing countries, however, the lack of adequate infrastructure means there is likely to be no filtering, posing a serious health threat.

The three Rs

The mantra of anti-waste campaigners at home – reduce, re-use and recycle – is a good philosophy to bear in mind when preparing for a trip; if you don't buy as much in the first place, dealing with the resulting rubbish will be less of a headache.

PACKING LIKE A PRO
The Travel Editor
Joanne O'Connor is travel editor of the *Observer* newspaper.

1. Elizabeth Arden Eight Hour Cream
'I try to take the bare minimum of toiletries away with me but this tiny tube is worth its weight in gold. Slap it on dry skin, sunburn, chapped lips, rashes, jellyfish stings...you name it. Oh, and it makes a good lip gloss too.'

2. Swiss Army Knife
'An essential item, even when I'm staying in a posh hotel. While most of its functions remain unfathomable to me, the tweezers and corkscrew have helped me out of many a tight spot.'

3. Phenergan
'As someone who suffers from hayfever, insomnia and seasickness, I wouldn't go anywhere without this multi-tasking medication. Available over the counter, it's basically an anti-histamine that works as a motion sickness tablet, a sedative and a treatment for hayfever allergies. The perfect companion for the travelling hypochondriac.'

4. A hefty Russian novel
'Even though I know I will not have the time or the inclination to read Dostoevsky's *Crime and Punishment*, I religiously pack several great and worthy works of literature in my suitcase on every trip – then I'll buy a trashy novel and a copy of *Hello!* at the airport and read those instead.'

5. A small radio
'I love to tune into local radio stations when I'm in far-off places.'

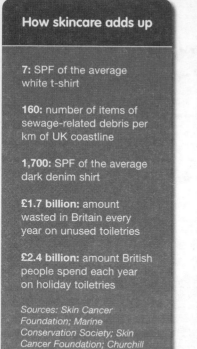
Disposable products, such as daily contact lenses and plastic razors are the most obvious no-no. Many women have also jettisoned disposable sanitary towels and tampons and turned to menstrual cups such as the Mooncup instead. Made from non-allergenic silicone, these are re-usable and contain no bleaches, deodorisers or absorbency gels. Menstrual cups aren't popular with everyone, however. If you prefer traditional sanitary products, always bin them rather than flush them and choose those made from unbleached, unperfumed organic cotton, certified by an independent body like the Soil Association or Ecocert. Natracare, the best-known natural sanitary protection brand, is certified by the Soil Association and is now stocked in many supermarkets, as well as by online retailers such as So Organic, the Natural Store and Natural Collection.

It's a similar story with nappies if you are travelling with small children. Even if you avoid disposables at home, it's likely you're going to use them on holiday. Minimise the environmental impact by opting for the biodegradable variety; if you're not sure you'll be able to source them at your destination, stock up from a company such as Spirit of Nature before you set off.

Try, also, to avoid unnecessary packaging. Re-wrapping toiletries in cling-film in case they burst open en route, for instance, is insanely un-environmentally friendly. So too, is stashing away the glamorous miniature travel toiletries laid on in some hotels – unless you can recycle them afterwards. Certainly don't leave half-used products behind. Opened bottles are often just thrown away and partly used soaps tend to get flushed down toilets. Carry a soap dish and bring your own soap instead.

It's not always possible to get by on suds and water alone, though. When you do need to buy toiletries, try to opt for natural, organic formulas in re-usable, biodegradable containers, or packaging that can be recycled when it has run its course (for an explanation of recycling symbols, see www.wasteconnect.co.uk).

Some cosmetics companies have taken this idea to a more extreme conclusion. Cargo Cosmetic's Plant Love range of lipsticks, for example, feature tubes made from compostable corn, while the boxes they're sold in are embedded with wildflower seeds; moisten them, plant them and watch them grow.

In destinations where there are no recycling facilities, wash out your empty bottles and take them home to dispose of there; this may make for additional air-miles but it is more responsible to recycle items back home than it is to leave them to fester on someone else's soil.

RIDING THE GREEN WAVE

'I'd heard about the impact harmful chemicals in toiletries and household cleaning products were beginning to have on the water environment in 1999. Male fish were getting gender confused and these chemicals just bypassed the sewage treatment works as they still do today, creating bio-accumulating chemical cocktails. I was heading to Costa Rica at the end of that year for a surf trip so I made sure that the toiletries I was going to take weren't going to impact on that pristine environment, especially as the sewage treatment infrastructure was pretty basic anyway.

'I've been using one hundred per cent green toiletries ever since, making sure I don't get duped by the potentially misleading labelling some companies use in marketing products as "natural" when they contain less than one per cent natural ingredients. It's really easy to find the clean, green, safer alternatives via the local health food/cosmetic shops and, increasingly, supermarket shelves, so there's really no excuse – and none whatsoever if you rely on the water environment to provide you with a clean playground to use day-in, day-out for wave-riding.

'Chemicals are expensive to take out once they're in the system so it makes sense not to add to the problem in the first place.'

Richard Hardy, Campaign Director, Surfers Against Sewage

Natural highs

Not long ago sourcing natural, organic beauty products meant rummaging around among shelves of lentils in a health food shop but these days green is chic. In June 2007 Harvey Nichols started stocking Nude, a natural, organic skincare range from the brains behind the hip Fresh & Wild organic supermarket chain. Its products aren't tested on animals, come in recyclable packaging made from recycled plastic and biodegradable starch and contain no parabens, sulphates, PEGs, propylene glycol, TEA or DEA.

Rival retailer Selfridges nailed its ethical colours to the mast a month later by snapping up retailing rights for Stella McCartney's Care range. Made from organic, natural, non-animal derived (or tested) ingredients, McCartney's line is free of petrochemicals, GM ingredients, chemical preservatives and synthetic fragrances.

Specifically designed to be as sexy as they are ethical, both of these ranges look as glamorous as any other luxury beauty brand – and are priced to match. Equally exclusive is the SheerinO'kho range of moisturisers, from France. Sold in the UK through branches of SpaceNK, these contain no parabens, artificial colourings or perfume, are not tested on animals and are sold in recyclable, non-polluting packaging. The range includes First Class Flight, a moisturising fluid specifically designed to offset the rigours of international travel.

But you don't need the salary of a Russian oligarch to jump on the natural bandwagon. There are plenty of affordable alternatives to the toxic norm, many of them available on the road; one of the most indulgent items in my bathroom cabinet is an organic apricot body oil, bought from a women's co-operative in India for a couple of pounds.

Make sure you double-check the ingredients before splashing out, though. Often products are labelled 'natural' or 'organic', when that's not actually the case, or when only some of the ingredients fall into those categories. If the labelling leaves you confused, one good place to get the lowdown on ingredients in popular brands – and what the effects of those might be – is the Skin Deep website. Although this is an American site, its ratings of thousands of products also give a rundown on many ingredients found in products sold closer to home.

Pale and interesting

Travel essentials for most people will include sun protection. Lessening the chemical load here doesn't mean letting your guard down. Skin cancer is mostly caused by damage from UV (ultraviolet) rays in sunlight, so it is vital to use some form of protection on sun-exposed skin. But, the more you can minimise contact with chemicals the better. Staying out of the sun when it is at its strongest (between 11am and 3pm), covering up with a t-shirt, hat and sunglasses and sticking to the shade should be the first step.

On occasions when you're likely to be more directly exposed to sunlight, look for organic, natural sunscreens with a sun protection factor (SPF) of at least 15, and which stop both UVA and UVB ultraviolet rays (bear in mind that most SPF ratings only take UVB rays into account). The most effective and least toxic of these are based on zinc oxide or titanium oxide, which physically block UVA and UVB rays. These mineral blocks traditionally gave a pasty Goth-like pallor when applied but transparent preparations are now available.

A 2006 survey of sunscreens by *Ethical Consumer* magazine named Green People's Edelweiss Sun Lotion and Weleda's Edelweiss Sun Lotion – both with an SPF of 15 – as best buys. Other reliable, affordable brands for natural sunscreens include Lavera, Ecolani, Aubrey Organics and Neal's Yard Remedies. Posher products include the Organic Pharmacy's own-brand sun cream, a clear zinc formula with an SPF of 25, and Dr Haushka's range of organic, biodynamic sun protection, which goes right up to a high-kicking SPF30. Some of these companies also produce natural after-sun skin products, the best of them based on nature's own healer: organic aloe vera.

While most of the companies mentioned above have their own websites, many of them are easy to track down on the high street, or you can buy through online organic beauty stores such as Love Lula, Mariposa Alternative Bodycare, White Ginger and My Being Well.

Travel bugs

Avoiding DEET is more problematic. Whatever its toxic side-effects, DEET is unarguably effective against mosquitoes, ticks and other biting insects. If you are travelling to an area where malaria, dengue fever, yellow fever, the West Nile virus or other serious insect-borne diseases are prevalent, it would be foolhardy not to use a powerful insect repellent. You should also contact your GP or a travel health advisory service such as MASTA to find out about necessary prophylactics.

As with sunscreens, the best course of action isn't to abandon DEET but to minimise exposure to it. From dusk till dawn, when the bugs are worst, try to stay inside and sleep under a well-maintained net. When outdoors, wear light-coloured, long-sleeved shirts and trousers and choose a product that contains 10 per cent or less DEET (if it's much stronger, only apply it to clothes or nets, rather than directly onto skin). Follow the manufacturers' guidelines especially carefully when using products containing DEET on children; their skin and still-developing nervous systems are particularly vulnerable to chemicals.

Where insects are more of a nuisance than a serious health threat, give the DEET a miss and choose products with naturally insect-repelling ingredients. Mosiguard, for instance, contains Citriodiol, an extract of lemon eucalyptus oil, while Mozzy Off, which is used by the Forestry Commission in Scotland, is a 100 per cent natural insect repellent based on eucalyptus. Several boutique hotels in the Caribbean stock Living Nature's natural insect repellent gel, made from lemon myrtle, calendula, almond oil and aloe vera.

Repellents containing neem tree oil and citronella are also popular; Neal's Yard sells a Citronella Organic Formula, made up mostly of organic ingredients, which has been shown to be effective in repelling mosquitoes by the London School of Hygiene and Tropical Medicine. Some travellers also swear that if you take vitamin B1 or fish oil capsules for a few days before your trip, potential biters will be put off by your smell, although this hasn't been scientifically proven.

If you do get bitten, Weleda produces a range of natural ointments, sprays and lotions containing combudoron, a combination of arnica and urtica, which relieves insect bites, stings and nettle rash.

PACKING LIKE A PRO
The Minimalist

Doug Dyment is the founder of www.onebag.com, a website dedicated to the 'art and science' of packing light.

1. **Credit card**
   'The only thing that comes close to being truly essential.'

2. **Passport**
   'Very important when you are crossing political borders.'

3. **A security pouch to hold passport, tickets and money**
   'For when you are travelling to areas where you are likely to be recognised as a non-local.'

4. **Travel clothesline**
   'For trips of more than a few days, where you will be washing clothes instead of carrying more of them around with you.'

5. **Toothbrush**
   'Important on all trips, though you can usually buy one when needed.'

Hop to it

Studies into alternatives to animal testing have been widely funded since the 1960s, although non-animal tests don't yet exist for all products and ingredients. In the meantime, if you want to ensure that the cosmetics you take on holiday with you haven't been tested on animals, choose products carrying the hopping bunny logo of the Humane Cosmetics Standard (HCS).

The world's only international standard for cosmetic products that are not animal tested, the HCS scheme was launched in 1996 by an international coalition of animal protection groups and is administered in the UK by the British Union for the Abolition of Vivisection (BUAV). To use the logo, a company must agree to exclude all ingredients tested after a fixed cut-off point – and prove this with independent audits.

No longer the preserve of a minority movement, these products are often easier to source than you might think – in June 2007 Marks & Spencer became the first mainstream retailer to adhere to cruelty-free standards on cosmetics with over a thousand own-brand beauty products receiving HCS approval.

For a comprehensive directory of companies whose products bear the HCS logo, the BUAV publishes a free listings booklet, the *Little Book of Cruelty Free*, or you can search through the list online.

Money worries

You're probably against supporting oppressive governments, arms sales and deforestation. Most people are. But the truth is that many of us fund these activities without realising it when we travel, through the purchase of financial services such as travel insurance.

These services are as much a part of the travel package as working out how to get to a place, or where to stay when you arrive. But, unless a financial institution has a policy stating otherwise, the money you spend on these services might be bankrolling social or environmental harm. Though buying a travel policy is not the same as investing directly in a company, the assets an insurer holds – including money made from insurance services – is usually invested, so it is a valid concern.

Good investments

The obvious answer to this conundrum would seem to be investment screening, where companies ensure that the profit from your transaction is invested in businesses not involved in activities such as animal testing, nuclear power, oil, pornography or tobacco but those which contribute positively to society and the environment, such as energy efficient technology firms, organic farming businesses, or those with a clear record of environmental auditing.

Plenty of financial products operate along these lines; according to the Ethical Investment Research Services (EIRIS), by the end of 2005, ethical investments in the UK were valued at £6.1 billion. However, the bulk of these products relate to stocks and shares, savings accounts and pensions. Straightforward investment screening by travel insurers is more difficult to source.

In 2005 the Co-operative Insurance Society (CIS) became the first major insurance company to launch a so-called ethical travel policy. Sister company to the Co-operative Bank, it is run along similar principles. However, its ethical insurance policy works not by screening out investments in certain sectors but by 'encouraging, and if necessary, bringing pressure to bear on the companies that we invest in to ensure that, for example, they take their environmental responsibilities seriously or do not engage in exploitative practices, such as child labour'.

This is the nearest travel insurance currently gets to being socially and environmentally responsible. The CIS's closest competitors are Naturesave, a small intermediary which donates a proportion of profit made by selling policies underwritten by Lloyd's of London to environmental and conservation projects, and the Environmental Transport Association, whose members can buy travel insurance (underwritten by UK Underwriting Ltd) which funds campaigns to 'make more people aware of ways to reduce their dependence on cars and lorries and create a sustainable transport system in Britain'.

Principles don't come cheap, however. I was quoted £102.70 and £108, respectively, from CIS and Naturesave for annual multi-trip insurance, with winter sports protection. While the cover both policies offer is generous, high street insurers offering similar levels of protection routinely charge around half those amounts. It is a similar, though not quite so expensive, story with green or other charity insurance schemes. Climate Sure, a sister business to the carbon-offsetting organisation Climate Care, offers a service similar to spending on a charity credit card where, if you buy travel insurance with the company, it will offset the greenhouse gases created by your travel. Other schemes offer travel insurance at a discount and donate an amount to charity.

Though none of these are bad ideas in principle, most of these schemes are underwritten by mainstream insurance companies, who inevitably profit from them. Neither do they offer the consumer great value for money. In many cases, it might make better financial sense to buy a policy from a mainstream insurer, which usually will be cheaper, and donate an amount to charity yourself.

If you go down this route, try to opt for an insurer with stated SRI policies, ideally one which is signed up to the United Nations' Environment Programme's (UNEP) Insurance Industry Initiative, 'Statement of Environmental Commitment by the Insurance Industry'. Signatories must pledge to 'seek to include environmental considerations in our asset management'. Although it's a pretty toothless assurance, it is at least a step in the right direction.

THE RESPONSIBLE TRAVELLER'S LITTLE GREEN (ADDRESS) BOOK

About the Little Green Book

The following section aims to provide easily referrable contact details for organisations relating to responsible travel. One of my reasons for writing this book was that I couldn't previously find clear information on 'eco-friendly' travel and on socially responsible travel initiatives in the same place. Yet, to me, these are inter-related elements of the responsible travel ethos.

This directory aims to address that gap. Included are contact details for all the businesses, forums and other institutions mentioned in the book – and also some which aren't. With a limited amount of space in each of the previous chapters and a subject area which is developing on a daily basis, it is likely that there will be some omissions. If the information you're searching for isn't here – or you want to look something up in more detail – I hope that this directory will point you in the right direction.

I have tried to group these listings under the most relevant sub-headings and to provide a brief description of each organisation. Some of these were more difficult to categorise than others, so it is worth checking under several headings if you don't immediately find the information you're looking for.

The Responsible Traveller's Little Green (Address) Book Contents

ACCOMMODATION

1 Hotels and Residences
Web: www.1residences.com

New 'earth-conscious' hotel and property brand

42 The Calls
Tel: 0113 244 0099
Web: www.42thecalls.co.uk

Leeds boutique hotel

70 Park Avenue
Tel: 00 1 212 973 2400
Web: www.70parkave.com

Kimpton hotel in New York, has an 'eco concierge' on staff

Adrère Amellal
Tel: 00 20 2738 1327
Web: www.adrereamellal.net

Eco hotel in Egyptian oasis

Agriturismo
Web: www.agriturismo.it)

Network of Italian farmhouses offering accommodation

Aislabeck Eco Lodges
Tel: 01612 422970
Web: www.naturalretreats.co.uk

Green self-catering in Yorkshire

The Albannach
Tel: 01571 844407
Web: www.thealbannach.co.uk

Lochinver restaurant with rooms

Al-Maha
Tel: 00 971 4 303 4222
Web: www.al-maha.com

Luxury resort in Dubai set within the Dubai Desert Conservation Reserve

Alt hotels
Tel: 00 1 514 849 2050
Web: www.althotels.ca

New budget hotel chain from trendy Canadian company, Groupe Germain

The Angel Inn
Tel: 01756 730263
Web: www.angelhetton.co.uk

North Yorkshire restaurant with rooms

Anjajavy
Tel: 00 33 144 691 500
Web: www.anjajavy.com

Madagascan hotel which funds community development projects

Apani Dhani
Tel: 00 91 159 422 2239
Web: www.apanidhani.com

Eco lodge in Rajasthan

Aqualogis
Tel: 00 33 3 85 78 64 63
Web: www.aqualogis.fr

Floating holiday cottage in France

Ardeonaig Hotel
Tel: 01567 820400
Web: www.ardeonaighotel.co.uk

Trossachs restaurant with rooms

At Home in London
Tel: 020 8748 1943
Web: www.athomeinlondon.co.uk

Upmarket London B&Bs

Babington House
Tel: 01373 812266
Web: www.babingtonhouse.co.uk

One of the first contemporary country house hotels in the UK

Baby Friendly Boltholes
Web: www.babyfriendlyboltholes.co.uk

An online directory of rental properties that combine 'taste with toddlers'

Baby Goes 2
Web: www.babygoes2.com

Specialist family travel website

Banyan Tree
Tel: 00 65 6849 5800
Web: www.banyantree.com

Fast-growing hotel group with sustainable tourism policies

Barnsley House
Tel: 01285 740000
Web: www.barnsleyhouse.com

Gloucestershire country house hotel

The Bed and Breakfast Homestay Association
Tel: 020 7385 9922
Web: www.bbha.org.uk

Upmarket London B&Bs

Bedruthan Steps
Tel: 01637 860555
Web: www.bedruthanstepshotel.co.uk

Large Cornish hotel big on the environment and children

The Bell at Skenfrith
Tel: 01600 750235
Web: www.skenfrith.co.uk

Monmouthshire gastropub with rooms

The Big Domain
Tel: 01326 240028
Web: www.thebigdomain.com

Large holiday rentals agency

Blancaneaux Lodge
Tel: 00 501 824 4912
Web: www.blancaneaux.com

Belizean hideaway owned by Francis Ford Coppola

Boda Farmhouse
Tel: Anna: 07946 587786
Swedish farmhouse holiday accommodation

Bulungula Lodge
Tel: 00 27 47 577 8900
Web: www.bulungula.co.za

Guest accommodation certified by FTTSA

Buffalo Ridge
Tel: 00 27 11 805 9995
Web: www.madikwecollection.com

Community-owned safari lodge in Kenya

Calcot Manor
Tel: 01666 890391
Web: www.calcotmanor.co.uk

Elegant and family-friendly country house hotel and spa in the Cotswolds

Can Marti
Tel: 00 34 971 333 500
Web: www.canmarti.com

Stylish holiday rentals on Ibiza

Canvas Chic
Tel: 00 33 46 624 2181
Web: www.canvaschic.com

Cool camping in France

Cartwheel
Tel: 01392 877842
Web: www.cartwheel.org.uk

Farm-based self-catering cottages and B&Bs in the southwest

Casa Camper
Tel: 00 34 933 426 280
Web: www.casacamper.com

Green hotel in Barcelona owned by the Camper shoe company

The CB Inn
Tel: 01748 884567
Web: www.cbinn.co.uk

Yorkshire gastropub with rooms

Celtic Castles
Tel: 01422 323200
Web: www.celticcastles.com

Castle rental agency

Cerro Da Fontinha
Tel: 00 351 282 949083
Web: www.cerrodafontinha.com

Portuguese holiday cottages

Chalalán Ecolodge
Tel: 00 591 2 231 1451
Web: www.chalalan.com

Bolivian community-run eco-lodge

Charlton House
Tel: 01749 342008
Web: www.charltonhouse.com

Somerset hotel that's strong on organics

Chhatra Sagar
Tel: 00 91 941 412 3118
Web: www.chhatrasagar.com

Cool camping in India

Chic Retreats
Tel: 020 7978 7164
Web: www.chicretreats.com

Specialist hotel-marketing company

Chic Treats
Tel: 0870 444 8890
Web: www.chictreats.co.uk

Characterful hotels on the Isle of Wight

Chumbe Island
Tel: 00 255 24 223 1040
Web: www.chumbeisland.com

Zanzibar resort and marine nature reserve

Classic Cottages
Tel: 01326 555555
Web: www.classiccottages.co.uk

UK cottage rental agency

Considerate Hoteliers Association
Web: www.consideratehoteliers.com

Nationwide membership scheme for sustainable hotels

Cowley Manor
Tel: 01242 870900
Web: www.cowleymanor.com

Gloucestershire country house hotel

Cumbria House
Tel: 01768 773171
Web: www.cumbriahouse.co.uk

Green Keswick B&B

Daintree Ecolodge
Tel: 00 61 7 4098 6100
Web: www.daintree-ecolodge.com.au

Australian resort, employs local Kuku
Yalanji guides

Design Hotels
Tel: 00 800 3746 8357
Web: www.designhotels.com

Specialist hotel marketing company

Discover Devon Naturally
Tel: 0870 608 5531
Web: www.discoverdevon.com/green

Council-run scheme which lists green
accommodation and attractions

Distinctly Different
Tel: 01225 866842
Web: www.distinctlydifferent.co.uk

Good for characterful B&Bs and
self-catering

The Drawing Room
Tel: 01982 552493
Web: www.the-drawing-room.co.uk

Powys restaurant with rooms

Eco Cabin
Tel: 01547 530183
Web: www.ecocabin.co.uk

Eco cottage in Shropshire

Ecosse Unique
Tel: 01835 822277
Web: www.uniquescotland.com

Scottish cottage rental agency

El Nido
Tel: 00 632 894 5644
Web: www.elnidoresorts.com

Two ecologically sensitive resorts
in the Philippines

The Eton Collection
Web: www.theetoncollection.com

A collection of UK boutique hotels

Fairmont
Tel: 00 1 888 499 9899
Web: www.fairmont.com

Luxury hotel company which also
publishes an industry handbook on
sustainability

Family Travel
Web: www.family-travel.co.uk

Specialist family travel website

Farm Stay UK
Tel: 024 7669 6909
Web: www.farmstayuk.co.uk

Lists a wide range of B&Bs, cottages,
caravans, campsites and bunkhouses on
farms

Feather Down Farm
Tel: 01420 80804
Web: www.featherdownfarm.co.uk

Provides posh, ready-equipped tents at
nine working farms throughout the UK

Gaia Napa Valley
Tel: 00 1 888 798 3777
Web: www.gaianapavalleyhotel.com

Californian hotel, first in a planned
green chain

Geenee
Tel: 020 0200 9340
Web: www.geenee.com

Home-swapping agency with a bit of
contemporary flair

Gleneagles
Tel: 0800 389 3737
Web: www.gleneagles.com

Scottish five-star hotel that's aiming
to go carbon-neutral

Good Cottage Guide
Tel: 01438 869489
Web: www.goodcottageguide.com

Independent directory of UK holiday
cottages

Good Hotel Guide
Tel: 020 7602 4182
Web: www.goodhotelguide.com

Independent annual guide to UK hotels

Great Escape Holiday Company
Tel: 08456 340511
Web: www.thegreatescapeholiday.co.uk

With-frills holiday rentals agency

Great Hotels of the World
Tel: 020 7383 2335
Web: www.ghotw.com

Specialist hotel marketing company

Great Small Hotels
Web: www.greatsmallhotels.com

Specialist hotel marketing company

Green Hotel
Tel: 00 91 821 425 5000
Web: www.greenhotelindia.com

Indian hotel that gives proceeds to local
causes and employs disadvantaged
people

Green Theme International
Tel: 00 33 55 508 4704
Web: www.gti-home-exchange.com

Home exchange agency

Guludo Beach Lodge
Tel: 01323 766655
Web: www.bespokeexperience.com

Fairtrade accommodation in northern
Mozambique

Helpful Holidays
Tel: 01647 433593
Web: www.helpfulholidays.com

Cottage rental agency

Higher Lank Farm
Tel: 01208 850716
Web: www.higherlankfarm.co.uk

Green family-friendly accommodation
in Cornwall

Hilton
Tel: 0870 590 9090
Web: www.hilton.co.uk

Hotel chain, part of International
Tourism Partnership

Himalayan Homestays
Tel: 00 91 1982 250 953
Web: www.himalayan-homestays.com

Socially responsible accommodation in
northern India

Holswap
Web: www.holswap.com

House-swapping agency

Homebase Hols
Tel: 020 8886 8752
Web: www.homebase-hols.com

House-swapping agency

Homelink
Tel: 01962 886882
Web: www.homelink.org

House-swapping agency

Hoopoe Yurt Hotel
Tel: 00 34 952 117 055
Web: www.yurthotel.com

Cool camping in Andalucia

Hope Street Hotel
Tel: 0151 709 3000
Web: www.hopestreethotel.co.uk

Liverpool boutique hotel

Hoseasons
Tel: 01502 502588
Web: www.hoseasons.co.uk

Cottage rental agency

Hotel du Vin
Tel: 01902 050070
Web: www.hotelduvin.com

UK boutique hotel chain

Hotelito Desconocido
Tel: 00 52 322 281 4010
Web: www.hotelito.com

Chic eco resort on Mexico's Pacific coast

I Escape
Tel: 0117 942 8476
Web: www.i-escape.com

UK-based website listing 'exciting and unusual places to stay'

Inter-Continental
Tel: 0870 400 9670
Web: www.ichotelsgroup.com

Hotel group, helped set up the International Tourism Partnership

Intervac
Tel: 0845 260 5776
Web: www.intervac.co.uk

House-swapping agency

Ionian Eco Villagers
Tel: 0871 711 5065
Web: www.relaxing-holidays.com

Greek self-catering with green credentials

Islas Secas
Tel: 00 1 805 729 2737
Web: www.islassecas.com

Cool camping in Panama

Jumeirah
Tel: 00 971 4 366 5000
Web: www.jumeirah.com

Properties include the iconic sail-shaped Burj Al Arab hotel in Dubai

Jungle Bay
Tel: 00 1 767 446 1789
Web: www.junglebaydominica.com

Dominican resort with environmental and social responsibility policies

Kahawa Shamba
Tel: 01728 685971
Web: www.tribes.co.uk

Tanzanian community tourism project, bookable through Tribes Travel

Kapawi
Tel: 00 593 4 251 4750
Web: www.kapawi.com

Remote ecolodge and reserve in Ecuador

Kasbah du Toubkal
Tel: 00 33 549 050 135
Web: www.kasbahdutoubkal.com

Berber 'hospitality centre' in Morocco

Kawaza Village
Web: www.kawazavillage.co.uk

Zambian community tourism project

Lace Market Hotel
Tel: 0115 852 3232
Web: www.lacemarkethotel.co.uk

Nottingham boutique hotel

Langdon Beck
Tel: 0870 770 5910
Web: www.yha.org.uk

Eco hostel in County Durham

Lapa Rios
Tel: 00 506 735 5130
Web: www.laparios.com

Costa Rican eco resort

Large Holiday Houses
Tel: 01381 610496
Web: www.lhhscotland.com

Scottish large holiday rentals agency

L'Ayalga Posada Ecológica
Tel: 00 34 616 897 638
Web: www.terrae.net/layalga

Environmentally sensitive B&B in Spain

Leading Hotels of the World
Tel: 00 800 1010 1111
Web: www.lhw.com

Specialist hotel marketing company

Loch Ossian Youth Hostel
Tel: 0870 155 3255
Web: www.syha.org.uk

Eco hostel in Scotland

Lockton
Tel: 0870 770 5938
Web: www.yha.org.uk

Eco hostel in North Yorkshire

Luxury Family Hotels
Web: www.luxuryfamilyhotels.co.uk

A collection of five decadent hotels with elaborate children's facilities

Malmaison
Tel: 0845 365 4247
Web: www.malmaison.com

UK boutique hotel chain

Mary Jane's Farm
Tel: 00 1 208 882 6819
Web: www.maryjanesfarm.com

Cool camping in the USA

Milia
Tel: 00 30 282 104 6774
Web: www.milia.gr

Mountain retreat in Crete

Mr & Mrs Smith
Tel: 0845 034 0700
Web: www.mrandmrssmith.com

Boutique and luxury hotel guide

Mr Underhill's
Tel: 01584 874431
Web: www.mr-underhills.co.uk

Michelin-starred restaurant with rooms in Ludlow

Mocking Bird Hill
Tel: 00 1 876 993 7267
Web: www.hotelmockingbirdhill.com

Small Jamaican hotel leading the way in sustainable tourism

Monachyle Mhor
Tel: 01877 384622
Web: www.monachylemhor.com

Trossachs restaurant with rooms

Next 6 Weeks
Tel: 0870 197 6964
Web: www.next6weeks.com

Specialises in short-notice holiday lets

Nihiwatu
Tel: 00 62 361 757 149
Web: www.nihiwatu.com

Luxury Indonesian hideaway which helps fund local communities

Old Chapel Forge
Tel: 01243 264380
Web: www.oldchapelforge.co.uk

Green Chichester B&B

Orchard Garden Hotel
Tel: 00 1 415 399 9807
Web: www.theorchardgardenhotel.com

San Francisco eco hotel

Organic Places To Stay
Tel: 01943 871468
Web: www.organicplacestostay.co.uk

Lists a wide range of organic accommodation

Paperbark Camp
Tel: 00 61 2 4441 6066
Web: www.paperbarkcamp.com.au

Cool camping in Australia

Patagonia Eco Camp
Tel: 0800 051 7095
Web: www.ecocamp.travel

Cool camping in Chile

Penrhos Court
Tel: 01544 230720
Web: www.penrhos.co.uk

Herefordshire hotel with an award-winning organic restaurant

Plas Bodegroes
Tel: 01758 612363
Web: www.bodegroes.co.uk

Gwynedd restaurant with rooms

Pride of Britain Hotels
Tel: 0800 089 3929
Web: www.prideofbritainhotels.com

Specialist hotel marketing company

The Punchbowl Inn
Tel: 01539 568237
Web: www.the-punchbowl.co.uk

Cumbrian gastropub with rooms

Relais & Chateaux
Tel: 00 800 2000 0002
Web: www.relaischateaux.com

Promotes small but sophisticated independent hotels and restaurants

Rick Stein
Tel: 01841 532700
Web: www.rickstein.com

Food and accommodation empire in Cornwall

Rural Retreats
Tel: 01386 701177
Web: www.ruralretreats.co.uk

UK cottage rental agency

Sawdays
Tel: 01275 395430
Web: www.sawdays.co.uk

A guide to special places to stay

Shinta Mani
Tel: 00 855 63 761 998
Web: www.shintamani.com

Cambodian hotel and hospitality training school

Small Luxury Hotels of the World
Tel: 01372 361873
Web: www.slh.com

Specialist hotel marketing company

Special Escapes
Web: www.special-escapes.co.uk

Sawdays' cottage rental website

The Star Inn at Harome
Tel: 01439 770397
Web: www.thestaratharome.co.uk

Yorkshire restaurant with rooms

Stately Holiday Homes
Tel: 01638 674749
Web: www.statelyholidayhomes.co.uk

Large holiday rentals agency

Strattons Hotel
Tel: 01760 723845
Web: www.strattons-hotel.co.uk

Green Norfolk boutique hotel

Summer Isles Hotel
Tel: 01854 622282
Web: www.summerisleshotel.co.uk

Scottish restaurant with rooms

The Sun Inn
Tel: 01206 323351
Web: www.thesuninndedham.com

Essex gastropub with rooms

Tablet Hotels
Web: www.tablethotels.com

Specialist hotel marketing company

Thakadu River Camp
Tel: 00 27 11 805 9995
Web: www.madikwecollection.com

Community-owned safari lodge in Kenya

The Three Chimneys
Tel: 01470 511258
Web: www.threechimneys.co.uk

Skye restaurant with rooms

Tiamo
Tel: 00 1 242 357 2489
Web: www.tiamoresorts.com

Luxury Bahamian resort with serious eco credentials

Tiger Mountain Pokhara Lodge
Tel: 00 977 1 436 1500
Web: www.tigermountain.com

Nepalese hotel with good responsible credentials

Torri Superiore
Tel: 00 39 0184 215 504
Web: www.torri-superiore.org

Italian eco village

Townhouse Company
Tel: 0131 274 7400
Web: www.townhousecompany.com

Boutique hotels and serviced apartments in Edinburgh and Glasgow

Travel Intelligence
Tel: 020 7580 2663
Web: www.travelintelligence.net

Specialist hotel marketing company

Treebones
Tel: 00 1 877 424 4787
Web: www.treebonesresort.com

Californian yurt resort

Trelowarren
Tel: 01326 222105
Web: www.trelowarren.com

Green holiday cottages in Cornwall

Tresanton Hotel
Tel: 01326 270055
Web: www.tresanton.com

Perennially popular Cornish boutique hotel

Tyddyn Llan
Tel: 01490 440264
Web: www.tyddynllan.co.uk

Denbighshire restaurant with rooms

Ulaa
Tel: 00 54 11 5918 6400
Web: www.ulaapatagonia.com

Cosy cabins and spa set on the edge of a lake in Chilean Patagonia

Under The Thatch
Web: www.underthethatch.co.uk

Responsibly minded holiday rental company in west Wales

Unusual Hotels of the World
Web: www.uhotw.com

Specialist hotel marketing company

Uptown Reservations
Tel: 020 7937 2001
Web: www.uptownres.co.uk

Upmarket London B&Bs

The Victoria at Holkham
Tel: 01328 711008
Web: www.holkham.co.uk/victoria

Smart bohemian hideaway on the north Norfolk coast

Vigilius Mountain Resort
Tel: 00 39 0473 556 600
Web: www.vigilius.it

High style meets sustainability in Italy's South Tyrol

The Village Pub
Tel: 01285 740421
Web: www.thevillagepub.co.uk

Gloucestershire gastropub with rooms

Welsh Rarebits
Tel: 01686 668030
Web: www.rarebits.co.uk

Markets stylish or characterful properties in Wales

Whatley Manor
Tel: 01666 822888
Web: www.whatleymanor.com

Wiltshire country house hotel

Whitepod
Tel: 00 41 24 471 38 38
Web: www.whitepod.com

Low impact mountain camp in Switzerland

Wolsey Lodges
Tel: 01473 822058
Web: www.wolseylodges.com

Good for finding upmarket B&Bs

The Zetter
Tel: 020 7324 4444
Web: www.thezetter.com

Green London boutique hotel

ATTRACTIONS AND ACTIVITIES

Bluebird Boats
Tel: 020 7262 1330
Web: www.solarshuttle.org

Solar boats on the Serpentine in London

The British Surfing Association (BSA)
Tel: 01637 876474
Web: www.britsurf.co.uk

Runs courses at the National Surfing Centre in Newquay

Bushcraft UK
Tel: 01239 711360
Web: www.bushcraftuk.com

Lists companies offering bushcraft courses in the UK

Cape Adventure
Tel: 01971 521006
Web: www.capeventure.com

Family – and other – activity holidays in the far northwest of Scotland

Centre for Alternative Technology
Tel: 01654 705950
Web: www.cat.org.uk

Aims to 'inspire, inform, and enable people to live more sustainably'

Chichester Harbour Conservancy
Tel: 01243 512301
Web: www.conservancy.co.uk

Solar boat trips in West Sussex

Coniston Ferry Services
Tel: 01539 436216
Web: www.conferry.co.uk

Solar boat trips in the Lake District

Craigencalt Ecology Centre
Tel: 01592 891567
Web: www.theecologycentre.org

Hosts the UK's first 'earthship', as well as green events and workshops

Dryad Bushcraft
Tel: 01792 547213
Web: www.dryadbushcraft.co.uk

Find out how to be more self-sufficient

The Eden Project
Tel: 01726 811911
Web: www.edenproject.com

Disused quarry turned botanical attraction in Cornwall

The Electric Boat Association
Tel: 01491 681449
Web: www.electric-boat-association.org.uk

Provides information on low-impact boating

ENCAMS
Tel: 01942 612621
Web: www.encams.org

Runs the Keep Britain Tidy campaign and oversees the Quality Coast Awards in England (www.cleancoastproject.org covers Wales and Ireland)

Farmer for a Day
Tel: 01606 853193
Web: www.farmer4aday.co.uk

Cheshire farm experience

Federation of City Farms and Community Gardens
Tel: 0117 923 1800
Web: www.farmgarden.org.uk

Information on urban farms and gardens

Garroch Glen
Tel: 01644 430349
Web: www.garrochglen.com

Informative farm and nature tours

The Genesis Centre
Tel: 01823 252934
Web: www.somerset.ac.uk/genesis05/

Somerset showcase of sustainable building

Highland Adventure Safaris
Tel: 01887 820071
Web: www.highlandadventuresafaris.co.uk

Wildlife tours in Scotland

London Zoo
Tel: 020 7722 3333
Web: www.zsl.org

Uses profits to fund conservation programmes

National Farm Attractions Network
Tel: 01536 513397
Web: www.farmattractions.net

Gives contact details for farm attractions by region

Norfolk Broads Authority
Tel: 01603 782281
Web: www.broads-authority.gov.uk

Includes information on solar boat trips

Northern Ireland Canoeing
Tel: 02890 303937
Web: www.nicanoeing.com

Includes information on Lough Erne
Canoe Trail

The Outsiders' Canoe Club
Tel: 00 353 86 387 0510

Runs canoe trips on the Lough Erne
Canoe Trail

The Outdoor Swimming Society
Web: www.outdoorswimmingsociety.com

Encourages taking a dip in clean lakes,
rivers and lidos in the UK

The Ramblers Association
Tel: 020 7339 8500
Web: www.ramblers.org.uk

Britain's biggest walking charity

River and Lake Swimming Association
Tel: 0151 428 3990
Web: www.river-swimming.co.uk

Advice and information on
swimming outdoors

Swimtrek
Tel: 020 8696 6220
Web: www.swimtrek.com

Organises specialist swimming holidays

Take The Family
Web: www.takethefamily.com

Specialist family travel website

Waterscape
Tel: 01923 201120
Web: www.waterscape.com

Ideas and information on trips around
Britain's waterways

What's On When
Tel: 020 7770 6050
Web: www.whatsonwhen.com

Worldwide events guide

Where Can We Go
Tel: 0118 984 1394
Web: www.wherecanwego.com

UK events guide

Whisby Natural World Centre
Tel: 01522 688868
Web: www.naturalworldcentre.com

Green café, gift shop and nature trails in
Lincolnshire

AWARDS AND ACCREDITATION SCHEMES

Ecotourism Australia
Web: www.ecotourism.org.au

Runs a certification scheme for Australian
ecotourism businesses

European Ecolabel
Web: www.ecolabel-tourism.eu

Accreditiation scheme for eco-friendly
accommodation in Europe

Green Globe
Web: www.greenglobe21.com

Well-known green certification scheme

The Green List
Web: www.condenast.com

An annual list of hotels and tour operators published by *Condé Nast Traveler* magazine

Green Tourism Business Scheme
Web: www.green-business.co.uk

Recognises over 1,000 sustainable businesses in England and Scotland

Paul Morrison Guide Award
Tel: 01753 620426
Web: www.wanderlust.co.uk

Launched by the travel magazine *Wanderlust* to recognise the value of good guides

Sustainable Tourism Certification Network of the Americas (see Rainforest Alliance)
Green certification scheme, launched in 2003

Sustainable Tourism Stewardship Council (STSC)
Web: www.stscouncil.org

Green certification scheme

Tourism for Tomorrow Awards
Web: www.tourismfortomorrow.com

Rewards best practice in four categories: destination, conservation, investor in people and global tourism business

Virgin Responsible Tourism Awards
Web: www.responsibletourismawards.com

Largest of such schemes, with 13 different categories

Voluntary Initiative for Sustainability in Tourism
Web: www.visit21.net

Brings together certification schemes and eco-labels across various European countries

CAMPING

Belle Tents
Tel: 01840 261556
Web: www.belletentscamping.co.uk

Boutique camping on the edge of Bodmin moor

Boutique Camping
Tel: 020 7871 1379
Web: www.boutiquecamping.net

Boutique camping at festivals

Camp Kerala
Tel: 01749 860077
Web: www.campkerala.com

Boutique camping at festivals

The Camping and Caravanning Club
Tel: 0845 130 7632
Web: www.campingandcaravanningclub.co.uk

The world's oldest and largest Club for all forms of camping. Also runs around 100 UK campsites

Camping Magazine
Tel: 01778 391180
Web: www.campingmagazine.co.uk

Good general source of camping information

Camping UK
Web: www.campinguk.com

UK camping directory

Cornish Tipi Holidays
Tel: 01208 880781
Web: www.cornish-tipi-holidays.co.uk

Boutique camping near St Kew

Eco Retreats
Tel: 01654 781375
Web: www.ecoretreats.co.uk

Boutique camping in Powys

Eweleaze Farm
Web: www.eweleaze.co.uk

Seasonal campsite in Dorset

Fisherground
Tel: 01946 723349
Web: www.fishergroundcampsite.co.uk

Cumbrian campsite that's family friendly

Glyn Y Mul Farm
Tel: 01639 643204
Web: www.glynymulfarm.co.uk

Campsite in West Glamorgan

The Happy Campers
Web: www.thehappycampers.co.uk

Accompanying website to the book (see 'Further Reading' page 181)

La Rosa
Tel: 07786 072866
Web: www.larosa.co.uk

Boutique camping outside Whitby

Northumbrian Wigwams
Tel: 01289 307107
Web: www.northumbrianwigwams.com

Northumbrian campsite

Shell Island
Tel: 01341 241453
Web: www.shellisland.co.uk

A tent-only campsite in Gwynedd

Tangerine Fields
Tel: 07821 807000
Web: www.tangerinefields.co.uk

Boutique camping at festivals

Tented Lodges
Tel: 07985 169101
Web: www.tentedlodges.co.uk

Boutique camping in Wales

Tresseck
Tel: 01432 840235
Web: www.tresseckcampsite.co.uk

Hereford campsite with canoeing

UK Campsite
Web: www.ukcampsite.co.uk

Useful general source of camping information

Vintage Vacations
Tel: 07802 758113
Web: www.vintagevacations.co.uk

Boutique camping on the Isle of Wight

CARBON OFFSETTING AND RATIONING

Atmosfair
Web: www.atmosfair.de

German-based non-profit carbon offsetting organisation

Best Foot Forward
Tel: 01865 250818
Web: www.bestfootforward.com

Analysis of carbon and ecological footprints

Carbon Clear
Tel: 0845 838 7564
Web: www.carbon-clear.com

For-profit carbon offsetting scheme

Carbon Counter
Web: www.carboncounter.org

American carbon offsetting scheme

Carbon Neutral Company
Tel: 020 7833 6000
Web: www.carbonneutral.com

Well-known British-based for-profit offsetting company

Carbon Offsets
Web: www.carbon-offsets.com

For-profit offsetting company

Carbon Rationing
Web: www.carbonrationing.org.uk

The low-carbon answer to Weight Watchers

Cheat Neutral
Web: www.cheatneutral.com

Spoof site for non-believers

Choose Climate
Web: www.chooseclimate.org/flying/

Click from point to point on a map and be shown the error of your flying ways

Climate Care
Web: www.climatecare.org

Well-known British for-profit offsetting company

Climate Friendly
Web: www.climatefriendly.org

Australian offsetting company with gold standard credentials

CO2 Balance
Web: www.co2balance.com

One of the few companies to offer emissions calculators for ferries, cars and trains as well as planes

Equiclimate
Web: www.ebico.co.uk

One of several offsetting schemes recommended by *Ethical Consumer* magazine

Global Cool
Web: www.global-cool.com

Pay £20 towards a mission to get a billion people to reduce their personal CO_2 emissions by at least a tonne

Gold Standard Foundation
Tel: 00 41 61 283 0916
Web: www.cdmgoldstandard.org

Offers a quality label to voluntary
offset projects

My Climate
Tel: 00 41 44 633 77 50
Web: www.myclimate.org

Swiss-based offsetting company with
gold standard credentials

NativeEnergy
Web: www.nativeenergy.com

One of *Ethical Consumer*'s top-rated
schemes for carbon offsetting

Pure
Tel: 020 7382 7815
Web: www.puretrust.org.uk

Non-profit, UK-based offsetting scheme
with gold standard credentials

Ticos
Tel: 01223 893907
Web: www.ticos.co.uk

British-based tourism industry carbon
offset service

Treeflights
Tel: 01570 493275
Web: www.treeflights.com

£10 buys you the planting of a tree
in Wales

Trees for Life
Tel: 01309 691292
Web: www.treesforlife.org.uk

Scottish charity trying to regenerate the
Caledonian forest

World Land Trust
Tel: 0845 054 4422
Web: www.carbonbalanced.org

Conservation charity which also
sells offsets

COSMETICS

ATM Organics
Tel: 01874 610667
Web: www.atmorganics.co.uk

Organic beauty retailer which stocks
Ecolani sunscreens

BUAV
Tel: 020 7700 4888
Web: www.gocrueltyfree.org

Information on animal testing and the
cosmetics industry. Also publishes
the *Little Book of Cruelty Free*, a free
directory of companies whose products
bear the HCS logo

Campaign for Safe Cosmetics
Web: www.safecosmetics.org

Calls for the removal of harmful chemicals
in cosmetics

Cargo Cosmetics
Tel: 00 1 416 847 0700
Web: www.cargocosmetics.com

Makers of compostable
Plant Love lipsticks

Dr Hauschka
Tel: 01386 791022
Web: www.drhauschka.co.uk

The grande dame of organic, biodynamic
beauty companies

EcoCert
Tel: 00 49 555 190 8430
Web: www.ecocert.com

Organic certification organisation

European Cosmetic Toiletry and Perfumery Association
Tel: 00 32 2 227 6610
Web: www.colipa.com

Trade association for the cosmetics industry

Green People
Tel: 01403 740350
Web: www.greenpeople.co.uk

Good range of chemical-free beauty products

Honesty Cosmetics
Tel: 01629 814888
Web: www.honestycosmetics.co.uk

Cruelty-free cosmetics

International Agency for Research on Cancer
Tel: 00 33 4 7273 8485
Web: www.iarc.fr

Carries out cancer research, part of the World Health Organisation

Lavera
Tel: 01557 870203
Web: www.lavera.co.uk

Good value natural toiletries

Living Nature
Tel: 01794 323222
Web: www.livingnature.com

Natural toiletries, including an insect repellent gel

Love Lula
Tel: 0870 242 6995
Web: www.lovelula.com

All the top brands in SLS and paraben-free organic skincare

Mariposa
Tel: 01273 242925
Web: www.mariposa-alternative-bodycare.co.uk

Good range of organic beauty products

MASTA
Web: www.masta-travel-health.com

Medical Advisory Services for Travellers Abroad, including travel health clinics

Menses
Web: www.menses.co.uk

Sells the 'Keeper' menstrual cups by mail order

Mooncup
Tel: 01273 673845
Web: www.mooncup.co.uk

Sells Mooncup menstrual cups

Mosiguard
Web: www.mosi-guard.com

Natural insect repellent

Mozzy Off
Tel: 08707 391591
Web: www.mozzyoff.com

More natural insect repellent

My Being Well
Tel: 01326 377555
Web: www.mybeingwell.com

Organic skincare and natural toiletries

Natural Collection
Tel: 0191 501 3878
Web: www.naturalcollection.com

Online supermarket for (almost) all things green

The Natural Store
Tel: 01273 746781
Web: www.thenaturalstore.co.uk

Natural, organic and Fairtrade clothing and cosmetics

Neal's Yard Remedies
Tel: 0845 262 3145
Web: www.nealsyardremedies.com

Classy natural beauty products in gorgeous blue glass bottles

NeemCo
Tel: 01294 204754
Web: www.neemco.co.uk

Neem-based insect repellent

Organic Pharmacy
Tel: 020 7351 2232
Web: www.theorganicpharmacy.com

Upmarket organic toiletries and sunscreens

Skin Cancer Foundation
Web: www.skincancer.org

US-based international organisation, educates about skin cancer. Also see SunSmart

Skin Deep
Web: www.cosmeticdatabase.com

Find out what exactly your favourite brand of shampoo is made of

Soil Association
Tel: 0117 314 5000
Web: www.soilassociation.org

Gives seal of approval on organic cosmetics and cotton

So Organic
Tel: 0800 169 2579
Web: www.soorganic.com

One-stop organic shop

SpaceNK
Tel: 020 8740 2085
Web: www.spacenk.co.uk

UK stockists for SheerinO'kho moisturisers

SunSmart
Web: www.cancerresearchuk.org/sunsmart

UK skin cancer prevention campaign

Surfers Against Sewage
Tel: 0845 458 3001
Web: www.sas.org.uk

Campaigns against marine pollution

There Must Be A Better Way
Tel: 0118 958 3917
Web: www.theremustbeabetterway.co.uk

Stockist for Aubrey Organics cosmetics and sunscreens

Weleda
Tel: 0115 944 8222
Web: www.weleda.co.uk

No-nonsense natural beauty products, including sunscreens

Women's Environmental Network
Tel: 020 7481 9004
Web: www.wen.org.uk

Aims to increase awareness of
environmental issues and create change

DIVING

PADI
Tel: 0117 300 7234
Web: www.padi.com

Professional Association of
Diving Instructors

Project AWARE
Tel: 0117 300 7313
Web: www.projectaware.org

Spin off charity from PADI which was set
up to encourage divers to help conserve
underwater environments

FAIR TRADE

British Association for Fair Trade Shops
Tel: 07882 680113
Web: www.bafts.org.uk

How to find the nearest Fair Trade shop

Ethical Trading Initiative
Tel: 020 7404 1463
Web: www.ethicaltrade.org

Promotes corporate codes of practice
over working conditions

Fair Labor Association
Tel: 00 1 202 898 1000
Web: www.fairlabor.org

Promotes respect for labour rights

Fairtrade Foundation
Tel: 020 7405 5942
Web: www.fairtrade.org.uk

Aiming for a better deal for producers in
the developing world

Fair Trade in Tourism South Africa (FTTSA)
Tel: 00 27 12 342 8307
Web: www.fairtourismsa.org.za

Certification scheme for Fairtrade tourism
businesses in South Africa

International Federation for Alternative Trade (IFAT)
Tel: 00 31 345 535 914
Web: www.ifat.org

Netherlands-based International
Fairtrade organisation

No Sweat
Web: www.nosweat.org.uk

Campaigns against sweatshop
exploitation

FINANCE

Climate Sure
Tel: 0845 600 3076
Web: www.climatesure.co.uk

Travel insurance with carbon offsets
built in

Co-operative Insurance Society
Tel: 0845 746 4646
Web: www.cis.co.uk

Sells 'ethical' travel insurance

Ethical Investment Research Services
Tel: 020 7840 5700
Web: www.eiris.org

Facts and figures on ethical investment

Naturesave
Tel: 01803 864390
Web: www.naturesave.co.uk

Donates a proportion of profit from travel insurance policies to environmental projects

FURTHER READING

All Things Eco
Web: www.allthingseco.co.uk

UK green pages

Bradt guides
Tel: 01753 893444
Web: www.bradt-travelguides.com

Publishes guides to interesting destinations. Has a firm responsible ethos

Condé Nast Traveler
Web: www.condenast.com

Luxury travel magazine, publishes an annual 'green list' (only in the States)

Eco Friendly Tourist
Web: www.ecofriendlytourist.com

Green holiday guide online

The Ecologist
Tel: 020 7422 8100
Web: www.theecologist.org

Environmental affairs magazine

Eco Escape
Web: www.ecoescape.org

A guide to 'responsible escapism' in the UK

Eco Travel
Web: www.ecotravel.com

Online eco travel magazine

Ethical Consumer
Tel: 0161 226 2929
Web: www.ethicalconsumer.org

UK magazine which analyses the ethical credentials of brands and runs www.ethiscore.org, an online ethical buying guide

Ethical Traveler
Web: www.ethicaltraveler.org

American green travel website

Green Futures
Tel: 01223 564334
Web: www.greenfutures.org.uk

Publishes *Centres of Inspiration* guide

Green Traveller
Web: www.greentraveller.co.uk

Tips for greener travels from author Richard Hammond

Guardian
Web: www.guardian.co.uk

National newspaper with dedicated green travel pages

International Centre for Responsible Tourism
Web: www.icrtourism.org

Post-graduate training and research into responsible tourism

Lonely Planet
Tel: 020 7841 9000
Web: www.lonelyplanet.com

Guidebook company which commits 5 per cent of its annual profit towards grass-roots charities

New Consumer
Tel: 0131 555 2594
Web: www.newconsumer.com

Hip ethical lifestyle magazine, includes some travel

No Fly Travel
Web: www.noflytravel.com

Getting from A to B by land and sea

Planeta
Web: www.planeta.com

Online ecotourism journal and forum

Responsible Tourism Partnership
Web: www.responsibletourismpartnership.org

Not-for-profit organisation that works to improve destinations for local people

Resurgence
Tel: 01237 441293
Web: www.resurgence.org

Ecology, art and culture magazine

Rough Guides
Tel: 020 7010 3000
Web: www.roughguides.com

Publishing company known for its responsible stance

Sawdays
Tel: 01275 395430
Web: www.sawdays.co.uk

Green publishing company that specialises in guides to accommodation which has 'a touch of fun and a touch of class'

Sustainable Travel
Web: www.sustainabletravel.com

Sells trips and offsets, has an eco certification scheme

Treehugger
Web: www.treehugger.com

Keep up-to-date on the latest green travel and lifestyle issues

Wanderlust
Tel: 01753 620426
Web: www.wanderlust.co.uk

Travel magazine with strong responsible travel slant

GOLF

Golf Environment Europe
Tel: 01620 850659
Web: www.golfenvironmenteurope.org

Promotes sustainable golfing

Scottish Golf Environment Group
Tel: 0131 660 9480
Web: www.sgeg.org.uk

Encourages environmental awareness on Scotland's golf courses

LUGGAGE AND EQUIPMENT

Berghaus
Tel: 0191 516 5600
Web: www.berghaus.com

Wide range of outdoor clothing and equipment

Brasher
Tel: 0191 516 5777
Web: www.brasher.co.uk

Footwear retailer, best known for walking boots

Ecocentric
Tel: 020 7739 3888
Web: www.ecocentric.co.uk

Stylish eco-friendly lifestyle products

Electronic Zone
Tel: 020 8447 1653
Web: www.electroniczone.co.uk

Voltaic™ backpack stockist

Entermodal
Tel: 00 1 503 224 0402
Web: www.entermodal.com

Sophisticated vegetable-tanned leather bags

ESC Outdoor
Tel: 01273 487509
Web: www.esc-outdoor.co.uk

Juice Bag stockists

Green Green Home
Tel: 01474 814158
Web: www.greengreenhome.co.uk

Recycled luggage tags and other green accessories

The Hemp Store
Tel: 01223 309993
Web: www.thehempstore.co.uk

Hemp rucksacks and bags

Millets
Tel: 0800 389 5861
Web: www.millets.co.uk

Look for the One Earth range of outdoor gear

Natural Collection
Tel: 0845 367 7001
Web: www.naturalcollection.com

Green online superstore

Patagonia
Tel: 0800 026 0055
Web: www.patagonia.com

Sportswear company with sound ethical credentials

Planet Silverchilli
Web: www.planetsilverchilli.com

Groovy recycled rubber bags and accessories

Pure Sativa
Tel: 020 8964 1717
Web: www.puresativa.com

Rustically chic hemp bags and rucksacks

Rohan
Tel: 0870 601 2244
Web: www.rohan.co.uk

One stop shop for travel clothing

Spirit of Nature
Tel: 0870 725 9885
Web: www.spiritofnature.co.uk

Hemp bags, organic clothing, natural cosmetics and biodegradable nappies

ORGANISATIONS AND CAMPAIGNS

Amnesty International
Tel: 020 7033 1500
Web: www.amnesty.org

Campaigns for human rights

Association of National Park Authorities
Tel: 029 2049 9966
Web: www.nationalparks.gov.uk

Information on National Parks in the UK

Blue Flag
Web: www.blueflag.org.uk

Awards beaches and marinas with good water quality and properly managed sewage treatment

Bluewater Network
Tel: 00 1 415 544 0790
Web: www.bluewaternetwork.org

American organisation that campaigns against environmental damage

The Born Free Foundation
Tel: 01403 240170
Web: www.bornfree.org.uk

Protests against holding animals captive for entertainment

The Burma Campaign UK
Tel: 020 7324 4710
Web: www.burmacampaign.org.uk

Publishes a list of 'dirty' companies which support the Burmese government

Cadw
Tel: 01443 336000
Web: www.cadw.wales.gov.uk

Welsh heritage organisation

The Campaign to Protect Rural England
Tel: 020 7981 2800
Web: www.cpre.org.uk

Works for a sustainable future for the English countryside

Captive Animals Protection Society
Tel: 0845 330 3911
Web: www.captiveanimals.org

Opposes the incarceration of animals

CIPRA
Tel: 00 423 237 4030
Web: www.cipra.org

The International Commission for the Protection of the Alps

The Civic Trust
Tel: 020 7539 7900
Web: www.civictrust.org.uk

Works to improve the quality of the built environment and its impact on people and runs annual Heritage Open Days each September, in conjunction with English Heritage

Climate Outreach and Information Network (COIN)
Tel: 01865 727911
Web: www.coinet.org.uk

UK charity aiming to educate about climate change

Convention on International Trade in Endangered Species
Tel: 0117 372 8749
Web: www.ukcites.gov.uk

Provides useful advice for travellers on buying animal products

Compassion in World Farming
Tel: 01483 521950
Web: www.ciwf.org.uk

Campaigns against cruelty to farm animals and the production of 'posh nosh' involving the inhumane treatment of animals

Coral Reef Alliance
Tel: 00 1 415 834 0900
Web: www.coralreefalliance.org

American reef protection organisation

The Countryside Access And Activities Network (CAAN)
Tel: 02890 303930
Web: www.countrysiderecreation.com

Helps manage the Northern Ireland countryside

The Countryside Code
Web: www.countrysideaccess.gov.uk

Lists countryside charities, organisations, activity providers and rural businesses

Countryside Council for Wales
Tel: 0845 1306 229
Web: www.ccw.gov.uk

The government's statutory advisor on 'sustaining natural beauty, wildlife and the opportunity for outdoor enjoyment in Wales'

Countryside Recreation
Web: www.countrysiderecreation.org.uk

Lists countryside charities, organisations, activity providers and rural businesses

DEFRA
Tel: 08459 335577
Web: www.defra.gov.uk

Department for environment, food and rural affairs

ECPAT
Tel: 020 7233 9887
Web: www.ecpat.org.uk

Children's rights organisation, focusing on the protection of trafficked children and children exploited in tourism

Endangered Fish Alliance
Tel: 00 1 416 323 9521
Web: www.endangeredfishalliance.org

Advises against eating certain fish on the grounds that they are being 'overfished, oversold and overeaten'

English Heritage
Tel: 0870 333 1181
Web: www.english-heritage.org.uk

Heritage properties and cottage rental agency

Environment and Heritage Service
Tel: 028 9054 3095
Web: www.ehsni.gov.uk

Northern Ireland heritage organisation

Environmental Change Institute
Tel: 01865 275848
Web: www.eci.ox.ac.uk

Part of Oxford University, undertakes research on environmental issues

Environmental Justice Foundation
Tel: 020 7359 0440
Web: www.ejfoundation.org

Aims to 'protect people and planet'

Forestry Commission
Tel: 0131 334 0303
Web: www.forestry.gov.uk

Government department responsible for the protection and expansion of Britain's forests and woodlands

Free Tibet Campaign
Tel: 020 7324 4605
Web: www.freetibet.org

Tibetan pressure group

Friends of the Earth
Tel: 020 7490 1555
Web: www.foe.co.uk

Environmental pressure group

Friends of Maldives
Tel: 01722 504330
Web: www.friendsofmaldives.org

Human rights NGO which calls for a boycott of resorts linked to members of the Gayoom regime

Global Sense
Web: www.globalsense.org.uk

Runs workshops on responsible tourism for young people

Greenpeace
Tel: 020 7865 8100
Web: www.greenpeace.org.uk

Environmental campaign group

Historic Scotland
Tel: 0131 668 8600
Web: www.historic-scotland.gov.uk

Scottish heritage organisation

Human Rights Watch
Tel: 020 7713 1995
Web: www.hrw.org

Human rights pressure group

Intergovernmental Panel on Climate Change
Tel: 00 41 22 730 8208
Web: www.ipcc.ch

Assesses and reports on the impact of climate change

International Fund for Animal Welfare
Tel: 020 7587 6700
Web: www.ifaw.org

Campaigns on animal welfare issues

International Porter Protection Group
Tel: 01229 586225
Web: www.ippg.net

Works to improve the conditions of mountain porters in the tourism industry

The Landmark Trust
Tel: 01628 825925
Web: www.landmarktrust.org.uk

Heritage and cottage rental organisation

Local Heritage Initiative
Tel: 020 7591 6042
Web: www.lhi.org.uk

Covers local heritage projects and organisations in the UK

Marine Conservation Society
Tel: 01989 566017
Web: www.mcsuk.org

UK charity dedicated to health of seas, shores and wildlife

Mark Lynas
Web: www.marklynas.org

Blog about climate change by the author of *Six Degrees of Hell*

Monbiot
Web: www.monbiot.com

Articles and information from campaigner George Monbiot

Mountain Wilderness
Web: www.mountainwilderness.org

Environmental pressure group

The National Trust
Tel: 0870 429 2429
Tel: 0870 458 4000
Web: www.nationaltrust.org.uk

Heritage properties and cottage rental agency

The National Trust for Scotland
Tel: 0131 243 9475
Tel: 0131 243 9300
Web: www.nts.org.uk

Scottish heritage properties and cottage rental agency

Natural England
Tel: 0845 600 3078
Web: www.naturalengland.org.uk

'Conserves and enhances' the English countryside

Natural Resources Defense Council
Web: www.nrdc.org

American environmental organisation

Rainforest Alliance
Tel: 00 1 212 677 1900
Web: www.rainforest-alliance.org

Conservation organisation

The Royal Society for the Protection of Birds (RSPB)
Tel: 01767 680551
Web: www.rspb.org.uk

Works to protect birds and the environment

RSPCA
Tel: 0870 555 5999
Tel: 0870 333 5999
Web: www.rspca.org.uk

Animal welfare charity

Scottish Natural Heritage
Tel: 01463 725000
Web: www.snh.org.uk

Works to conserve Scottish wildlife and the environment

Stuff Your Rucksack
Web: www.stuffyourrucksack.com

Links travellers with space in their bags to charities and schools overseas that need books, clothes or other items

Sustrans
Tel: 0845 113 0065
Web: www.sustrans.org.uk

Sustainable transport charity

Travel Operators for Tigers (TOFT)
Tel: 01285 643333
Web: www.toftiger.org

Supports tigers and other Indian wildlife

Tyndall Centre for Climate Change Research
Tel: 01603 593900
Web: www.tyndall.ac.uk

Working to develop sustainable responses to climate change

UNESCO World Heritage Centre
Tel: 00 33 1 45 68 15 71
Web: whc.unesco.org

848 properties of special cultural or natural value

The Vivat Trust
Tel: 0845 090 0194
Web: www.vivat.org.uk

Heritage and cottage rental organisation

Voices for Burma
Web: www.voicesforburma.org

Encourages responsible travel to Burma

The Wildlife Trusts
Tel: 0870 036 7711
Web: www.wildlifetrusts.org

'Working for an environment rich in wildlife for everyone'

The Woodland Trust
Tel: 01476 581135
Web: www.woodland-trust.org.uk

Working to protect native woodland in the UK

World Monuments Fund
Tel: 00 646 424 9594
Web: www.worldmonumentswatch.org

The world's 100 most endangered architectural and cultural sites

WWF
Tel: 01483 426444
Web: www.wwf.org.uk

World's largest independent conservation organisation

SKIING

National Ski Areas Association
Tel: 00 1 303 987 1111
Web: www.nsaa.org

American organisation with a 'Sustainable Slopes' charter for ski areas

Respect The Mountain
Web: www.respectthemountain.com

Environmental campaign run by the Ski Club of Great Britain

Ski Club of Great Britain
Tel: 020 8410 2000
Web: www.skiclub.co.uk

Lots of useful information online, including its Green Resort Guide

Ski Dubai
Tel: 00 971 4 409 4000
Web: www.skidxb.com

Indoor ski centre surrounded by desert

SPAS

Budock Vean
Tel: 01326 250288
Web: www.budockvean.co.uk

Cornish hotel with an earth-friendly spa

The Hay Barn
Tel: 01608 731700
Web: www.daylesfordorganic.com

Gloucestershire organic spa

Monty's Spa
Tel: 01749 342008
Web: www.montyspa.com

Somerset hotel spa which uses natural products

Thermae Bath Spa
Tel: 01225 331234
Web: www.thermaebathspa.com

Relatively green spa complex utilising the only hot springs in the UK

Titanic Spa
Tel: 0845 410 3333
Web: www.titanicspa.com

West Yorkshire 'eco' spa set in a former textile factory

Senspa
Tel: 01590 623551
Web: www.senspa.co.uk

New Forest spa which sources its energy from a green supplier

TOUR OPERATORS AND TRAVEL AGENTS

Adventure Alternative
Tel: 02890 701476
Web: www.adventurealternative.com

Trekking holidays, mountaineering expeditions, teaching placements and safaris

Association of Independent Tour Operators (AITO)
Tel: 020 8744 9280
Web: www.aito.co.uk

Members must sign up to responsible tourism

Andante Travels
Tel: 01722 713800
Web: www.andantetravels.co.uk

Archaeological and historical journeys

Archipelago Azores
Tel: 01768 775672
Web: www.azoreschoice.com

Azores specialist

ATG Oxford
Tel: 01865 315678
Web: www.atg-oxford.co.uk

Walking and cycling holidays in Europe

Audley Travel
Tel: 01933 838000
Web: www.audleytravel.com

Tailor-made trips worldwide

Baobab Travel
Tel: 0870 382 5003
Web: www.baobabtravel.com

Africa ecotourism specialist

Big Apple Greeter
Tel: 00 1 212 669 8159
Web: www.bigapplegreeter.org

'See New York through the eyes of a New Yorker'

Bushbaby Travel
Tel: 0870 850 9103
Web: www.bushbaby.travel

South Africa and Mauritius specialist with a family slant

Cazenove & Loyd
Tel: 020 7384 2332
Web: www.cazenoveandloyd.com

Tailor-made travel worldwide

Charity Challenge
Tel: 020 8557 0000
Web: www.charitychallenge.com

Fund-raising trips

Chinatown Alleyway Tours
Tel: 00 1 415 984 1478
Web: www.chinatownalleywaytours.org

Not-for-profit two-hour walking tours in San Francisco

City Sherpa
Web: http://blogit.hs.fi/citysherpa

Summer-only tours of Helsinki taken by locals

Classic Tours
Tel: 020 7619 0066
Web: www.classictours.co.uk

Fund-raising trips

Cox & Kings
Tel: 020 7873 5000
Web: www.coxandkings.co.uk

Claims to be the world's oldest travel company

Couchsurfing
Web: www.couchsurfing.com

Pairs up travellers with like-minded locals – also see www.yoursafeplanet.co.uk

CPH Cool
Tel: 00 45 2980 1040
Web: www.cphcool.dk

Private guided walks in Copenhagen

Discover Adventure
Tel: 01722 718444
Web: www.discoveradventure.com

Fund-raising trips and school expeditions

Discovery Initiatives
Tel: 01285 643333
Web: www.discoveryinitiatives.co.uk

Specialist wildlife package operator

Dive Worldwide
Tel: 0845 130 6980
Web: www.diveworldwide.com

Specialist dive holiday operator

Dragoman
Tel: 01728 861133
Web: www.dragoman.uk.com

Responsible overlanding

Equatorial Travel
Tel: 01335 348770
Web: www.equatorialtravel.co.uk

'Fair trade' holidays in India, Morocco
and Ecuador

Erna Low
Tel: 0845 863 0525
Web: www.ernalow.co.uk

Ski operator with membership of AITO

Expert Africa
Tel: 020 8232 9777
Web: www.expertafrica.com

Specialist tour operator

Explore
Tel: 0870 333 4001
Web: www.explore.co.uk

Small group adventure holidays

Federation of Tour Operators
Tel: 01444 457900
Web: www.fto.co.uk

Represents much of the package
holiday industry

Fingal of Caledonia
Tel: 01397 772167
Web: www.fingal-cruising.co.uk

A hotel barge which cruises Loch Ness
and the Caledonian Canal

Gane & Marshall
Tel: 020 8445 6000
Web: www.ganeandmarshall.co.uk

Tailor-made safaris and treks

Go Differently
Tel: 01799 521950
Web: www.godifferently.com

Ethical holidays in Thailand, Cambodia,
Laos, India, Bhutan and Bali

Green Visions
Tel: 00 387 033 717 290
Web: www.greenvisions.ba

Locally led 'eco tours' in Bosnia and
Herzegovina

High Places
Tel: 0845 257 7500
Web: www.highplaces.co.uk

Worldwide trekking and walking holidays

Himalayan Kingdoms
Tel: 01453 844400
Web: www.himalayankingdoms.com

Small group adventures, not only in
the Himalayas

Inntravel
Tel: 01653 617949
Web: www.inntravel.co.uk

Cycling, walking and other holidays

Insider Tour
Web: www.insidertour.com

Locally run city tours of Berlin

Insider Tours
Tel: 01233 811771
Web: www.insider-tours.com

Family-run tours of Peru, India and
Sri Lanka

Into Africa
Tel: 0114 255 5610
Web: www.intoafrica.co.uk

Ethically minded safaris and treks in
East Africa

Journey Latin America
Tel: 020 8747 8315
Web: www.journeylatinamerica.co.uk

Central and South America specialists

KE Adventure Travel
Tel: 01768 773966
Web: www.keadventure.com

Trekking, climbing and biking trips
worldwide

Kooljaman
Tel: 00 61 8 9192 4970
Web: www.kooljaman.com.au

Aboriginal-owned wilderness camp on
Australia's northwest coast

Last Frontiers
Tel: 01296 653000
Web: www.lastfrontiers.com

Tailor-made travel to Latin America

Like A Local
Tel: 00 31 20 530 1460
Web: www.like-a-local.com

Insider city tours (mainly of Amsterdam)

Long Travel
Tel: 01694 722193
Web: www.long-travel.co.uk

Specialists in southern Italy, Sicily and
Sardinia

Meet the People Tours
Tel: 0191 265 1110
Web: www.traidcraft-tours.com

Specialist holidays run by Fairtrade
retailers Traidcraft, and the tour operator
Saddle Skedaddle

Muir's Tours
Web: www.nkf-mt.org.uk

Worldwide holidays where profits go
to charity

My Genie In Paris
Tel: 00 33 1 43 18 18 46
Web: www.mygenieinparis.com

Pick a local's brain – for a fee – in Paris

Naturetrek
Tel: 01962 733051
Web: www.naturetrek.co.uk

Offers a wide range of wildlife trips

Nomadic Thoughts
Tel: 020 7604 4408
Web: www.nomadicthoughts.com

Tailor-made travel worldwide

On the Go Tours
Tel: 020 7371 1113
Web: www.onthegotours.com

Holidays and overland tours

Out of the Blue Holidays
Tel: 01249 449533
Web: www.wdcs.org/outoftheblue

The travel side of the Whale and Dolphin Conservation Society (WDCS)

Rainbow Tours
Tel: 020 7226 1004
Web: www.rainbowtours.co.uk

Responsible Africa and Indian Ocean specialists

Reality Tours and Travel
Tel: 00 91 22 228 338 72
Web: www.realitytoursandtravel.com

Takes tourists into the 432-acre Dharavi squatter settlement in Mumbai

Responsible Travel
Tel: 01273 600030
Web: www.responsibletravel.com

Ethical holiday supermarket, selling 2,500 trips from 200 companies

Serenity Holidays
Web: www.serenity.co.uk

AITO member with several different brands

Shacklabank
Tel: 01539 620134
Web: www.shacklabank.co.uk

Family farm in Cumbria that also offers 'free range' walking holidays

Simply Tanzania
Tel: 020 8986 0615
Web: www.simplytanzania.co.uk

Tanzania specialists

Ski Beat
Tel: 01243 780405
Web: www.skibeat.co.uk

Ski operator with AITO membership

Skyline Overseas
Tel: 0870 905 5577
Web: www.skylineoverseas.co.uk

Fund-raising trips

Tim Best Travel
Tel: 020 7591 0300
Web: www.timbesttravel.com

Tailor-made holidays

Travelling Naturalist
Tel: 01305 267994
Web: www.naturalist.co.uk

Bird-watching and wildlife holidays

Travel Roots
Web: www.travelroots.com

Small ethically minded travel agency

Tribes Travel
Tel: 01728 685971
Web: www.tribes.co.uk

Fair trade and responsible holidays and safaris

Tyred Out
Tel: 01690 760181
Web: www.tyred-out.com

Runs beginners mountain biking courses in Snowdonia

Village Ways
Tel: 01223 750049
Web: www.villageways.com

Walking holidays between rural Indian villages in the foothills of the Himalayas

Wildlife Worldwide
Tel: 0845 130 6982
Web: www.wildlifeworldwide.com

Specialises in tailor-made wildlife-viewing holidays

Wind, Sand and Stars
Tel: 0870 757 1510
Web: www.windsandstars.co.uk

Bedouin-led trips to Sinai

World Primate Safaris
Tel: 0870 830 9092
Web: www.worldprimatesafaris.com

Brighton-based company doing what it says on the tin

TRANSPORT (AVIATION)

Air Fleets
Web: www.airfleets.net

Get the lowdown on different planes

Airport Watch
Tel: 020 7248 2227
Web: www.airportwatch.org.uk

Opposes airport expansion

Association of European Airlines (AEA)
Tel: 00 32 26 398 989
Web: www.aea.be

Represents 31 European airlines

Aviation Environment Federation
Tel: 020 7248 2223
Web: www.aef.org.uk

UK non-profit making environmental association concerned with the environmental effects of aviation

Civil Aviation Authority
Tel: 020 7379 7311
Web: www.caa.co.uk

UK aviation regulator

Greener By Design
Web: www.greenerbydesign.org.uk

Aviation's environmental taskforce

Green Skies Network
Tel: 020 7248 2223
Web: www.greenskies.org

NGO campaigning to control and reduce the impact of air transport

International Air Transport Association (IATA)
Tel: 00 41 22 770 2525
Web: www.iata.org

Represents the airline industry

LowFlyZone
Web: www.lowflyzone.org

Pledge to limit the number of flights you take each year

North South Travel
Tel: 01245 608291
Web: www.northsouthtravel.co.uk

Flight ticket agency which donates profits to charity

OAG
Tel: 01582 695050
Web: www.oag.com

Flight information company, useful for aviation statistics and trends

Plane Stupid
Web: www.planestupid.com

Campaigning to 'bring the aviation industry down to earth'

TRANSPORT (CYCLING)

Bicing
Tel: 00 34 902 31 55 31
Web: www.bicing.com

Barcelona bike-sharing scheme

Bicycle Beano Holidays
Tel: 01982 560471
Web: www.bicycle-beano.co.uk

UK cycling tour operator

Bike Events
Tel: 0870 755 8519
Web: www.bike-events.com

UK organisation offering information on bike rides and holidays

Bike Sharing blog
Web: http://bike-sharing.blogspot.com/

Lists lots of – but not all – city bike sharing schemes

Bike Week
Web: www.bikeweek.org.uk

Annual UK cycling event

Byways Breaks
Tel: 0151 722 8050
Web: www.byways-breaks.co.uk

Guided and self-guided cycling holidays in Shropshire, Cheshire and the Welsh borders

Call a Bike
Tel: 00 49 70 005 225 522
Web: www.callabike-interaktiv.de

German bike-sharing scheme

City Bike, Tallinn
Tel: 00 37 26 836 383
Web: www.citybike.ee

Estonian bike tour company

City Bikes
Tel: 00 45 36 16 42 33
Web: www.bycyklen.dk

Copenhagen bike-sharing scheme

Company of Cyclists
Tel: 01904 778080
Web: www.companyofcyclists.com

Promotes cycling in the UK

Country Lanes
Tel: 0845 370 0622
Web: www.countrylanes.co.uk

UK cycling tour operator, also does guided mountain biking

Cycle Breaks
Tel: 01449 721555
Web: www.cyclebreaks.com

Suffolk cycling tour operator

Cycling Around The World
Web: www.cyclingaroundtheworld.nl

Useful independent information on cycling in various countries

Cyclists' Touring Club
Tel: 0870 873 0060
Web: www.ctc.org.uk

Useful information on cycling in the UK

European Bike Express
Tel: 01430 422111
Web: www.bike-express.co.uk

Shuttles cyclists – and their bikes – to France and Spain by coach

Fat Tire Bike Tours
Tel: 00 33 1 56 58 10 54
Web: www.fattirebiketoursparis.com

Bike tours in Paris (also run in Berlin and Barcelona)

Galloway Cycling
Tel: 01556 502979
Web: www.gallowaycycling.co.uk

Cycling holidays in southwest Scotland

The International Mountain Biking Association (IMBA)
Tel: 01562 864771
Web: www.imba.org.uk

Provides information on responsible mountain biking

Laid Back Bikes
Web: www.laid-back-bikes.co.uk

Recumbent bike tours in Edinburgh

London Bicycle Tour Company
Tel: 020 7928 6838
Web: www.londonbicycle.com

Daily tours around the capital

Natural Discovery
Tel: 0845 458 2799
Web: www.naturaldiscovery.co.uk

Rents out electric bikes in the Surrey Hills

OYBike
Tel: 0845 226 5751
Web: www.oybike.com

London bike-sharing scheme

Saddle Skedaddle
Tel: 0191 265 1110
Web: www.skedaddle.co.uk

Cycling holiday specialist

Two Wheels Tours
Tel: 00 46 709 843 802
Web: www.twowheeltours.se

Stockholm bike tours

Urban Biking
Tel: 00 54 11 4568 4321
Web: www.urbanbiking.com

Bike tours of Buenos Aires

Volib
Tel: 00 33 1 30 79 79 30
Web: www.velib.paris.fr

Parisian bike-sharing scheme

Vélo'v
Web: www.velov.grandlyon.com

Lyon bike-sharing scheme

Yellow Zebra Bike Tours
Web: www.yellowzebrabikes.com

Budapest bike tour company

TRANSPORT (GENERAL)

Department for Transport
Tel: 020 7944 8300
Web: www.dft.gov.uk

Oversees UK government's transport strategy and policies

Traveline
Tel: 0871 200 2233
Web: www.traveline.org.uk

Useful service for working out routes on public transport in the UK

TRANSPORT (MOTORING)

Bio Beetle
Tel: 00 1 808 873 6121
Web: www.bio-beetle.com

Biodiesel-fuelled VW Beetle rental in Maui and LA

Car Plus
Tel: 0113 234 9299
Web: www.carplus.org.uk

Website listing car share and other 'green' car schemes

City Car Club
Tel: 0845 330 1234
Web: www.citycarclub.co.uk

Membership scheme, giving pay-as-you-go car rental in various UK cities

Climate Cars
Tel: 020 8968 0440
Web: www.climatecars.com

London-based taxi service using hybrid cars and offering a 'bicycle rescue' service – if you've cycled to work but don't fancy the journey home it will drive you and your bike home (each car has a bike rack stored in the boot)

Compartir
Tel: 00 34 93 789 1106
Web: www.compartir.org

Global car-share network

Eco Igo
Tel: 0800 032 6446
Web: www.ecoigo.com

Decadent 'green' London-based minicab service

Eco Limo
Tel: 00 61 1300 326 546
Web: www.ecolimo.com.au

Does roughly the same in Melbourne, Australia

Evo Limo
Tel: 00 1 310 642 8600
Web: www.evolimo.com

Runs a fleet of CNG-run SUVs in LA

Environmental Transport Association
Tel: 0800 389 1010
Web: www.eta.co.uk

Campaigns for greener motoring and sells alternative breakdown cover

Eurolines
Tel: 0870 514 3219
Web: www.eurolines.com

Biggest long-distance coach operator
in Europe

Future Vehicles
Web: www.electriccarhire.com

Offers weekly electric car hire
from London

Green Tomato Cars
Tel: 020 8568 0022
Web: www.greentomatocars.com

London minicab service running a fleet of
Toyota Prius cars

Hertz
Tel: 0870 850 2677
Web: www.hertz.co.uk

Recently launched a 'green collection'
of hire cars

Hitchsters
Web: www.hitchsters.com

Airport taxi-sharing scheme in New York
and Boston

Is Anyone Going To
Web: www.isanyonegoingto.com

Puts travellers in touch with each other in
an aim to reduce the number of cars on
the road

Lift Pool
Web: www.liftpool.co.uk

Car-sharing scheme

Liftshare
Tel: 0870 078 0225
Web: www.liftshare.org

Organised hitching

Megabus
Tel: 0901 331 0031
Web: www.megabus.com

Cheap Intercity coach services in the UK
and US

My Lifts
Web: www.mylifts.com

Car-sharing scheme

National Express
Tel: 0870 580 8080
Web: www.nationalexpress.com

The largest coach network in the UK

PlanetTran
Tel: 00 1 617 475 1665
Web: www.planettran.com

Serves New England and San Francisco
with a fleet of hybrid taxis

Scottish Citylink
Tel: 0870 550 5050
Web: www.citylink.co.uk

Scottish coach services

Segway Guided Tours
Web: www.segwayguidedtours.com

Find a list of companies running
Segway tours

Share A Car
Web: www.shareacar.com

UK car-sharing scheme

Society of Motor Manufacturers and Traders
Tel: 0870 751 8270
Web: www.smmt.co.uk

Represents the motor industry

Translink
Tel: 028 90 66 66 30
Web: www.ulsterbus.co.uk

Coach and rail services in Northern Ireland

Tuctuc
Tel: 020 7735 5059
Web: www.tuctuc.co.uk

CNG-run tuc-tuc taxi services worldwide

Ze Bus
Web: www.ze-bus.com

Seasonal hop-on, hop-off service in the west of France

Zipcar
Tel: 0207 960 6421
Web: www.zipcar.com

Pay as you go car rental in London and across North America.

TRANSPORT (RAIL)

Amtrak
Tel: 00 1 800 872 7245
Web: www.amtrak.com

For US train tickets

Christian Wolmar
Tel: 07931 504555
Web: www.christianwolmar.co.uk

Informative website of well-known UK transport commentator

Deutsche Bahn
Tel: 0870 243 5363
Web: www.bahn.co.uk

Sells tickets to Germany, Austria, Scandinavia and Eastern Europe (also see www.nachtzug.de for German night trains)

Elipsos
Web: www.elipsos.com

Runs 'trainhotel' overnight services from Paris, Milan and Zurich to Spain

European Rail
Tel: 020 7387 0444
Web: www.europeanrail.com

Rail ticket agency

Eurostar
Tel: 0870 518 6186
Web: www.eurostar.com

Cross-channel tickets and beyond

Eurotunnel
Tel: 0870 535 3535
Web: www.eurotunnel.com

Cross-channel motorail service

International Rail
Tel: 0870 084 1410
Web: www.international-rail.com

Tickets for Australia, North America and Japan

Irish Rail
Tel: 00 353 1 703 4070
Web: www.irishrail.ie

Tickets for Ireland

National Rail
Tel: 0845 748 4950
Web: www.nationalrail.co.uk

Details of UK services

Optima Tours
Tel: 00 49 89 5488 0111
Web: www.optimatours.de

Sells Motorail tickets from Austria to
Bulgaria, Macedonia, Turkey and Greece

Rail Australia
Tel: 01572 768022
Web: www.railaustralia.com

Tickets for Australian railways

Railbookers
Tel: 0844 482 1010
Web: www.railbookers.com

Rail ticket agency

Railchoice
Tel: 0870 165 7300
Web: www.railchoice.co.uk

Rail ticket agency

Rail Europe
Tel: 0870 584 8848
Web: www.raileurope.co.uk

Sells tickets to France, Spain, Italy or
Switzerland

Rail Pass Direct
Tel: 0870 084 1413
Web: www.railpassdirect.co.uk

Rail ticket agency

Rail Savers
Tel: 0870 750 7070
Web: www.railsavers.com

Rail ticket agency

Renfe
Tel: 00 34 902 24 0202
Web: www.renfe.es

Spanish rail service

Seat 61
Web: www.seat61.com

A one-stop source of information on
getting from place to place overland

Simply Rail
Tel: 0870 084 1410
Web: www.simplyrail.com

Rail ticket agency

SNCF
Web: www.voyages-sncf.com

French rail service

Thomas Cook
Tel: 01733 416477
Web: www.thomascooktimetables.com

Contact for rail timetables

Tour Vacations to Go
Tel: 00 18 00 680 2868
Web: www.tourvacationstogo.com

Rail ticket agency

Trainline
Web: www.thetrainline.com

Book UK rail and Eurostar tickets (see
www.internationaltrainline.com for
further afield)

Trenitalia
Web: www.trenitalia.com

Italian rail service (also see www.italiarail.co.uk)

Tranzscenic
Tel: 00 64 4 495 0775
Web: www.tranzscenic.co.nz

For New Zealand services

Via Rail
Tel: 00 1 888 842 7245
Web: www.viarail.ca

For Canadian rail services

TRANSPORT (SHIPPING)

A Ferry To
Web: www.aferryto.co.uk

Ferry agency

All Ferries
Web: www.allferries.co.uk

Ferry agency

Brittany Ferries
Tel: 0870 907 6103
Web: www.brittanyferries.co.uk

Services from Plymouth to Roscoff (France) and Santander (Spain), Poole to Cherbourg (France) and Portsmouth to Caen and St Malo (both France)

Caledonian MacBrayne
Tel: 0870 565 0000
Web: www.calmac.co.uk

For crossings around Scotland's west coast

Cheap4Ferries
Tel: 0870 111 0634
Web: www.cheap4ferries.com

Ferry agency

Condor Ferries
Tel: 0870 243 5140
Web: www.condorferries.com

Services from Poole to St Malo (France), Weymouth to St Malo and Portsmouth to Cherbourg (France). Also to Guernsey and Jersey in the Channel Islands

Cruise Junkie
Web: www.cruisejunkie.com

Seeing cruising from a new perspective

Cruise People
Tel: 020 7723 2450
Web: www.cruisepeople.co.uk

Freighter and cruise agency

DFDS Seaway
Tel: 0871 522 9955
Web: www.dfdsseaways.co.uk

Services from Newcastle to Stavanger, Haugesund and Bergen (Norway), Newcastle to Ijmuiden (Holland) and Harwich to Esbjerg (Denmark)

Dutch Flyer
Tel: 0870 545 5455
Web: www.dutchflyer.co.uk

Combination sail and rail fares on UK–Holland trips

Ferry Booker
Tel: 0870 442 2418
Web: www.ferrybooker.com

Ferry agency

Ferry Green
Tel: 0870 264 2644
Web: www.ferrygreen.com

Ferry agency linked with carbon offsetting scheme

Ferry Savers
Tel: 0870 066 9612
Web: www.ferrysavers.com

Ferry agency that offers offsets when you book

Freighter Trips
Web: www.freightertrips.com

Information on travelling by cargo ship

Hovertravel
Tel: 01983 811000
Web: www.hovertravel.co.uk

Services from Southsea to the Isle of Wight

Irish Ferries
Tel: 0870 517 1717
Web: www.irishferries.com

Services from Holyhead to Dublin, Pembroke to Rosslare and Rosslare to Cherbourg and Roscoff (France)

Isle of Man Steam Packet Company
Tel: 0870 552 3523
Web: www.steam-packet.com

Services from the Isle of Man to Liverpool, Heysham, Belfast and Dublin

Isle of Sark Shipping Company
Tel: 01481 724059
Web: www.sarkshipping.info

Services between Guernsey and Sark

Isle of Scilly Steamship Group
Tel: 0845 710 5555
Web: www.ios-travel.co.uk

Services between Penzance and the Scillies

John o'Groats Ferries
Tel: 01955 611353
Web: www.jogferry.co.uk

Services from John o'Groats to Orkney

LD Lines
Tel: 0870 428 4335
Web: www.ldlines.co.uk

Services from Portsmouth to Le Havre (France) and Newhaven to Le Havre and Dieppe (France)

Norfolkline
Tel: 0870 870 1020
Web: www.norfolkline.com

Services from Dover to Dunkirk (France) and from Heysham and Birkenhead to Belfast and Dublin

NorthLink Ferries
Tel: 0845 600 0449
Web: www.northlinkferries.co.uk

Services from Scrabster and Aberdeen to Orkney and Shetland

P&O Ferries
Tel: 0870 598 0333
Web: www.poferries.com

Services from Hull to Zeebrugge (Belgium), Dover to Calais (France), Hull to Rotterdam (Holland) and Portsmouth to Bilbao (Spain)

P&O Irish Sea
Tel: 0870 242 4777
Web: www.poirishsea.com

Services between Liverpool and Dublin and between Larne and Troon or Cairnryan

Passenger Shipping Association
Tel: 020 7436 2449
Web: www.the-psa.co.uk

Represents UK cruise and ferry companies

Red Funnel
Tel: 0870 444 8898
Web: www.redfunnel.co.uk

Services from Southampton to the Isle of Wight

Sail Rail
Tel: 0845 075 5755
Web: www.sailrail.co.uk

Sells combination rail and ferry tickets between the UK and Ireland

SeaFrance
Tel: 0870 571 1711
Web: www.seafrance.com

Services from Dover to Calais (France)

Smyril Line
Tel: 00 298 34 59 00
Web: www.smyril-line.com

Connects the UK (Shetland) with Norway, Iceland and the Faroes

Speed Ferries
Tel: 0870 220 0570
Web: www.speedferries.com

Services from Dover to Boulogne (France)

Stena Line
Tel: 0870 570 7070
Web: www.stenaline.co.uk

Services from Harwich to Hook of Holland (Holland), Fishguard to Rosslare, Fleetwood to Larne, Holyhead to Dun Laoghaire or Dublin Port and Stranraer to Belfast.

Strand Voyages
Tel: 020 7766 8230
Web: www.strandtravel.co.uk

Cargo ship agency

Superfast Ferries
Web: www.superfast.com

From Rosyth to Zeebrugge (Belgium)

Transeuropa
Tel: 01843 595522
Web: www.transeuropaferries.co.uk

Services from Ramsgate to Ostend (France)

Transmanche
Tel: 0800 917 1201
Web: www.transmancheferries.com

Services from Newhaven to Dieppe (France)

Wightlink
Tel: 0870 582 7744
Web: www.wightlink.co.uk

Services from Portsmouth and Lymington to the Isle of Wight

TRAVEL & TOURISM ORGANISATIONS

Association of Independent Tour Operators (AITO)
Tel: 020 8744 9280
Web: www.aito.co.uk

Includes a commitment to Responsible Tourism in its business charter

Association of National Tourist Offices
Web: www.antor.com

Contacts for many tourist offices worldwide

Ecoclub
Web: www.ecoclub.com

Listings for some ecolodges, hotels and resorts by country

Eco Friendly Tourist
Web: www.ecofriendlytourist.com

A directory of green travel services and operators

Environmentally Friendly Hotels
Web: www.environmentallyfriendlyhotels. com

American site containing links to green hotels, B&Bs and villas

Ethical Escape
Tel: 01244 570336
Web: www.ethicalescape.com

Lists some green hotels, holidays and tour operators

Fair Trade in Tourism South Africa (FTTSA)
Tel: 00 27 12 342 8307
Web: www.fairtourismsa.org.za

Certification scheme for businesses in South Africa

Foreign and Commonwealth Office
Web: www.fco.gov.uk

Travel advice and warnings by country

Green Hotels Association
Web: www.greenhotels.com

Lists green accommodation (some more so than others), mainly in the States

International Centre for Responsible Tourism
Tel: 07738 297057
Web: www.icrtourism.org

Post-graduate training and research centre based at Leeds Metropolitan University. Director Harold Goodwin also co-founded www.responsibletravel.com

International Ecotourism Society (TIES)
Tel: 00 1 202 347 9203
Web: www.ecotourism.org

Promotes responsible travel

International Tourism Partnership
Tel: 020 7467 3600
Web: www.tourismpartnership.org

Puts together guides on sustainable hotel management. Members include Hilton, Four Seasons, Marriott, Hyatt, City Inn, Rezidor, Six Senses, Starwood, Taj and Scandic

Minority Rights Group
Tel: 020 7422 4200
Web: www.minorityrights.org

Works to secure the rights of minorities and indigenous communities

Planeta
Web: www.planeta.com

Ecotourism forum with worldwide reach and a vast online catalogue of information

Sustainable Travel International
Tel: 00 1 720 273 2975
Web: www.sustainabletravelinternational.org

Includes a useful 'eco directory' of hotels and other green travel businesses

Tourism Concern
Tel: 020 7133 3330
Web: www.tourismconcern.org.uk

British-based charity fighting exploitation in tourism

The Travel Foundation
Tel: 0117 927 3049
Web: www.thetravelfoundation.org.uk

Sustainable tourism charity set up to work with the UK travel industry

Travel Watch
Tel: 07973 384496
Web: www.travelwatch.org.uk

Environmental travel consultancy

The UN Environment Programme (UNEP)
Tel: 00 25 42 076 21 234
Web: www.uneptie.org

Promotes sustainable tourism among government agencies and the industry

World Tourism Organisation
Tel: 00 34 91 567 81 00
Web: www.unwto.org

Part of the UN, serves as a global forum for tourism policy issues

World Travel and Tourism Council (WTTC)
Tel: 0870 727 9882
Web: www.wttc.org

Voice of the travel industry

VOLUNTEERING

Biosphere Expeditions
Tel: 0870 446 0801
Web: www.biosphereexpeditions.org

Environmental conservation holidays

Blue Ventures
Tel: 020 8341 9819
Web: www.blueventures.org

Conservation holidays

British Trust for Conservation Volunteers
Tel: 01302 388888
Web: www.btcv.org.uk

Runs volunteering holidays in the UK

Coral Cay Conservation
Tel: 020 7620 1411
Web: www.coralcay.org

Marine and forest projects

Different Travel Company
Tel: 02380 669903
Web: www.different-travel.com

Volunteering and charity fund-raising trips

Earthwatch
Tel: 01865 318838
Web: www.earthwatch.org

Scientific and research-based projects

Ethical Volunteering
Tel: 0131 346 8929
Web: www.ethicalvolunteering.org

Download Kate Simpson's Ethical
Volunteering Guide

Gap Year For Grown Ups
Tel: 01892 701881
Web: www.gapyearforgrownups.co.uk

Long- and short-term volunteering
projects

Global Vision International
Tel: 0870 608 8898
Web: www.gvi.co.uk

Community and conservation projects

Hands Up Holidays
Tel: 0800 783 3554
Web: www.handsupholidays.co.uk

Volunteer holidays worldwide

International Voluntary Service
Tel: 01206 298215
Web: www.ivs-gb.org.uk

Wide range of projects and offices
throughout the UK

International Volunteering
Tel: 0845 601 4008
Web: www.intervol.org.uk

Volunteering projects

i-to-i
Tel: 0800 011 1156
Web: www.i-to-i.com

Volunteer travel company, now owned by
First Choice

The Leap
Tel: 01672 519922
Web: www.theleap.co.uk

Short- or long-term volunteering,
including some family trips

National Centre for Volunteering
Tel: 0845 305 6979
Web: www.volunteering.org.uk

A good one-stop shop for information on
volunteering in the UK

Original Volunteers
Tel: 0800 345 7582
Web: www.originalvolunteers.co.uk

Volunteering organisation, with
placements worldwide

People and Places
Tel: 01795 535718
Web: www.travel-peopleandplaces.co.uk

Responsible volunteering specialist,
which matches people to projects

Volunteering Options
Tel: 00 353 1 478 3490
Web: www.volunteeringoptions.org

Download Comhlámh's volunteer charter

VSO
Tel: 020 8780 7200
Web: www.vso.org.uk

Well-established organisation offering
short- and long-term placements

WWOOF
Web: www.wwoof.org

Worldwide Opportunities on
Organic Farms

Working Abroad
Tel: 00 33 4 68 26 41 79
Web: www.workingabroad.com

Offers a range of volunteering projects,
including grass-roots organisations

Worldwide Volunteering
Tel: 01935 825588
Web: www.worldwidevolunteering.org.uk

A non-profit making organisation which
matches volunteers with projects

Bibliography

Code Green (Lonely Planet, 2006)
Ethical Travel: 25 Ultimate Experiences (Rough Guides, 2007)
Pure Living by Sally Bevan (BBC Books, 2005)
EcoEscape, Laura Burgess (www.ecoescape.org, 2007)
The Rough Guide to Ethical Living, by Duncan Clark (Rough Guides, 2006)
How To Live A Low-Carbon Life by Chris Goodall (Earthscan, 2007)
Green Places to Stay: Eco-lodges and Other Green Places to Stay by Richard
     Hammond (Alastair Sawday Publishing, 2006)
A Good Life by Leo Hickman (Eden Books, 2005)
The Final Call by Leo Hickman (Eden Project Books, 2007)
Ethical Tourism: Who Benefits? Institute of Ideas (Hodder & Stoughton, 2002)
Six Degrees: Our Future On A Hotter Planet by Mark Lynas (Fourth Estate, 2007)
The Community Tourism Guide by Mark Mann (Earthscan, 2000)
The Good Alternative Travel Guide by Mark Mann (Earthscan, 2002)
The No-Nonsense Guide to Tourism by Pamela Nowicka (New Internationalist
     2007)
Tourism Concern's Ethical Travel Guide, by Orely Minelli and Polly Pattullo
     (Earthscan, 2006)

Other Sources

Air and Rail Competition and Complementarity, case study report for the European
     Commission by Steer Davies Gleave, August 2006
     (http://ec.europa.eu/transport/air_portal/internal_market/studies/doc/2006_08_
     case_study_air_rail_competition_en.pdf)
Aircraft Emissions, the Economist, 8 June 2006
     (http://www.economist.com/business/displaystory.cfm?story_id=7033931)
Air Transport White Paper, UK Government, 2003
     (http://www.dft.gov.uk/about/strategy/whitepapers/air/)
Arms Without Borders: Why a globalised trade needs global controls, Amnesty
     International, 2 October 2006
     (http://web.amnesty.org/library/Index/ENGPOL340062006?open&of=ENG-2M4)
A Strategy Towards Sustainable Development of UK Aviation by Sustainable
     Aviation, June 2005
     (http://www.sustainableaviation.co.uk/doc/summarydocument.pdf)
Aviation and the Global Atmosphere, IPCC, 1999
     (http://www.grida.no/climate/ipcc/aviation/064.htm)
Beware the Ecotourist, New Scientist, 6 March 2004
     (http://www.newscientist.com/article/mg18124371.100-beware-the-ecotourist.
     html)

Brown Is The New Green For Golf In Parched Spain, Planet Ark, 5 September 2005
(http://www.planetark.com/dailynewsstory.cfm/newsid/32331/newsDate/5-Sep-2005/story.htm)

CO2 output from shipping twice as much as airlines, the Guardian, 3 March 2007
(http://www.guardian.co.uk/transport/Story/0,,2025723,00.html)

Decarbonising the UK: Energy for a Climate Conscious Future, the Tyndall Centre, 2005
(http://www.tyndall.ac.uk/media/news/tyndall_decarbonising_the_uk.pdf)

Derek Walcott's Poetics of the Environment in The Bounty, George Handley, Callaloo 28.1 (2005) 201–215
(http://muse.jhu.edu/demo/callaloo/v028/28.1handley01.pdf)

Economic Impacts of Tourism, UNEP Tourism, October 2001
(http://www.uneptie.org/pc/tourism/sust-tourism/economic.htm)

Ecotourism Champion: A Conversation with Hector Ceballos-Lascurain, Ron Mader, Planeta, October 2005
(http://www.planeta.com/ecotravel/weaving/hectorceballos.html)

Ethiscore Report into Carbon Offsetting, Ethical Consumer Magazine issue 106, May/June 2007

European Commission Plans Emissions Trading for Aviation Industry, Aerlines magazine, issue 36 (spring 2007)
http://www.aerlines.nl/issue_36/36_Grimme_Emmission_Trading.pdf

Holidays From Hell, Tourism Concern, TSSA Journal, July/August 2004
(http://www.tourismconcern.org.uk/downloads/pdfs/TSSA-Article.pdf)

Hotels Get More Eco Friendly, CNN, 19 September 2005
(http://edition.cnn.com/2005/TRAVEL/09/14/eco.hotels/index.html)

How Coldplay's green hopes died in the arid soil of India, The Telegraph, 29 April 2006
(http://www.telegraph.co.uk/news/main.jhtml?xml=/news/2006/04/30/ngreen30.xml)

How Does Air Travel Compare, Aviation Environment Federation
www.aef.org.uk/downloads//Howdoesairtravelcompare.doc

How Toxic is Your Bathroom? The Independent, 24 October 2005
(http://environment.independent.co.uk/article321838.ece)

Huge Artificial Islands Destroy Dubai's Coral Reefs, CDNN, 27 February 2005
(http://www.cdnn.info/news/eco/e050227.html)

IATA Annual Report 2007

I'm All for Putting More Vehicles on Our Roads. As Long as They're Coaches, George Monbiot in the Guardian, 5 December 2006
(http://www.guardian.co.uk/commentisfree/story/0,,1963958,00.html)

India's Aviation Growth Phenomenon, OAG press release, 5 June 2007
(http://www.oag.com/oag/website/com/en/Press+Room/Press+Releases+2007/Indias+aviation+growth+phenomenon+05060701)

Information Paper on The Potential Use of Alternative Fuels for Aviation, Committee on Aviation Environmental Protection (CAEP), February 2007
(http://web.mit.edu/aeroastro/partner/reports/caep7/caep7-ip028-altfuels.pdf)

James Lovelock: Nuclear power is the only green solution, The Independent, 24 May 2004
(http://comment.independent.co.uk/commentators/article61727.ece)

Making all-inclusives more inclusive, a research project on the economic impact of the all-inclusive hotel sector in Tobago, The Travel Foundation (February 2004)
(http://64.233.183.104/search?q=cache:Ry8ztHCk0v4J:www.thetravelfoundation.org.uk/assets/project%2520summaries/all-inclusives%2520final%2520report.doc+travel-foundation+tobago+cruise&hl=en&ct=clnk&cd=1&gl=uk)

Managing Tourism at World Heritage Sites: a Practical Manual for World Heritage Site Managers, UNESCO World Heritage Centre (2002)
(http://whc.unesco.org/documents/publi_wh_papers_01_en.pdf)

Mintel Holiday Lifestyle Report, January 2007

Nitrogen Limitation Constrains Sustainability of Ecosystem Response to CO2, Nature, Volume 440, Issue 7086, pp. 922-925 (2006)

OAG Quarterly Airline Traffic Statistics, May 2007
(http://www.oag.com/oag/website/com/en/Home/Travel+Magazine/Executive+Travel/News+Briefing/Aviation+growth+hits+all+time+high+020507)

Perhaps Flying Turboprop Isn't Dying, Treehugger, 16 December 2006
(http://www.treehugger.com/files/2006/12/perhaps_flying_1.php)

Predict and Decide: Aviation, Climate Change & UK Policy, Environmental Change Institute, September 2006
(http://www.eci.ox.ac.uk/research/energy/downloads/predictanddecide.pdf)

Santa's Container Ship Heralds a Greener Christmas, the Guardian, 9 November 2006
(http://www.guardian.co.uk/comment/story/0,,1942795,00.html)

Ship It, Ship It Good: How Companies are Driving Down the Impacts of Shipping, Grist, 23 May 2006
(http://www.grist.org/biz/tp/2006/05/23/shipping/)

Ships, Planes and Carbon Emissions, New Scientist blog, 5 March 2007
(http://www.newscientist.com/blog/environment/2007/03/ships-planes-and-carbon-emissions.html)

Snowmobile Position Paper, the Bluewater Network, 1999 (updated 2002)
(http://www.bluewaternetwork.org/reports/rep_pl_snow_snowposition.pdf)

Summaries & Evaluations on Formaldehyde, International Agency for Research on Cancer (IARC), 1995 (updated 1997)
(http://www.inchem.org/documents/iarc/vol62/formal.html)

The Deadly Chemicals in Cotton, Environmental Justice Foundation, 2007
(www.ejfoundation.org/pdf/the_deadly_chemicals_in_cotton.pdf)

The Impact of Dolphin-Watching Boats on Resident Bottlenose Dolphins in the Sado Estuary, Portugal. Paper presented at Measuring Behavior 2002, 4th International Conference on Methods and Techniques in Behavioral Research, 27-30 August 2002
(http://www.noldus.com/events/mb2002/program/abstracts/cascao.html)

The Impact of High-Altitude Ski-Runs on Alpine Grassland Bird Communities, Journal of Applied Ecology, Volume 44, Number 1, February 2007, pp. 210-219(10) (http://www.ingentaconnect.com/content/bsc/jappl/2007/00000044/00000001/art00022;jsessionid=1ocdddqu2qs29.alice?format=print)

The Importance of the Diurnal and Annual Cycle of Air Traffic for Contrail Radiative Forcing by Nicola Stuber, Piers Forster, Gaby Rädel, and Keith Shine (Department of Meteorology, The University of Reading), Nature, June 2006

The Stern Review Report on the Economics of Climate Change, UK Government, October 2006 (http://www.hmtreasury.gov.uk/independent_reviews/stern_review_economics_climate_change/stern_review_report.cfm)

Tourism Certification Schemes Still Leave Much To Be Desired, WWF, 29 August 2000 (http://www.wwf.org.uk/News/n_0000000132.asp)

Tourism Concern International Network on Fair Trade in Tourism (http://www.tourismconcern.org.uk/downloads/pdfs/fairtrade-introduction.pdf)

Transport Statistics Bulletin, National Travel Survey 2005 (http://www.dft.gov.uk/162259/162469/221412/221531/223955/223958/coll_nationaltravelsurvey2005/nationaltravelsurvey2005a)

Trash Landings: How Airlines and Airports Can Clean Up Their Recycling Programs, NRDC, December 2006 (http://www.nrdc.org/cities/recycling/airline/airline.pdf)

Travel News: Too Little Rain, Too Late, The Times, 11 September 2005 (http://travel.timesonline.co.uk/tol/life_and_style/travel/article564561.ece)

Travel: The New Tobacco, the Observer, 6 May 2007 (http://www.guardian.co.uk/travel/2007/may/06/travelnews.climatechange)

UCR Scientist Finds Key to Sex Alterations in Fish, The Press Enterprise, 15 November 2005 (www.pe.com/breakingnews/local/stories/PE_News_Local_H_fish15.cf49b98.html)

We Are All Killers, George Monbiot, 28 February 2006 (http://www.monbiot.com/archives/2006/02/28/we-are-all-killers/#more-977)

What is a Good Personal Carbon Target, by George Marshall. Coinet (the article originally appeared in Clean Slate, the Journal of the Centre for Alternative Technology) (http://coinet.org.uk/projects/challenge/target)

Why Environmental Benchmarking Will help Your Hotel, The Prince of Wales International Business Leaders Forum (IBLF), 2005 (http://www.tourismpartnership.org/downloads/WWF%20Benchmarking.pdf)

Acknowledgements

I am very grateful to the many people who generously gave me advice, time, support, inspiration and even, occasionally, a bed for the night while I was writing this book. I would especially like to thank the following for their help:

Benedict Allen; Camilla Baker; Bill, Barbara and Rachel Batten; Gemma Bowes and Joanne O'Connor at the *Observer*; Hilary Bradt, Janice Booth and Caroline Mardall at Bradt Guides; Angus Bremner; Carmen Bruegmann and Sarah Gooding at *She*; Georgina Butler; Shaun Bythell of The Bookshop; Simon Calder, Sophie Lam, Ben Ross and Jo Ellison at the *Independent*; Tess Carr and Kat Heyes of *The Happy Campers*; Anna and Mike Christopherson and family; Sally Coulthard; Jennifer Cox; Sofia De Meyer of Whitepod; Judith De Witt of Rainbow Tours; Doug Dyment of Onebag.com; Justin Francis of ResponsibleTravel.com; Lucy Gillmore; Guy Grieve; Barbara Haddrill; Richard Hammond of GreenTraveller.co.uk; Richard Hardy of Surfers Against Sewage; Mike and Petagay Hartman of Tiamo Resorts; Martin Hepworth; Jessa Latona at the Centre for Alternative Technology; Rory MacLean; Amanda Marks of Tribes Travel; Finn and Ella McCreath; Ginny McGrath; Marjorie Middleton; Paul Miles of Paul Miles Photography; Sarah Milne; Linda Moss of Organic Places To Stay; Harriet O'Brien; Aoife O'Riordain; the Outsiders' Canoe Club; Himanshu Pande and Dinesh Pande of Village Ways; Alastair and Toby Oawday; Mark Smith of Seat61.com; Graham Thompson of Plane Stupid; Pamela Timms and Dean Nelson; Sue Ward-Davies.

Thanks also for the unwavering enthusiasm and encouragement of Lucy Luck – especially in moments of panic – and to the team at Virgin – not least Ed Faulkner for believing in *Higher Ground* and Davina Russell for her dedication and hard work.

My deepest thanks are reserved for Adrian Turpin, without whose guidance and encouragement I couldn't have finished this book.

Index